BEAUFIGHTER STRIKE

Dedicated to the fallen – not for how they fell, but for why they stood.

Authors

History must be shared to be appreciated – and only in the sharing does it truly live.

Ethos of the authors' website ww2stories.org

Disclaimer

This publication utilises historical materials and publicly available sources in good faith and with due regard for existing rights and legacies. All reasonable efforts have been made to verify the accuracy of the information and to identify and contact copyright holders. The inclusion of quotations, images, and personal accounts is made under fair dealing and in the public interest. Any unintentional infringement, upon notification, will be duly acknowledged and rectified in subsequent editions.

BEAUFIGHTER STRIKE

THE UNTOLD STORY OF A PILOT'S SURVIVAL AND LRDG RESCUE

ROSS J. ROBERTSON & KONSTANTINOS GIANNAKOS

WITH THE ORIGINAL WORDS OF F/LT W.E.J. 'BILL' HAYTER, WWII RAF PILOT

AIR WORLD

AIR WORLD

BEAUFIGHTER STRIKE
The Untold Story of a Pilot's Survival and LRDG Rescue

First published in Great Britain in 2026 by
Air World
An imprint of
Pen & Sword Books Ltd
Yorkshire – Philadelphia

Print ISBN 978 1 03619 905 0
ePUB ISBN 978 1 03619 907 4
ePDF ISBN 978 1 03619 908 1

A CIP catalogue record for this book is available from the British Library.

Typeset by SJmagic DESIGN SERVICES, India.

Printed and bound in the UK by CPI Group (UK) Ltd.

The Publisher's authorised representative in the EU for product safety is Authorised Rep Compliance Ltd., Ground Floor, 71 Lower Baggot Street, Dublin D02 P593, Ireland. www.arccompliance.com

For a complete list of Pen & Sword titles please contact

PEN & SWORD BOOKS LIMITED
George House, Units 12 & 13, Beevor Street, Off Pontefract Road,
Barnsley, South Yorkshire, S71 1HN, England
E-mail: enquiries@pen-and-sword.co.uk
Website: www.pen-and-sword.co.uk

or

PEN AND SWORD BOOKS
1950 Lawrence Rd, Havertown, PA 19083, USA
E-mail: uspen-and-sword@casematepublishers.com
Website: www.penandswordbooks.com

FSC
www.fsc.org
MIX
Paper | Supporting responsible forestry
FSC® C013604

CONTENTS

MAPS

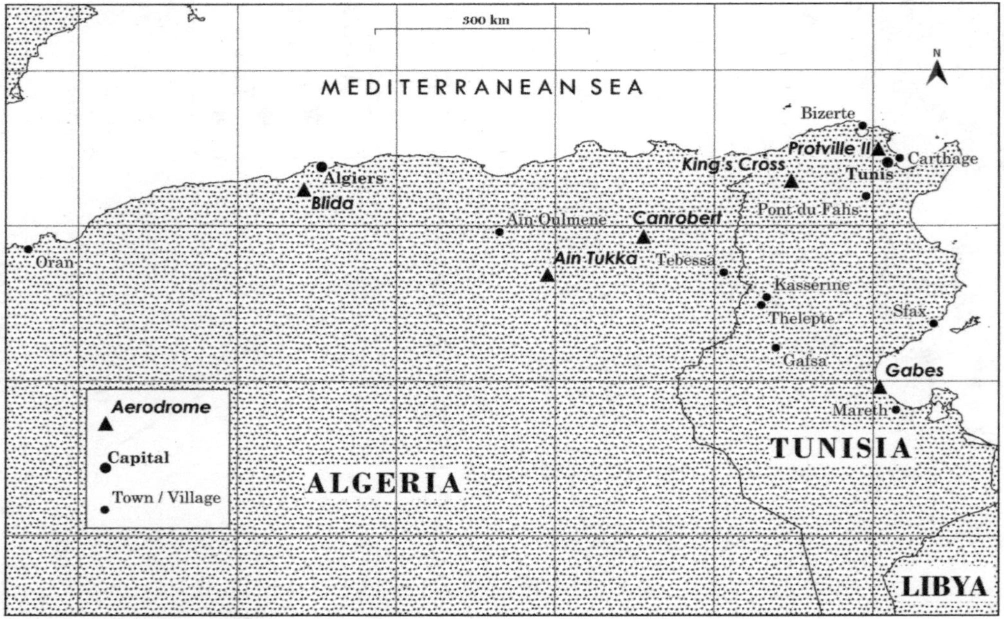

Bill Hayter's operational area (Nos. 114 & 13 Sqdns RAF), Nov. 1942 to Sept. 1943, incl. Tunisia Campaign. (Kimon Papadimitriou)

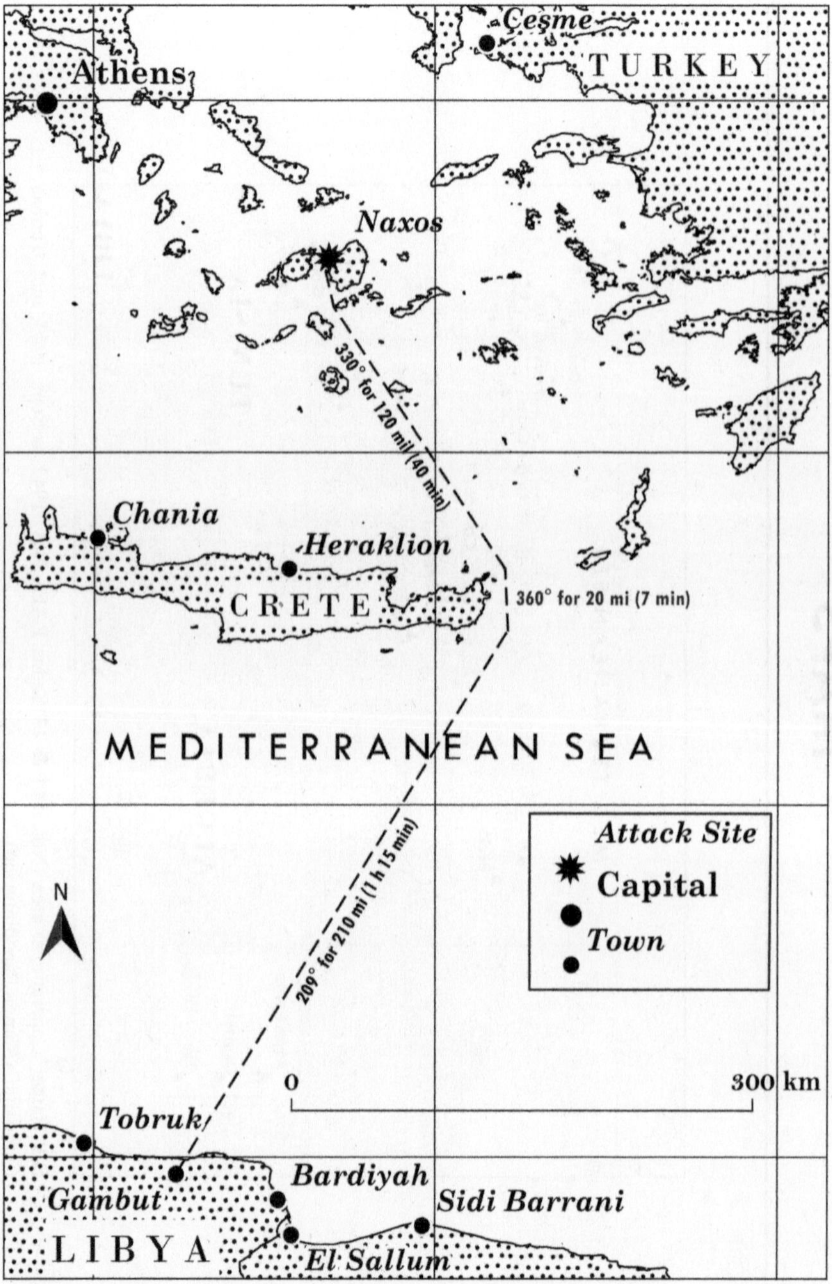

Beaufighter Strike, 30 Oct 1943: Flight path of low-level incursion from Cyrenaica (modern Libya) to the Greek island of Naxos. (Kimon Papadimitriou)

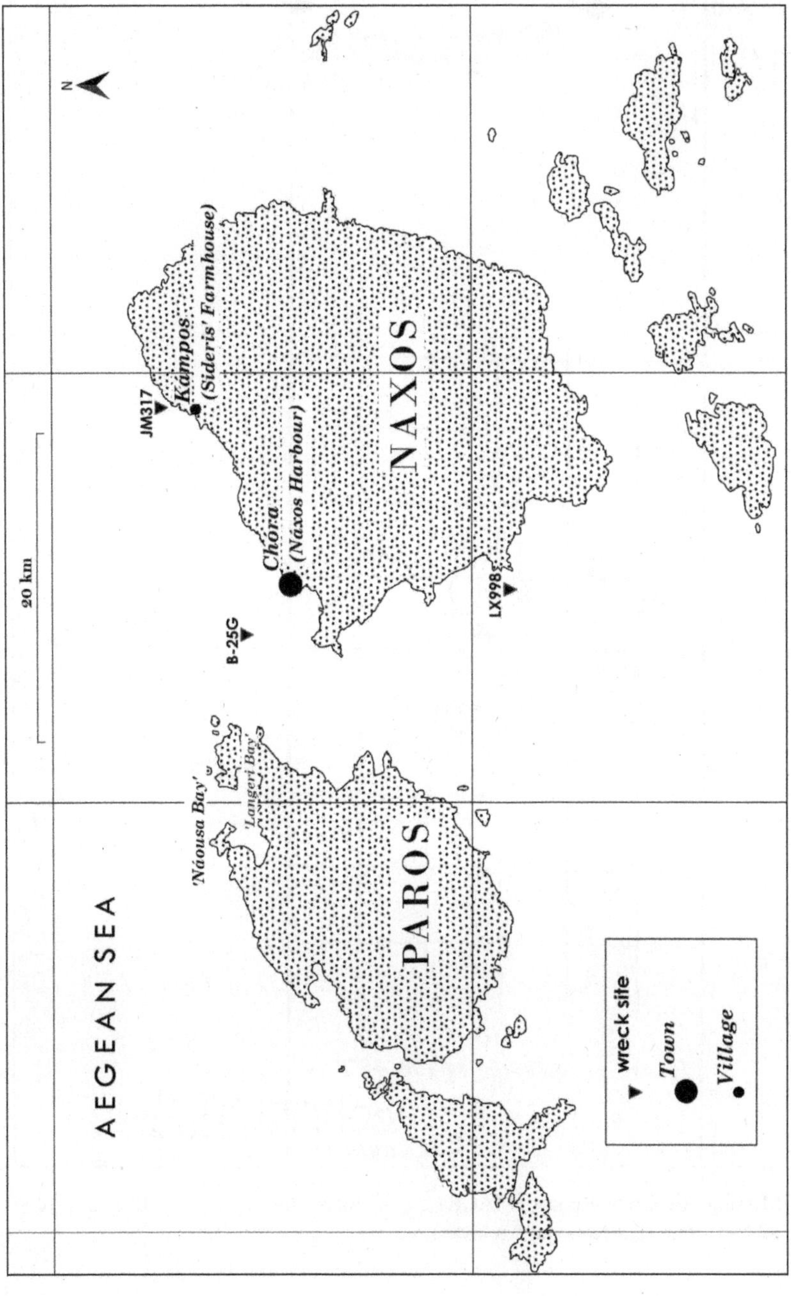

Aircraft wreck sites off Paros and Naxos (Cyclades, Aegean Sea): Beaufighters *'S' for Sugar* ('JM317') and 'LX998', and B-25G *Flying Caisson*. (Kimon Papadimitriou)

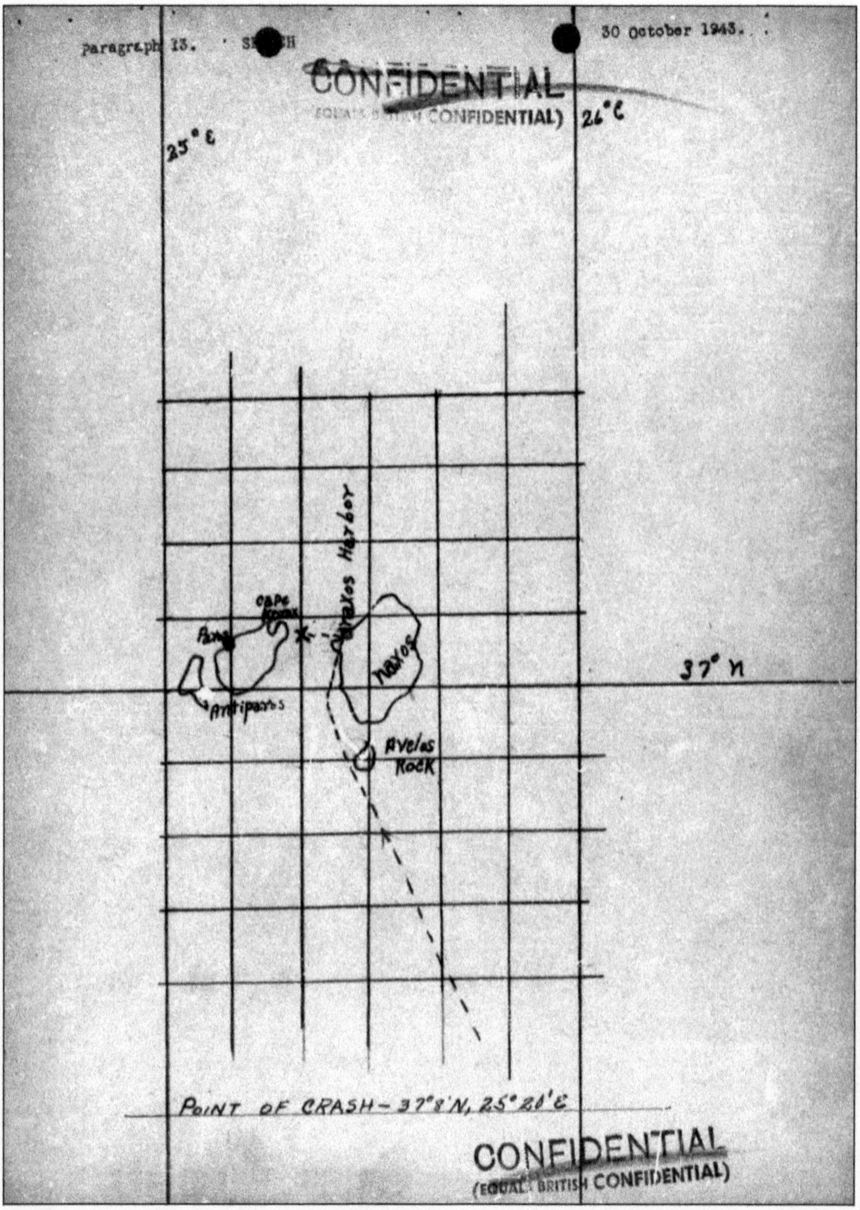

USAAF Missing Air Crew Report (MACR) #1137 map showing loss of B-25G *Flying Caisson*, 30 Oct 1943. (US National Archives)

LIST OF ILLUSTRATIONS

13. Lt D.J. 'Jack' Aitken (on chair) and his LRDG men training at the Cedars, Lebanon (background photo). On back: '*Missing links in Lebanese Mts. R1 Patrol after a 10-day scheme, August '43*'. (Brendan O'Carroll archive)
14. Crew of the RN motor launch *ML-359*, which ferried the R1 LRDG to and from Naxos, enabling Hayter and Harper's escape. (Brendan O'Carroll archive)
15. George Sideris and Bill Hayter, Cairo mid-1944, in a studio portrait celebrating their friendship. (Hayter family archive)
16. Bill Hayter steps into the cockpit of a legendary Spitfire while serving as a flight instructor in the UK. (Hayter family archive)

FOREWORD

It started with the want of a perch on a hot summer morning and a conversation I almost didn't have.

I'd known Ross for years – ever since he taught my elder daughter English – but until that day in 2022, we'd exchanged little more than inane pleasantries. Then, while waiting for my younger daughter at the exam centre, I spotted him cracking jokes among other waiting parents and took the empty seat beside him. We started talking.

To my surprise, Ross wasn't just a teacher with a questionable sense of humour – he was also an author, SCUBA diver, and keen amateur historian. That last part caught my attention.

Back in 2020, I'd completed a PhD on the Greek Civil War and the role of the British Military Mission in rebuilding the Greek National Army. Since then, my research had shifted to the occupation – and the shadow war waged by SOE, MI9 and other Allied irregulars alongside Greek resistance fighters. I'd just returned from the archives at Kew and was eager to share my excitement at what I'd found.

What began as a chat soon became collaboration. When Ross mentioned the rescue of two injured Allied airmen by George Sideris – stitched up by Dr Emmanuel Bardanis in a farmhouse – I thought it just one compelling tale among many. But he insisted it was more, and the idea of a book eventually emerged.

We divided the work. Ross would follow the airmen and the Allied side, while I, being Greek, would explore the local context. I focused on the life of Sideris, his niece Varvara, and the broader Greek situation.

The more I uncovered, the more I was astounded. Sideris didn't just take risks – he defied reason. Hunted, condemned, he was willing to surrender himself to protect those he loved. He sheltered strangers, knowing discovery meant death. His actions were neither calculated nor grandiose – just quietly, stubbornly brave.

Today, 'hero' is used so casually it has lost meaning. A goalkeeper makes a save – hero. A driver avoids a pothole – hero. So how do we label someone like George Sideris?

And yet, he was not unique. Across occupied Europe and the Pacific, countless others risked everything to help fugitive Allies – often paying with their lives. Rarely, if ever, did anyone take such risks for Axis soldiers. Even viewed through the most critical modern lens, the conclusion is hard to escape: the Allies must have stood for something better than their fascist enemies.

As the story unfolded, it became clear we weren't just documenting one man's courage. We were honouring a broader legacy – of ordinary Greeks who resisted extraordinary evil. The Aegean provided the setting. Greece, our shared ground, gave the story its weight.

Before the war, these men and women led quiet lives. When the time came, they rose. They suffered, fought, endured – not for glory, but because it was right.

As Konstantinos Kavafis wrote in *Thermopylae*:

> Honour to those who in the life they lead, define and guard a Thermopylae.
> Never betraying what is right …
> And even more honour is due to them when they foresee
> That in the end Ephialtis will appear,
> And the Medes will break through after all.

Sideris did not wait to see who would win. He joined the resistance when Greece was crushed and Britain stood alone. He believed that hubris would be met by nemesis – that injustice would one day face justice. So, when two strangers needed help, he acted – moved by the spirit of mighty Zeus, king of the Olympian gods, whose many epithets included Zeus *Xenios*, protector of strangers and sacred guardian of hospitality. Sideris offered shelter to two foreign souls in need. For that simple act of grace, he was betrayed by those he may once have trusted. Driven from his birthplace, he did not falter. He carried on the fight.

Others joined later, when the tide turned. Sideris stood firm from the beginning. His sense of honour would not allow otherwise – in a sense, Sideris was already free.

In the *dráma* (drama) of WWII, the *Ellinikí* (Hellenic) resistance became a *sýmbolo* (symbol) of *dimokratía* (democracy), *hērōismós* (heroism), and *strategía* (strategy). The *íroes* (heroes) of this *istoría* (history, story) were not guided by abstract *theoría* (theory) or *filosofía* (philosophy), but by a powerful sense of *ethikí* (ethics), *filía* (friendship, love), and *patriōtismos* (patriotism). Their *páthos* (emotion, suffering) was both *fysikó* (physical) and *psychikó* (psychological), their *kátharsis* (catharsis) forged in *krísi* (crisis).

This technique – using Latinised Greek with English equivalents – was made famous by Xenophon Zolotas, Greek economist and former prime minister, to illustrate Greece's enduring influence on Western thought and language. It also reminds us that because we share the same ideas embodied in the same words, the war Greece fought was not merely local – it was civilisational.

Yes, those in Britain, the US, Canada, or Australia and New Zealand suffered, but they were never occupied. Their families were not rounded up and executed, their villages not burned to the ground. Their children did not starve. So I used the story of George Sideris as a vehicle, a way to explore what occupation meant. The cruelty, the courage, the impossible choices.

Some say younger generations no longer care – that they prefer selfies and influencers to history or sacrifice.

Perhaps.

However, I will keep trying.

This book is my own small *Thermopylae* – with fewer swords, a few more footnotes, and the same stubborn belief: that history matters.

Major Konstantinos Giannakos HA (ret'd), PhD

Preamble

THREADS OF SURVIVAL

Μόνο οι νεκροί έχουν δει το τέλος του πολέμου.
'Only the dead have seen the end of war.'

Modern aphorism, often falsely attributed
to the Greek philosopher Plato

47 Squadron RAF Operational Record Book, October 1943

30/OCT/43.

Beaufighter 'L' F/O. Fletcher J.
F/O. Jones T.E.

Beaufighter 'S' F/O. Hayter W.E.
W/O. Harper (W/O. Harper from 603 Squadron)

Strike Naxos harbour with 2 B-25Gs 310th [sic] Bombardment Group. Up 1347 hrs. Down 1812 hrs.

1545 hrs. Naxos harbour. The B25s crossed the neck of land south of the harbour. One was hit in S/B side during run-in and crashed 1 or 2 miles north-west of the harbour. The A/C [aircraft] broke up and nothing was seen of the crew, and the other B25 completed his attack and broke off to port. 3 ships 500 tons were lying close together halfway between North and South ends of the harbour. 'L' scored hits on one ship with

> a 5 second burst. 'S' attacked another ship, and as a result 2 flashes were observed on the superstructure. He was hit in the engine and climbed away towards the hills. Intense heavy and light flak from the ships. 'S' crashed near Naxos, and the crew have since made their escape and have rejoined their respective squadrons. (AIR-27-464-30)

Like countless reports gathering dust in the archives, this Royal Air Force (RAF) record from WWII appears stark and impersonal – yet within its brevity lies a unique story of survival. On that fateful day, F/O Bill Hayter (pilot) and W/O Tom Harper (navigator/observer) faced withering flak, catastrophic damage, and a forced ditching at sea – and somehow lived. The official account records only that they escaped; it cannot capture the fear that gripped them, the split-second choices they had to make, or the agonising uncertainty of whether they would ever escape alive.

Fortunately, Hayter – equally adept with pen and propeller – documented the ordeal not once, but twice. First in an old RAF Sight Log Book, then in a 1945 Agenda. Both were lost and forgotten over time. As he had shared little of his wartime service, discovering these accounts 80 years later in an attic in France was an absolute revelation for his children.

Hayter's photographic memory made the accounts nearly identical, though subtle additions enriched the story's texture. Both were transcribed and combined into a single journal brimming with detail, insight, and the quiet tension of men confronting death. Together with official records, a unique and authentic narrative of a long-lost wartime experience has finally come to light.

The story of Hayter and Harper's ordeal might have remained untold were it not for a physical connection to their circumstance that also emerged.

In 2007, Manolis Bardanis discovered the well-preserved wreck of Beaufighter Mk X serial LX998 off Naxos, lying at just 105ft (32m). Vasilis Mentogiannis visited the site shortly afterwards with Panagiotis Niflis, photographing and documenting the wreck, and later wrote an article in Greek. Several years later, I translated it into English for Dr Kimon Papadimitriou's *wreckhistory* website and shared it online.

This caught the attention of Hayter's eldest daughter, Anne Timsit-Hayter, whose interest in Beaufighters was only inspired by the rediscovery of the first of her father's writings. She reached out from France, and I was contacted.

Meanwhile, Tom Harper's son, Richard, had been pursuing his own research, contributing to a chapter in a book by New Zealander Brendan O'Carroll, a Long Range Desert Group (LRDG) specialist and personal friend whose works are also coincidentally published by Pen & Sword. Richard even visited Naxos, yet despite these efforts, contact with Bill Hayter's family remained elusive.

Then, in another twist of fate, a fellow shipwreck enthusiast, George Karelas, noticed that in 2020 Richard had posted an otherwise obscure inquiry on the Royal Canadian Air Force Association website. Incredibly, a reply came from a lady who turned out to be the daughter of Bill Hayter's former girlfriend during his pilot training in Canada. Her 97-year-old mother was still alive then, though sadly suffering from dementia. Nevertheless, it was a major breakthrough accompanied by a wealth of information and photographs, for which we have the kindness of Patricia Staunton (née Heintzman) and her brothers to thank.

By April 2023, I was able to connect the Hayter and Harper families directly. In a flurry of ensuing emails, the wayward strands of the story were finally coming together, illuminating for both families the hidden details that had eluded them for decades.

This all led to my article '"S" for Sugar, "S" for Survival', which appeared as the cover feature in the August 2023 issue of *Britain at War* magazine in the UK. The strong reader response, together with a later discovery of Hayter's 1945 Agenda, pushed the investigation further. A serendipitous encounter eventually brought retired Hellenic Army major and military historian Dr Konstantinos Giannakos into the project. His expertise was to prove both insightful and invaluable.

So, what began as a terse wartime report has become a richly detailed chronicle of a single sortie – its perils, its aftermath, and the lives it touched. By preserving the Hayter and Harper story, we also shed light on WWII events in Greece and its truly beautiful Aegean islands – a wartime theatre far too often left in the shadows.

History, once scattered and silenced by time, now comes full circle – fragments of lives, deeds, and documents woven into one enduring narrative.

This is the miracle that drives historical discovery and deepens our understanding of our own times.

This is why we are all still here.

Ross J. Robertson

ABBREVIATIONS

a/c	aircraft
ACM	Air Chief Marshal
Adm.	Admiral
AG	air gunner
AI	air interception
AM	Air Marshal
AVM	Air Vice-Marshal
B-17	Boeing Flying Fortress, heavy bomber
B-24	Consolidated Liberator, heavy bomber
B-25G	North American Mitchell gunship
Bf 109	Messerschmitt (Me 109) fighter
Brig.	Brigadier
Capt.	Captain
CO	Commanding Officer
col.	column
Col.	Colonel
EFTS	Elementary Flying Training School
e/a	enemy aircraft
F/Cdr	Flight Commander
F/Lt	Flight Lieutenant
F/O	Flying Officer (RAF), Flight Officer (USAAF)
F/Sgt (Sgt)	Flight Sergeant

Fw 190	Focke-Wulf fighter/fighter-bomber
He 111	Heinkel medium bomber
hrs	hours
HSL	High Speed Launch
Ju 52	Junkers tri-motor transport
Ju 87	Junkers 'Stuka' dive-bomber
Ju 88	Junkers multirole aircraft
LAC	Leading Aircraftman
L/Cpl	Lance Corporal
LRDG	Long Range Desert Group
Lt	Lieutenant
Lt Col.	Lieutenant Colonel
Lt Gen.	Lieutenant General
Maj.	Major
Me 109	Messerschmitt (Bf 109) fighter
ME	Middle East
Mk	mark/type
MT	motor transport (vehicle)
M/V	merchant/motor vessel
nav	navigator
nav/obs	navigator/observer
NFT	night flying training
obs	observer
P-38	Lockheed Lightning, long-range fighter
P/O	Pilot Officer
p	pilot
Pte	Private
RAF	Royal Air Force
RAFVR	Royal Air Force Volunteer Reserve

SAAF	South African Air Force
SFTS	Service Flying Training School
S/L (Sqn Ldr)	Squadron Leader
Sng	signalman
Sqdn (Sdn)	squadron
TF	Torpedo Fighter (variant of Beaufighter)
Tpr	Trooper
USAAF	United States Army Air Force
VHF	very high frequency radio
W/AG	Wireless Operator and Air Gunner
W/Cdr	Wing Commander
W/O	Warrant Officer
W/Op	Wireless Operator
W/T	wireless telegraphy

Chapter 1

RABBLE ROUSING

Ἐν ταῖς στάσεσι τοῖς μὲν βελτίστοις ἐναντιοῦνται οἱ δημαγωγοί, τοὺς δὲ πονηροὺς εἰς δύναμιν ἀνάγουσιν.
'In civil strife, demagogues oppose the best citizens and raise the worst to power.'

Thucydides, *History of the Peloponnesian War* 8.1 (c. 411 BCE)

A quick bash at context seems in order.

Arguably, most modern conflicts are proxy wars – bankrolled by sovereign states or other players with vested interests, whether political, religious, financial, or a toxic mix of all three. Each operates within its own ideological frame – its version of the 'truth' – to rally support while fighting for territory, resources, and influence. Ostensibly, it's all for the good of their citizens, devotees, or investors; in reality, it keeps decision-makers safe, comfortable, and in charge.

Cynical as that may sound, it suits most involved. Although brutal for those in the firing line, proxy wars are always regional and contained – they have to be, or we'd all end up in nuclear ashes, which is neither fun nor profitable.

Most of us never call the shots – even in democracies – but nor do we usually get shot. Our role is passive: unwitting contributors, insulated from danger, free to watch amusing cat videos, cure cancer, or anything in between. Oil prices might spike, shipping delays might undermine Christmas gift plans, but nuclear deterrence and strategic balance keep the damage contained. Modern wars are mostly fought by proxies, sparing the rest of us from humanity's second favourite pastime – perpetual conflict.

Take Europe's latest war. Before troops massed at the border, how many Ukrainians really expected Russia's 2022 invasion, despite Crimea's annexation in 2014? Once war arrived, they had a choice: resist one of the world's largest armies or surrender. They resisted, with NATO's open backing, turning it into a proxy war. In the face of sanctions, Vladimir V. Putin sought his own suppliers and cut-price oil buyers. Without invasion, Ukrainians would likely have stayed as passively compliant as the rest of us. And had Putin attacked Finland instead – as in WWII – how many Ukrainians would have volunteered to fight there?

Interestingly, all this unfolds despite Russia's ample deterrent, abundant resources, and status as the planet's largest country.

Guess there's no pleasing some people.

WWII was a different animal entirely – like an internal explosion, erupting from within and consuming everything in its path. It was not a proxy war; it was entirely home-grown.

Few moments capture this better than the 'Total War' speech delivered by Dr Joseph Goebbels, the inventor of modern propaganda, at the Berlin Sportpalast on 18 February 1943. In the wake of the disastrous defeat at Stalingrad, Goebbels told Germans that survival depended on greater sacrifice and total mobilisation, erasing any line between civilian and military. His question – *'Wollt ihr den totalen Krieg?'* ('Do you want total war?') – was met with the roar he had scripted in advance.

It's hard to argue with your own captive audience.

But fate often has its reckoning. Broadcast nationwide and replayed in cinemas, the event rallied a population already steeped in Nazi ideology. Accustomed to Berlin's bright streets and well-stocked shops, they were suddenly thrust onto a war footing far more fitting to their grim reality. As everyone knows, the Germans fought on until utter ruin – a truth caught in a 1945 photograph of bombed-out Aachen, where an Allied soldier had posted a sign bearing an old boast from *Der Führer*: 'Give me five years, and Germany will be unrecognisable!'

The lesson? The boldest boasts and grandest plans often come crashing down, drenched in irony.

Japan showed the same suicidal resolve – from *banzai* charges on the ground to *kamikaze* attacks in the air – until the atomic destruction of Hiroshima and Nagasaki forced surrender.

The point being that such events remind us how, in the early twentieth century, populations were far more obedient to a common cause. In 1914, men flocked to the banners from many parts of the world. The ensuing slaughter understandably tempered their enthusiasm for dying for any king or kaiser. Meanwhile, economic collapse in the late 1920s and early 1930s further eroded faith in liberalism and capitalism.

Germany, crippled by the Treaty of Versailles, proved fertile ground for a failed Austrian artist turned beerhall agitator and self-styled leader. Fascism had first been served up by Benito A.A. Mussolini in 1919, but Adolf Hitler took it to new extremes. Tellingly, *Mein Kampf* (My Struggle) – initially an utter flop – became a huge bestseller after his rise to power in 1933. Germany was swiftly militarised, Europe's political divides deepened, and peace grew fragile.

Like all despots, the dictators of the age had no use for free speech or self-determination. Hitler's antisemitic campaigns, Mussolini's imperial daydreams, and Joseph V. Stalin's paranoid purges wielded propaganda, violence, and fear with skill. In Western Europe, the new tools of radio and film amplified nationalist fervour, much as social media does today – a stark reminder that we ignore these lessons at our own peril.

In 1936, Hitler and Mussolini backed the Spanish nationalists, turning the war into a fascist proving ground. In 1937, Japan launched its imperial rampage in China, threatening European colonial interests. Yet Western democracies clung to appeasement, wherever the threat. When British Prime Minister Arthur Neville Chamberlain brandished Hitler's Sudetenland agreement in 1938 at Heston aerodrome, declaring '*Peace for our time*', it was already too late.[1]

It fell to Winston L.S. Churchill to shatter the otherwise understandable pacifism born of WWI's horrors – a culmination of events that tested everyone, from leaders to ordinary citizens.

So, what was it like to be an ordinary civilian in such extraordinary times – especially a young person like Bill Hayter, with his whole future ahead of him?

There is no single answer; there were as many perspectives as people who lived through it.

However, one striking account comes from 18-year-old Patricia K.G. Sandbach. After finishing at St Teresa's Convent School in Surrey, she went to Vienna on a year-long exchange to improve her German – just months after Hitler annexed Austria in March 1938. From modest English country roots, at one stage she suddenly found herself a house guest of Princess Eleonore of Liechtenstein at the family estate near Graz.

In spring 1939, Patricia witnessed something few English people of the time ever could – and because of her language skills, she understood every word:

> There was a time of great excitement – Herr Hitler was coming to Vienna! He was to come out onto the balcony of his hotel and speak. Should I go or not? Well I did, in a party of young people. The city was covered in swastikas, flags, bunting and posters with extra police, soldiers, SS and SA uniformed patrols.[2] The crowds were thick and we fought our way through nearly to the front. Directly above us was the centre of the balcony of the hotel, where party members were waiting. Soldiers were standing shoulder to shoulder before us, armed, immobile, alert. It was a silent, expectant crowd that waited and then eventually he was standing there, backed up presumably by bodyguards. The crowd surged forward but we had linked arms and stood our ground. Not for long because everyone's right arm shot up (except mine) in the Nazi salute and there were deafening shouts of '*Heil Hitler!*' and '*Sieg Heil!*' and then an intense silence as the Führer began his speech.

The fervour surrounding the man driving Europe towards war was undeniable:

> I cannot remember much of it – I was totally absorbed in the man himself. This little man, not so many years previously a humble house-painter, now the author of *Mein Kampf*, the leader of Germany, the most powerful man in Europe, in his eyes, and in the world. There he was, up on that balcony, gesticulating, his well-known voice proclaiming the principles of fascism and what it meant for his beloved Austria.

> As he was speaking, I felt an extraordinary tension taking hold of the crowd around me, which communicated itself to me too. I felt that I was being swayed against my will and I recognised the danger of it. I forced myself to think of home, my war-wounded father, my mother who had also experienced front-line horrors, of the concentration camps and the fears of so many of my friends. It has been said that Hitler had an hypnotic aura about him, and this I believe to be true and I certainly felt a wave of near-hysteria in the crowd about me. I clasped my bag with my ID card (my icon) close to me and willed myself not to join in the '*Heil Hitlers!*', '*Sieg Heils!*' and '*Deutschland über Alles!*' with my delirious companions.[3]
>
> If we had not been dispersed by the storm-troopers, we would have stayed there all night. I was glad to be back safe in my own little bed, even if not to sleep.

Her relief is oddly echoed in Chamberlain's 'Peace for our time' speech, six months earlier:

> My good friends, for the second time in our history, a British Prime Minister has returned from Germany bringing peace with honour. I believe it is peace for our time. We thank you from the bottom of our hearts. And now I recommend you to go home and sleep quietly in your beds.

Given this prime ministerial advice, along with Patricia Sandbach's first-hand experience, we might ask: how much security did one's bed really offer?

After taking the Sudetenland, Hitler moved swiftly, occupying all of Czechoslovakia in March 1939. Then, on 22 August, Berlin stunned the world with news of a non-aggression pact with Stalin's Soviet Union – an alliance between ideological arch-enemies.

Signed the next day, the Nazi-Soviet Pact doomed Poland.[4] On 1 September, Hitler invaded; 35 days later, it was divided between the fascists and communists. Britain and France had declared war on 3 September – the unimaginable now starkly real.

Put simply, there were no longer any covers under which to hide.

Well, almost none.

An eight-month lull coined the 'Phoney War' followed. Hitler's armies were stretched east; Anglo-French forces were unready in the west. It was as if both sides feared the fight they had already chosen.

That illusion ended in April 1940, when the *Wehrmacht* (German armed forces) unleashed *blitzkrieg* (lightning war) on Norway and Denmark. Despite the Royal Navy's strength, Britain's bid to pre-empt the German occupation of Norway with an amphibious assault was a farce.

The Fall of France began on 9 May 1940 as Nazi forces swept through Luxembourg, the Netherlands and Belgium, outflanking the Maginot Line, on which the French mindset had depended so much. Tanks punched through the 'impassable' Ardennes – there were so many vehicles that a 160-mile (250km) traffic jam stretched from the Meuse to the Rhine. The stalled convoy was known to the French and could have been destroyed from the air. Instead, nothing was done.

C'est la vie! (Such is life!)

Merciless resolve, reinforced by superior weaponry and precise battlefield coordination via state-of-the-art military radio – all supercharged on the front line by methamphetamine tablets – proved unstoppable. Western Europe crumbled, leaving death, destruction, and legions of displaced innocents in its wake. France fell in astonishingly short order, with Paris taken unopposed on 14 June 1940.

However, *la Tour Eiffel* (the Eiffel Tower) and the *Arc de Triomphe* (Arch of Triumph) still stood, allowing Nazi propagandists to film Hitler parading his conquests – now horrifically rebranded as '*der Eiffelturm*' and '*der Triumphbogen*'. The German newsreel public never knew that his dawn sightseeing tour was less about avoiding crowds and more about evading assassins – a growing absurdity entirely lost on the soon-to-be drug-addled *Führer und Reichskanzler* (Leader and Chancellor of the Reich), who was no one's idea of an early riser.

At Dunkirk, the core of the British Army was nearly wiped out. Dubbed a 'successful failure', the rushed evacuation (26 May to 4 June 1940) was trumpeted by newly installed Churchill and his propagandists, drowning out the reality of a major defeat. The Nazi war machine seemed unstoppable – simply because it was.

U-boat *Rudel* (wolf packs) choked vital supply lines, while the *Luftwaffe* (German Air Force) fought for air supremacy to bring Britain to its knees. The Battle of Britain (10 July to 31 October 1940) was so fiercely contested that the nation's independence – the very bedrock of its identity since the Norman Conquest of 1066 – hung in the balance.

Toppling the Anglo-French order so swiftly vindicated Nazi fascism beyond its leaders' wildest dreams, inflating egos to dangerous new heights. For the defeated, the Blitz (7 September 1940 to 11 May 1941) brought 40,000 civilian deaths, the destruction of over a million homes and countless factories, and the constant spectre of defeat.

If Britain's plight was bleak, the Continent's was catastrophic. Fascism unleashed some of history's worst atrocities – war crimes, genocide, and the wrecking of entire families and futures.

Yet in doing so, it encountered a growing nemesis that would strike back at every level.

Ironically, fascism would be destroyed using one of its own creeds – the subordination of the individual to the needs of the nation. In liberal democracies, shaped by ideals from classical Greece, the right to pursue one's own path, free from state control, is fundamental. But to preserve those freedoms, they had to be set aside to forge a collective strong enough to fight.

Whether conscript or volunteer, boffin or factory hand, commando or cannon fodder, millions in Britain, its dominions, and eventually North America, saw their rights suddenly made alienable. Like their fascist foes, they were swept up in a whirlwind of politics, propaganda, and expectation – and almost all of them went willingly.

Among them was a young man named Bill Hayter, whose own journey was about to be shaped – and tested – by the war.

Chapter 2

FITTING THE BILL
Part I

Dulce bellum inexpertis.
'War is sweet to those who have never experienced it.'
Erasmus, *Adagia* (c. 1500)

Amid the relentless *Luftwaffe* bombing of the UK and mounting societal pressure, Bill Hayter arrived at the RAF 1st Recruit Receiving Centre, Uxbridge, on 25 October 1940 to enlist in the Royal Air Force Volunteer Reserve (RAFVR). As we shall see, he had to run – or at least cycle – a marathon mile to get there.

His service record carries one of two bold lies told to officialdom. First, that he was born on 1 July 1922, making him 18 and eligible to enlist. In truth, William 'Bill' Edward Jocelyn Hayter was born in Barnby Dun, Yorkshire, on 11 December 1922. Falsifying age was common – young men swept up by boyish enthusiasm, patriotism, and the lure of adventure sought to join the fight.

For boys growing up between the wars, aviation was a thrilling dream. News of flying feats and speed records filled the papers, tin toy aeroplanes sparked early imaginations, and the Biggles books by former RAF pilot Captain (Capt.) W.E. Johns – 15 titles published between 1932 and 1938 – romanticised the skies and inspired countless teenagers, including Bill.

With war came urgent recruitment, driven by stirring propaganda and speeches. Churchill's famous 20 August 1940 address, praising the Battle of Britain with '*Never in the field of human conflict was so much owed by so many to so few*', made flying for the RAF seem both heroic and glamorous.[1]

WWII was unlike any war Britain had known. Technological advances brought devastation to civilians' doorsteps, making the horrors of battle a daily reality. Bill and his family resided at Spaynes Hall, Great Yeldham, an Elizabethan country house in Essex, which spared them the worst of the Blitz. No doubt he witnessed some of the aerial battles of the Battle of Britain, but had little real idea of what awaited him in combat. Still, he volunteered – driven by duty, courage, and a strong sense of purpose.

The second lie Bill told concerned his medical examination. His service record notes he was 5ft 10in (178cm), with a 31in (79cm) chest, brown hair, brown eyes (although actually green),[2] a tanned complexion (debatable), and a vaccination mark on his left arm. He appeared robust and healthy but concealed a secret with quiet cunning – a serious colour-blindness that should have barred him from pilot training.

Distinguishing red from green is critical for reading cockpit instruments, navigation lights, signal flares, and runway markers, especially in poor visibility. The RAF's strict Ishihara test routinely rejected those who failed. Undeterred, Bill likely substituted another candidate's results (someone with brown eyes) to hide his condition. This deception, born of determination, secured his acceptance into the RAF pilot training scheme as an aircraftman second class (AC2) – the most junior rank – marking his official entry into military aviation.

Physical fitness was critical – especially for RAF pilots, who, apart from keen eyesight, needed quick reflexes and sharp minds, given the huge investment in their training. Losing an aircraft meant not only wasted time but also the loss of skilled crew and scarce resources. This is why the RAF's largest bombers, such as the Handley Page Halifax and Avro Lancaster, had no co-pilots, but relied on flight engineers trained in technical systems, easing crew training and replacement.

Such rigorous pilot selection raises a question: did these demands align with Bill Hayter's upbringing and ambitions? For him, the answer lay deeper – in a strong family tradition.

His father, Capt. Mark C. Hayter, a Harrow man, had served with the Middlesex Hussars before joining the Royal Flying Corps during WWI, prior to its transformation into the RAF. He had a distinguished record, piloting and testing Airco DH.9 light bombers and the rare Westland Wagtail fighter prototypes, of which only three were ever built.

The Hayters' military service ran deep. Four of Bill's paternal uncles enlisted during the Great War, all surviving the conflict. His grandfather, Canon Harrison Goodenough Hayter, rector of Elmdon, Essex, from 1892 to 1934, had five sons. The eldest, George Theodore Meynell Ingram Hayter, became a chaplain to the forces; John Grenville Hayter rose to acting major in the Royal Field Artillery, earning the Military Cross; and James Benedict Arden Hayter served as a captain in the Machine Gun Corps. Duty defined the family, a legacy that would shape Bill's own path.

On 22 April 1919, Capt. Mark Cholmondeley Hayter married Joshuanna 'Anna' Skinner, a glamorous and cosmopolitan American. Their secret registry office marriage in Hartley Wintney,[3] Southampton, scandalised both families – worsened by religious differences, as she was Catholic and he Anglican. A formal church ceremony soon followed. The couple divided their time between England and an estate near the picturesque Villefranche-du-Périgord in southwestern France, purchased in 1928, when Bill was 6 years old.

He had two sisters: Margaret Patricia Sarah (born 1920) and Mary Concilia Boumeester (born 1924). Though somewhat distant – Bill was sent to boarding school – their childhoods were privileged, cultured, and well connected, reflecting their class and heritage.

Decades later, a very different story emerged. After their mother's death, it was revealed that Joshuanna 'Anna' Skinner was a fiction. Her real name was Dora Skinner, and she had married under the false identity of Joshuanna Sirian Howard. Only then did her family history come into focus – until that point, it had been erased.

Some facts were true: she fled abroad with an aunt, a nurse, and a suitcase full of money. She lived extravagantly in Paris, travelled on the Orient Express, and joined the Royal Flying Corps as a nurse in 1914. But these were woven into a carefully constructed persona – an altered name, a false age, and a flamboyant lifestyle underpinned by escape, secrets, and parental disapproval.

Years later, a cousin confessed to having destroyed a box of her papers and photographs. Whether shame, scandal, or something graver lay hidden is unknown. 'Joshuanna' was a shield hiding a troubled past – the source of her wealth and the secrets she fled remain a mystery to this day.

Bill may have sensed the tension. His daughter, Anne Timsit-Hayter, later remarked: '*Communication between my father and my grandmother was strained, but the house was big enough for them to avoid each other.*'[4]

Yet Bill's awareness came much later, if at all. As a boy, he remained in the UK, attending Weymouth College before beginning classical studies at Oundle in 1935, then continuing at the École des Roches in Normandy in 1938.

When war broke out, Bill acted decisively, cycling some 480 miles (770km) south to the family estate in Villefranche-du-Périgord. Amid the turmoil, the family secured passage on the final boat from Bordeaux to England. Mark C. Hayter immediately sought to rejoin the RAF but was deemed too old. Bill, as we know, circumvented age restrictions to enlist early. Both sisters joined as nurses, carrying forward the family's ethos of service.

Bill Hayter spent the first half of 1941 in the UK undergoing basic military and aviation training. It began on 4 January 1941 at No. 9 Receiving Wing, No. 54 Group, Stratford-upon-Avon, where recruits endured early rises, drills, inspections, roll calls, and lights out.

On 5 March, he moved to No. 10 Initial Training Wing, No. 54 Group, Scarborough. As a 'pilot U/T' (pilot under training), Bill laid the foundations of aviation – trigonometry, navigation, meteorology, aircraft recognition, and flight theory. On 14 May, he was promoted to leading aircraftman (LAC), the equivalent of an army private.

Bill's journey then took him far from home. Under the British Commonwealth Air Training Plan (BCATP), a vast network across Australia, Canada, New Zealand, and the UK trained aircrew.[5] Bill arrived in Canada on 21 June 1941, joining No. 20 Elementary Flying Training School (EFTS) in Oshawa, Ontario.[6]

At the outbreak of war, Canadian flying clubs unified under the Dominion Companies Act to meet Royal Canadian Air Force (RCAF) standards. Oshawa's aerodrome and No. 20 EFTS were purpose-built, fully operational a year before their official opening in June 1942 by Prince George, Duke of Kent, then an air commodore (A/Cdre) in the RAF. Around 3,600 pilots trained there during the war, a vital Allied contribution.

Here, Bill first took control of an aircraft – a Tiger Moth. Designed by Geoffrey de Havilland in the early 1930s, the biplane was WWII's iconic trainer. Its robust build, forgiving handling, and manoeuvrability made it ideal for novices. The open cockpit and tandem seating gave instructors clear oversight, while its simple, durable design ensured easy maintenance, crucial in wartime. It was indispensable in the BCATP, helping pilots like Bill gain skills and confidence for more advanced aircraft.

Its durability is shown by Tiger Moth 4080 at No. 5 EFTS, High River, Canada. After 158 hours, it suffered taxi damage late in 1940, a hard landing in January 1941, a propeller-damaging crash into a barrier in April, and the near destruction of its undercarriage in July. Yet it was repaired and flew until replaced by a Cornell in spring 1943, logging 2,359 training hours, 16,000 US gallons (60,567l) of fuel, and over 200 pilots – none fatally injured.

Oshawa played a vital, if often overlooked, wartime role. Beyond pilot training, it was a hub of espionage, industry, and service. Just outside town, No. 103 Special Training School, Camp X, opened in 1941. Created by Canadian spymaster Sir William Stephenson, who came to be known as 'A Man Called Intrepid',[7] and run by Britain's Special Operations Executive (SOE), it trained hundreds in sabotage, secret communications, and covert warfare.

Among those drawn into this shadowy world was F/O Roald Dahl. A No. 80 Squadron RAF fighter pilot in the Middle East until a crash fractured his skull and caused temporary blindness, Dahl briefly returned to combat in Greece in 1941 before migraines forced his withdrawal. Recruited by British Intelligence, he served in Washington, DC, with links to Camp X. He would later become a beloved author, best known for *Charlie and the Chocolate Factory*.

Within Oshawa, General Motors shifted from civilian production to wartime manufacturing. Factories once making domestic cars churned out tanks, armoured vehicles, and aircraft parts – including fuselages for the de Havilland Mosquito, the legendary wooden twin-engine aircraft prized for speed, versatility, and the ability to avoid interception by enemy fighters.

For 18-year-old Bill Hayter, the Canadian experience must have been otherworldly. He was not just learning to fly, thereby gaining profound purpose, but living in a country largely untouched by the deprivations or war, yet fully mobilised. Oshawa's aerodrome and No. 20 EFTS, purpose-built and operational from June 1941, employed around 400 civilians, including 70 instructors. The base bustled with life. Students lodged in on-site bunkhouses, with a bowling alley and swimming pool adding comfort and routine.

The local community warmly welcomed the influx of new students to the area. Among the residents were Robert 'Bob' and Kathleen 'Kay' Mills, who owned a cottage where they hosted Bill Hayter and five other trainee pilots during one of their leaves in the summer of 1941.

One of these trainees was Charles R.C.A. Allberry, a distinguished 30-year-old Cambridge academic specialising in Coptic and Syriac studies. Allberry had authored the influential *A Manichaean Psalm Book, Part II*[8] in 1938, and had an impressive résumé that included participating in excavations at Medinet Madi in Egypt and collaborating with Professor Hans Heinrich Schaeder in Berlin. He also briefly served as the editor of the Egypt Exploration Society's *Journal of Egyptian Archaeology*.

Despite his prominent academic career, Allberry felt compelled to contribute to the war effort. With his academic expertise and fluency in German, he was swiftly recruited for intelligence work at Bletchley Park in Buckinghamshire, England, the central site for British codebreakers during WWII. Operated by the Government Code and Cypher School (GC&CS), it played a crucial role in deciphering encrypted communications, particularly those encrypted by the German Enigma and Lorenz machines.

As is well known today, the most crucial intelligence produced at Bletchley Park was code-named ULTRA, and its effects were far reaching. It provided the Allies with crucial insights into German military plans and operations, allowing them to anticipate and counteract German moves, most famously in the Battle of the Atlantic against U-boat packs – thereby helping to shorten the war and save countless lives. It also contributed significantly to the development of early computing, notably through the creation of the Bombe and Colossus electro-mechanical computers.

Due to high levels of security and a lack of detailed operational records, it is impossible to determine Allberry's exact role at Bletchley. Given his skill set, it is likely that his contributions were significant. Nevertheless, in a surprising turn of events, he decided to become a pilot and joined the RAF on 4 November 1940.

'*The move was largely inexplicable*,' comments Charles' son, David C.A. Allberry. '*He had met my mother at Bletchley, and a relationship quickly followed. They had only a few short months together before he was dispatched to Canada for training. It must have been difficult for both of them.*'[9]

In an era when women were largely relegated to a supporting role, David Allberry's mother was a person worthy of interest, not least as she has already been mentioned as having experienced the fervour of one of Hitler's speeches first hand. After war was declared, Patricia Sandbach hastily returned to the UK and volunteered her services. She was recruited at Bletchley Park, where her first assignment in Hut 4 – the Naval Station – involved translating a sea-soaked, blood-stained captured U-boat logbook.

Their relationship stemmed from a casual conversation in the dining room during which Patricia asked Charles what his peacetime occupation was.

'*I write hymns*,' was his earnest reply.

The response was taken facetiously as Patricia wrote: '*That nearly ended our budding relationship, but for the sight of Professor Bruford sitting opposite us, choking with laughter on his biscuits and cheese*.'

'*On one of our evening walks*,' Patricia later recounted, '*Charles took me to a vantage point and we stood and watched the glowing red sky, far away, where London was burning*.'[10]

Indeed, many a love story unfolded under the surreal backdrop of WWII – a fact too often ignored in history books. The intensity of these relationships was heightened by the uncertainty of the times, where every moment was precious, especially as it could be the last. Couples, even if separated by countless miles, found solace in each other, their bonds strengthened by a shared determination to hold on to normalcy and create moments of joy amidst the turmoil. Romance was a quiet resistance against the war – a small but significant triumph of the human spirit.

One of Cupid's arrows – or those of Eros, if you prefer the Greek mythology on which the idea is based – also struck Bill Hayter. His invitation to the Mills' cottage would prove far more significant than providing a good home-cooked meal, warm company, and a little rest and recreation. Here, he met Bob and Kay's 17-year-old daughter, Catherine 'Ann' Mills.

A strong romantic connection formed between them, a bond that would endure through the turbulence of war and beyond. Throughout his service, Bill sent Ann letters, postcards, and photographs – expressions of affection and longing that are still preserved in Canada, along with a photo album.

'*After the war, Bill returned to Canada in late 1946, writing "C/o G.P.O., Oshawa" as his contact address on official release forms – clearly planning to see my mother and grandparents,*' recalls Ann's daughter, Patricia Staunton.

'*Indeed, Bill must also have been fond of my grandparents in the brief six months he was here. He gave my grandfather a sterling silver cigarette box engraved "RGM from WEH" when he returned.*'[11]

All that, however, lay ahead. In 1941, Bill completed his initial 50 hours of aviation training at No. 20 EFTS. For those who qualified, the next step was advanced instruction at a different facility. Cadets were then streamed – one path for fighter pilots, the other for bomber, coastal, or transport roles – while those who did not qualify could still serve in other capacities such as flight engineers or bombardiers.

For Bill, there was no question. Having graduated from elementary training, he now stood at the threshold of his next great challenge – one that would take him into the heart of the war if he succeeded.

Chapter 3

FITTING THE BILL

Part II

Οὐ γὰρ ἐν τῷ πλήθει τῆς δυνάμεως, ἀλλ᾽ ἐν τῇ εὐταξίᾳ καὶ τῇ ἀσκήσει τοῦ στρατοπέδου τὸ κρατεῖν ἐστίν.

'Victory does not lie in the number of troops, but in their discipline and training.'

Polybius, *Histories* 6.42 (c. 150 BCE)

On 20 August 1941, Bill Hayter, with classmates including Allberry, was posted to No. 5 Service Flying Training School (SFTS) in Brantford, Ontario. The self-contained complex featured runways, hangars, support buildings, and its own swimming pool. Like his previous school, it had been built from scratch in about five months, opening on 11 November 1940. As part of the second stream, he would now fly multi-engine aircraft.

He trained on twin-engine Avro Anson Mk Is, with a mostly fabric-covered fuselage and a one-piece wooden wing. Commissioned in 1935 for reconnaissance, by WWII their 188 miles per hour (302km/h) speed, poor manoeuvrability, and lack of hard points for bombs made them unsuitable for combat, but ideal for training.

Hayter's arrival at No. 5 SFTS coincided with a tragic event, as the institution's logbook noted:

> August 27, 1941. This morning at 1050 hrs two Ansons collided in midair as they were approaching number three runway. Both aircraft crashed to the ground and LAC Davis

> and LAC Switzer, the pilots of the two respective aircraft, were instantly killed. The crash tender and the ambulance lost no time in getting to the scene of the crash but both pilots were beyond aid. The two planes were completely wrecked.[1]

The incident underscored the razor-thin margin between competence and disaster. Ironically, many fatalities arose not from lack of courage but from excessive daring. Trainees' impetuosity, youthful overconfidence, and rivalry often proved lethal, and unauthorised low flying remained common despite lectures, reprimands, and court-martials.

Boys will always be boys – but at what cost?

In 1941 alone, Canada's BCATP training exercises claimed 170 lives: 40 from low flying, 37 from stalls, 31 during night drills, 20 from mid-air collisions, including Davis and Switzer, 15 from instrument or propeller failures, and 27 from other causes. Non-fatal mishaps ranged from minor wingtip damage to ground-looping or overturned aircraft. Overall, 856 students died in flight-training accidents.

Learning to fly was undeniably perilous. Yet, for those who endured, the next milestone offered the recognition they dearly sought.

On 21 November 1941, Hayter's class graduated in a Wing Parade. A proud moment it must have been as each trainee stepped forward to have the highly coveted two-winged pilot badge pinned to his chest by Group Captain (Gp Capt.) Bertram F. Johnson RCAF, officer commanding. The ceremony was more than a rite of passage; it also marked immediate promotion to flight sergeant (F/Sgt), a rank from which most would later become commissioned officers.[2]

Allberry, however, was not among the recipients. He had washed out of the SFTS course at the last moment for unknown reasons. He opted to retrain as an observer and navigator, but not before making the most of his circumstances. Ever the academic, he toured American Ivy League institutions such as Harvard and Yale, liaising with leading scholars before completing his training.

'*When my father eventually returned from Canada and the States as a qualified navigator, he and my mother married on 27 August 1942,*' David Allberry says. '*Their whole lives must have seemed ahead of them.*'[3]

But it was not meant to be.

Tragically, Flying Officer (F/O) Charles Allberry was killed over Holland on 3 April 1943 during his very first combat sortie for Bomber Command.[4] The No. 78 Squadron Halifax II JB845 he was navigating was shot down by 24-year-old night-fighter ace *Oberleutnant* (Flying Officer) Eckart-Wilhelm von Bonin in a Messerschmitt Bf 109.[5] The Halifax exploded and broke apart, as witnessed by 15-year-old Lei Breukers from the ground. Wreckage was found the next morning near Colusdiki in Nederweert; Allberry's body was recovered from a large section of fuselage. The tail gunner, Sergeant (Sgt) Webb, was found alive, still strapped into his position with his wristwatch stopped at 2340 hrs. He was taken to a hospital in Weert but succumbed to his severe injuries shortly afterwards.

Despite their age difference, Hayter and Allberry shared intelligence and purpose. At No. 5 SFTS, they photographed each other around an Avro Anson Mk I, smiling with pride. Lamentably, Hayter would not learn of his friend's fate until much later, if at all. Allberry's transfer to navigator/observation training separated him from his classmates, most of whom returned to England for final specialisation and assignment. Even before friends began dying in combat, recruits like Hayter faced the challenge of leaving behind those with whom they had spent their days laughing, training, and smoking endless cigarettes.

War brought them together and tore them apart with equal suddenness.

A photograph Hayter took of F/Sgt J. Redman in North Africa, late 1942 or early 1943, reflects this bond. Redman, also a No. 20 EFTS graduate who earned his wings at No. 5 SFTS, is identified on the back by Hayter: '*Jimmy Redman, one of my best friends, and the only one from Oshawa I still know about.*'

Such is the too-often unrecognised cruelty of war.

After qualifying, Bill Hayter returned to the UK on 23 December 1941 and was immediately posted to No. 3 Personnel Reception Centre (PRC) in Bournemouth. Nestled on England's south coast, the seaside town might have seemed an unlikely waypoint on the road to war – genteel, quiet, and far from the front lines. Yet for thousands of newly trained airmen arriving from Canada, Bournemouth was both a place of anticipation and transition – the last brief spell of normality before deployment.

At No. 3 PRC, aircrew were billeted in requisitioned hotels and flats. They queued for meals, swapped training stories, and awaited assignment. Even this in-between world offered no real safety. Although Hayter passed through well before the worst of the danger reached it, Bournemouth would later show how vulnerable even 'safe' zones could be.

On Sunday, 23 May 1943, it became a target. At lunchtime, 26 Focke-Wulf Fw 190 fighter-bombers crossed the Channel at sea level, evading British radar before rising over the coast and unleashing a devastating raid. In minutes, 22 buildings were destroyed and over 3,000 damaged. The Metropole Hotel, housing Allied aircrew, was hit hardest. Estimated casualty figures amounted to 130.

The attack highlighted just how precarious life had become for airmen – not only in the skies but even in towns once thought secure. For Hayter, the front-page news must have been a chilling reminder: danger began the moment they donned the uniform. Soon, those risks would multiply tenfold as inexperienced airmen joined operational squadrons.

Hayter was destined for Bomber Command – arguably the RAF's most dangerous allocation, with an overall death rate of around 44 per cent (over 55,000 of 125,000 aircrew killed by war's end). He stayed in Bournemouth for a month before transferring to No. 3 SFTS in South Cerney, Gloucestershire, for advanced flying training and orientation to local conditions and standards. On 4 March 1943, he attended Beam Approach School (BAS), learning to use airfield radio beacons that guided aircraft safely to runways in poor visibility and at night.[6]

On 24 June 1942, Hayter was assigned to No. 21 Squadron, based at Bodney, a satellite of RAF Watton in Norfolk. This squadron – part of No. 2 Group, Bomber Command – operated medium bombers, including Bristol Blenheim Mk IVs and Venturas. At the time of his arrival, the squadron focused on training, aircraft testing, and air-sea rescue missions. If Hayter flew with No. 21 Squadron – and no records confirm it – it would not have been in combat.

Just ten days later, he was reassigned to No. 114 Squadron, also part of Bomber Command, flying Bristol Blenheim Mk IVs from West Raynham, Norfolk. Unlike his previous posting, this squadron flew sorties against the enemy.

Having qualified and joined a combat squadron, William 'Bill' Edward Jocelyn Hayter had proven beyond doubt that he could 'fit the bill' – but his ultimate test awaited.

At the time, No. 114 Squadron was primarily engaged in night-intruder operations, attacking German night-fighter bases in the Ruhr and along the bomber stream in support of Bomber Command's broader strategic campaign. It participated in Operation Millennium, the RAF's first 1,000-bomber raid, targeting Cologne on the night of 30–31 May 1942. Launched just after a full moon in favourable weather, the raid was described in squadron records as '*the largest in the history of aerial warfare*'.[7] High-explosive bombs tore roofs from buildings, followed by incendiaries that created a devastating firestorm. Later raids would match the numbers, but none equalled the scale or symbolic impact of this first strike.[8] The civilian toll was unprecedented.

'*They sowed the wind, and now they are going to reap the whirlwind*,' Sir Arthur T. 'Bomber' Harris, Air Officer Commanding-in-Chief of RAF Bomber Command, famously stated.[9]

On the night of 28–29 July 1942, Bill Hayter flew his very first combat mission. It was meant as continual harassment – a small raid – but ended in an ill-fated triumph. He joined an eight-aircraft sortie against enemy aerodromes also targeted in Operation Millennium. Three Blenheim Mk IVs attacked Vechta, three attacked Rheine/Salzbergen, and the remaining two, piloted by Hayter and Jimmy Redman, were assigned to Twente in the Netherlands.[10]

The flight took off around 2200 hrs but was recalled via W/T (wireless telegraphy) near the Dutch coast. With hallmark brevity, RAF records noted: '*6 aircraft were recalled owing to U/W [unserviceable weather], F/Sgt Hayter's undercarriage collapsing on landing at base.*'[11]

Only one of the recalled aircraft jettisoned its load – eight 40lb (18kg) high-explosive and eight 30lb (13.6kg) incendiary bombs – before returning. The others, including Hayter's, came back still carrying their full payload – standard procedure, but potentially perilous. The bombs were unarmed, their arming wires pulled only when released over a target, yet almost anything could have triggered disaster during Hayter's impromptu belly landing at one minute to midnight, guided only by Beam Approach, a wing, and a proverbial prayer.

Through a mix of skill and sheer luck, Hayter and his crew, Sgts D. Jeffery and R. Almond, walked away uninjured from what must have been a hair-raising – if not utterly terrifying – ordeal.

As the old WWII wartime adage goes: '*Any landing you can walk away from is a good one!*'

The other two aircraft, including Squadron Leader (S/Ldr) G. Gauthier's, continued their attack on Vechta and returned successfully, though Gauthier was injured by shrapnel near Lowestoft.

On 24 August 1942, No. 114 Squadron officially reverted to non-operational status. Night-intruder operations had already been reduced to '*if required*' to allow conversion to the newer Blenheim Mk V (Bisley), in preparation for Operation Torch, the Anglo-American invasion of French North Africa.

Hayter was offered a commission as pilot officer (P/O) on probation, effective 13 September 1942, and was officially reposted to No. 114 Squadron on 20 October.

It was a proud achievement – following in his father's footsteps into the officer ranks – and all the more remarkable given that, with his 20th birthday still months away, he was still just a teenager.

Chapter 4

DARKENED TORCH

Οὐδὲν γὰρ οὕτω τρέμει στρατόπεδον ὡς καινοτομίαν πολέμου καὶ τὸ ἀπειροπόλεμον.
'Nothing causes more fear in an army than a new and unfamiliar form of warfare – and inexperience in war.'

Thucydides, *History of the Peloponnesian War* 4.126 (c. 424 BCE)

Operation Torch on 8 November 1942 saw US and British forces land in Vichy French-controlled Morocco at Casablanca and in Algeria at Oran and Algiers, shortly after the British Eighth Army's victory at the Second Battle of El Alamein in Egypt. With Vichy opposition virtually absent, the Allies could now mount a pincer from east and west to seize all of North Africa – securing the fiercely contested Mediterranean. In response, Axis troops swiftly occupied Tunisia, a defensible prize just across the water from their Sicilian bases. The Vichy French forces there, hesitating through circumstance, did not initially resist, giving the Italians and Germans a growing foothold.

Although anticipated, the occupation still found the Allies slow to react. When they did, the Royal Navy – with limited air support – struggled to block Axis troops, supplies, and materiel from flooding into Tunisia. In desperation, the Allies launched the 'Run for Tunis', a 500-mile (800km) dash to the capital before Axis reinforcements could dig in.

Two roads ran east from Algeria into Tunisia – one along the coast, the other through the Atlas foothills. In Greek mythology, Atlas bore the heavens for eternity; in reality, he only shouldered a mountain range stretching 1,600 miles (2,500km) through Morocco, Algeria, and Tunisia.

The Allied plan was to advance along both routes to capture the deep-water ports at Bizerte and Tunis. However, poor roads, winter rains, and Axis defensive positions exploiting the terrain slowed progress to a crawl. For the inexperienced US troops, this was the first trial against battle-hardened Axis – especially German – forces, and the cost would be steep in the months ahead.

Amid these events, No. 114 Squadron RAF moved to Blida, Algeria, joining Eastern Air Command under No. 326 Wing. Ground crews and reserves sailed on 8 November, reaching Algiers on the 23rd. Most of the squadron's 18 aircraft left on 13 November for Portreath, then flew via Gibraltar to Blida.

Bill Hayter's first combat sortie in the North African theatre came on 22 November 1942. At 1255 hrs, he took off in Bisley BA729 with a navigator and a W/T operator/air gunner to bomb two ships in Bizerte harbour. The damage was unconfirmed; his was the only aircraft in the raid, making for a solitary and exacting debut. After some 1,000 miles (1,600km), BA729 landed back at base at 1830 hrs.

Drinks in the officers' mess all round then.

Over the next weeks, Hayter flew in formations of at least four aircraft, mostly against Bizerte and Tunis (see Appendix 1 for full sortie list). Distances shortened in early December when the operational echelon moved to Canrobert aerodrome, 2.5 miles (4km) south of Oum El Bouaghi, sharing the base with No. 18 Squadron RAF.

Unlike the Germans, masters of daytime tactical air support with aircraft such as the Junkers Ju 87 'Stuka' *Sturzkampfflugzeug* (dive bomber), the Allies in Algeria and Tunisia struggled to match their coordination and capability. No. 114 Squadron's bombing raids were thus confined to night operations, with round trips of about 600 miles (965km) from Canrobert aerodrome.

For many, 'aerodrome' suggests a tidy provincial airfield. In wartime North Africa, it often meant a rough strip cut from desert sand, with no buildings, hangars, or even toilets – and certainly no technical refinements like Beam Approach. These were crude tented camps ringed with anti-aircraft guns, their dugouts doubling as air-raid shelters. Unlike Canadian training bases with bowling alleys and swimming pools, such outposts trucked in drinking and washing water and offered few comforts.

Survival demanded stoicism, or outright heroism. Ground crews bore the burden of perfection, knowing one error could be fatal. Aircrews, despite privation and constant danger, were expected to fly at peak performance. They also had to contend with luck – which, as every combat aviator knew, could turn either way.

One notable incident occurred on the night of 4–5 December 1942, shortly before the move to Canrobert, when four aircraft were dispatched to raid Bizerte harbour. The squadron's Operations Record Book (ORB) noted that F/Sgt Bailie's Bisley BA983: '*Took off from Blida, had engine trouble so jettisoned bombs in sea & ordered a bailout. Sgt G.R. Acheson & J. Cummings bailed out successfully, landing 10 miles S. [south] of Maison Blanche. F/Sgt Bailie's chute failed to open & he was killed.*'[1]

Another came ten days later, on the night of 14–15 December, when four aircraft took off around 0430 hrs to raid Tunis docks. Bill Hayter, in Bisley BA817, bombed the target successfully and returned at 0745 hrs. P/O J.L. Steele and crew were less fortunate:[2] '*Crash landed 10 miles S. of A/D [aerodrome] in Lake Guerrah et Tarf through engine failure. Crew uninjured.*'[3]

On the nights of 26–27 and 28–29 December, two missions of four aircraft each were flown against motor transport (MT). Hayter took part in the latter, leaving at 0434 hrs and returning at 0725 hrs after attacking vehicles somewhere on the Pont du Fahs-Tunis or Tunis-Massicault roads (the report does not specify).

From New Year until 15 January 1943, all aircraft were grounded due to '*persistently unfavourable weather*'.[4] On 16 January, a detachment began operating from a satellite airfield in the desert at Ain Tukka, about 80 miles (129km) south. Tactics shifted permanently to targeting road and rail traffic to aid the army in Tunisia by striking the enemy's lines of communication. Bridges, rail junctions, and lorries were bombed or machine gunned. For the first time in the campaign, aircraft returned with flak damage, though none were shot down outright. Encounters with the *Luftwaffe* were avoided – wisely, given the Bisley's lacklustre performance – as operations remained night only.

On 19–20 January, returning from a sortie against enemy road transport (Tunis, Tebourba, Bir Mecherga, Cheylus), Bisley BA744 was forced to belly-land when its undercarriage failed to deploy; the crew was unhurt.[5]

An earlier mission was less fortunate: F/Sgt D.F. Gilbert's BA991: '*Failed to return. Crew subsequently reported prisoners of war.*'[6]

No sorties by Bill Hayter are recorded for January 1943. This is unsurprising, as only eight combat flights took place between the resumption of operations on 16–17 January and their suspension after 21–22 January. As No. 114 Squadron's records note: '*As each Squadron in the Wing was by now very short of aircraft and a redistribution took place, as a result of which all our aircraft were handed over to No. 614 Squadron and three crews are also attached to them. The Squadron then went on rest and many of the crews were sent on leave.*'[7]

Even as the squadron remained idle until 18 February, '*awaiting re-equipment with a new type of aircraft*', things were heating up on the ground.[8]

The tactical situation was complex. In northern and central Tunisia, *Generaloberst* (Colonel General) Hans-Jürgen von Arnim's *5. Panzerarmee* (5th Panzer Army), equipped with new 54-ton Tiger I tanks, mounting their formidable 3.46in (88mm) guns, held the line. These Tigers, from *Schwere Panzerabteilung 501* (501st Heavy Tank Battalion), first saw local action at Tebourba on 3 December 1942 as part of *Kampfgruppe Lueder* (Task Force Lueder). In the south, *Generalfeldmarschall* (Field Marshal) Erwin Rommel commanded *Heeresgruppe Afrika* (Army Group Africa), including the remnants of the *Deutsches Afrikakorps* (Afrika Korps), along the Mareth Line – a French-built fortification against invasion from Cyrenaica (modern Libya). Rivalry between Arnim and Rommel meant the Tigers were not shared. However, Axis strategy aimed to hold key passes and natural approaches into Tunisia to block converging Allied forces.

Meanwhile, US II Corps, under Maj. Gen. Lloyd Fredendall, advanced into western Tunisia, securing positions around Kasserine Pass. This strategic gap offered a route eastward, threatening Axis supply lines. In response, Rommel devised a spoiling attack, using mobility and firepower to strike the inexperienced Americans and disrupt Allied positions and logistics.

On 19 February 1943, Rommel pounced with elements of the *Deutsches Afrikakorps*, including the *10. Panzer-Division* and *21. Panzer-Division* (10th and 21st Panzer Divisions), plus the Italian *Divisione Corazzata*

'Centauro' (Centauro Armoured Division). His first assaults captured the Faid Pass and opened the way to Kasserine, driving the unprepared Americans back.

That day, four Bisleys were urgently dispatched to No. 114 Squadron to bomb the railway station at Gafsa. Poor weather forced two aircraft to drop blindly, while the others returned with bombs intact.

On 20 February, Rommel's forces entered the Kasserine Pass. The rugged terrain favoured the defenders, but Fredendall's poorly coordinated troops were scattered, hampered by inexperience, communication failures, and an inability to support one another: all of which played into Rommel's hands.

For aspiring battle commanders, Lesson 101 in *Rommel's Master Class of Battle Tactics* is to fully exploit every available opportunity.

No. 114 Squadron recorded: '*The military position deteriorated further during the day – the enemy breaking into the KASSERINE PASS and a menacing situation being thereby created.*'[9] Four aircraft were ordered to strike a convoy moving toward the Pass from Thelepte. One was grounded by a burst tyre, and the remaining three, hampered by mist and fog, dropped bombs blindly on roads and railways.

The next night, 21–22 February, was worse: all operations were scrubbed due to unfavourable weather.

Rommel, having broken through and inflicted heavy casualties, split his forces: one column moved north to Thala, the other west toward Tebessa, just over the Tunisia-Algeria border, aiming to seize badly needed US supplies. The Americans teetered on the edge of collapse.

The promise of relief came on 22 February: '*During the day a number of new Bisleys which had just arrived from England were delivered to the Squadron, and maximum effort was planned for the night.*'[10]

That same night, Hayter flew in a mission with eleven Bisleys in two flights against armoured vehicles and motor transport on the road from Thala to Kasserine Pass. Mist, confusion, and mechanical problems made the raid highly improvised.

The first flight of four took off around 2230 hrs. Thick clouds obscured the target; only two aircraft hit vehicles – one striking a group of 16 parked near a wood, the other six on the road near Kasserine Pass. The other two bombed the town of Kasserine and '*a fire resembling a flare or incendiary on the ground near the reported position of the target, so bombed this*'.[11]

The second flight of seven, departing around 0430 hrs, was equally improvised. Hayter, in BA733 with Sgt D.L. Jeffery (navigator) and P/O R. Almond (W/T operator/air gunner), bombed vehicles in Kasserine square, though it was not the intended target. Other crews struck Kasserine, a railway, or the town of Feriana, while one returned with bombs intact, fearing they might hit their own troops. Two aircraft suffered technical failures: one aborted early, the other lost an engine.

Flying his Bisley on a single engine, F/O R.C. Newcomb faced a harrowing choice: attempt a forced landing on unknown terrain or risk the perilous return to base. Choosing the latter, he jettisoned his bombs and carefully nursed the crippled aircraft home. As he lined up for landing, a faulty intercom left W/T operator/air gunner Sgt R. Gratrex '*presumably misunderstanding the situation*', and he bailed out at low altitude over the aerodrome, where he was instantly killed in the darkness.[12] Newcomb belly-landed at 0510 hrs with minor damage; he and navigator Sgt M.O. Dunne survived, but not happily.

Although the next effort, on the night of 23–24 February, lacked the earlier tragedy, it was just as make-do – their targets were hard enough to hit by day, let alone in darkness. A flight of ten Bisleys swept the Kasserine-Feriana-Gafsa and Kasserine-Sbeitla-Faid roads. Hayter, now in BA882 with the same crew, took off at 0455 hrs and returned at 0700 hrs, failing to find the intended target: '*Found no MT, so bombed a road junction.*'[13] Others attacked what they could: one '*bombed objects which might have been a cluster of M.T. or huts*',[14] another '*bombed a railway and bridge*',[15] while the rest struck roads or junctions, and one brought its bombs back.

It had become a game of hit or miss, with Miss Fortune clearly prevailing.

Poor weather, with '*widespread ground mist or fog over most of the target area*', made success almost impossible to observe.[16] In all cases – except for the 22–23 February attack on 16 vehicles parked at the edge of a wood, where '*bombs were seen to burst near the fire which then began to throw up debris*' – the results went unobserved, making it impossible to assess the effectiveness of their efforts.[17] Enemy resistance was absent, yet every flight remained a gamble, threatened by mechanical failure, navigational error – and the fickle favour of Lady Luck.

Despite their haphazard nature, these night sorties kept Rommel's forces under constant pressure. No. 114 Squadron was not alone; other units conducted similar operations, collectively blunting the Axis advance through relentless, unpredictable attacks.

Meanwhile, with his feet firmly on the ground, General (Gen.) Dwight D. 'Ike' Eisenhower, Allied Commander in North Africa, grasped the gravity of the situation and acted. Fredendall got the proverbial army boot, replaced by Maj. Gen. George S. 'Blood and Guts' Patton – aggressive, capable, and charismatic. His trademark look – ivory-handled revolvers slung at the hips, polished boots, riding breeches, all topped off with a steel helmet – was a masterstroke of personal branding, decades before the term even existed.

British reinforcements from the First Army were rushed forward. The 26th Armoured Brigade's stand at Thala was pivotal, blocking the Germans from exploiting their breakthrough. Then fresh troops, tighter coordination, and concentrated defensive fire stopped the Axis advance cold. Allied guns on the Kasserine heights tore into exposed German armour, while the mountains hemmed them in.

Rommel – facing stubborn resistance, fraying supply lines (Lesson 102 in *Rommel's Master Class*, always learnt the hard way), and Gen. Bernard L. 'Monty' Montgomery pressing from the east – heard the death knell. Within days, Axis forces were in retreat, and by 25 February the Allies had reclaimed lost ground.

On the night of 24–25 February 1943, No. 144 Squadron recorded the turn: '*A further big improvement in the military situation took place and the enemy now began to withdraw from KASSERINE PASS.*'[18] Nine aircraft struck Gafsa and enemy transport in clear weather; all found their mark, with incendiaries lighting the targets. The next night, the record noted, '*The military situation was now well in hand, with the enemy retreating,*' but heavy rain shut the aerodrome, ending operations for the month.[19]

The Battle of Kasserine Pass was over. Bill Hayter had played his part, though his squadron had been hamstrung by foul weather and too few aircraft. The US Army paid dearly in the debacle: over 3,300 killed or wounded, nearly as many captured, and around 180 tanks lost.

The Axis toll was far lighter: fewer than 1,000 killed or wounded, some 600 captured, and a scant 20 tanks and 70 vehicles destroyed. The Americans had met Rommel at their cost. Earlier nicknamed the 'Desert Fox' by the British press, this was no mere tabloid flourish – he remained a genuine legend of the war.

In the immediate and wider view, the battle was a bracing wake-up call for the US Army, laying bare raw inexperience and tactical flaws. To their credit, they adapted fast, becoming more disciplined, aggressive, and tactically astute.

For Hayter, these changes were no distant ripple – yet, for the moment, they brought an unexpected lull amid the relentless grind of the Algeria-Tunisia campaign.

Chapter 5

FLYING HIGH

Πολλὰ νικῶντες καὶ ἀεὶ μαχόμενοι καμόμεν.
'Though often victorious and constantly fighting, we grew weary.'
Xenophon, *Anabasis* 3.1.41 (c. 370 BCE)

While the battle against Axis forces in Tunisia raged throughout March 1943, for Bill Hayter it was a rare period of stand down. According to No. 114 Squadron records: '*News was received that the Squadron was definitely to be re-equipped with Bostons immediately, and crews were ordered to standby, with all Bisley aircraft being transferred to other squadrons.*'[1] As many as 16 pilots and air gunners returned to England to collect the new aircraft, though it is unclear whether Hayter was among them.

This reshuffle was part of a wider Allied reorganisation in North Africa after Operation Torch and the Allied advance into southern Tunisia. The RAF and United States Army Air Force (USAAF) merged into the North African Air Force (NAAF), with the Tactical Air Force (TAF) under Air Marshal (AM) Arthur Coningham CB, DSO, MC, DFC, AFC.[2] Within the TAF, light bomber squadrons – including No. 326 Wing's No. 114 Squadron – were grouped into the Tactical Bomber Force (TBF), led by Gp Capt. Laurence F. Sinclair GC, CBE, DSO.[3]

If nothing else, the reorganisation revealed just how deeply the military treasured organised confusion – liberally punctuated with forgettable acronyms.[4] Indeed, the command structure remains opaque even eight decades later, yet for anyone curious about just how the rank and file came to sport an acronym after their name, the following episode proves revealing.

On 15 March 1943, No. 114 Squadron hosted the air marshal. Coningham outlined the roles of aircrews and ground staff in expelling the enemy from Africa. It was informal – he was an Australian nicknamed 'Mary' after all – yet stirring, a rallying call. Tactics were shifting. The Americans, contributing A-20s[5] and B-25 Mitchells to the TBF, abandoned low-level attacks for high-altitude bombing. Nos. 114 and 18 Squadrons, soon with Douglas Boston Mk IIIs, would follow suit, while Nos. 13 and 614 Squadrons were stuck with the inadequate Bisleys.

While most of No. 114's aircrews were in England collecting the new aircraft, several gunners and observers were loaned to the American 47th Bombardment Group (BG) for sorties over central Tunisia. The Americans drew on British expertise in fighting control, map reading, and the British IXE bombsight – not a particularly innovative device, but entirely unfamiliar to their bombardiers. RAF observers led each box formation as part of the familiarisation.

On 5 April 1943, F/O R.J. Phillips flew as lead observer on a raid by the 85th Squadron USAAF from La Fauconnerie, Tunisia. The success of the entire box formation depended on his precision – a single mistake could cause him and the five following aircraft to miss their objective or even hit friendly lines.

As they approached the target, flak shredded the sky, and a fragment tore through Phillips' foot. Despite the searing pain, he released the bombs with deadly accuracy, completing the mission. The injury later required amputation, yet his mettle was swiftly recognised. Squadron records noted: '*His courage and splendid example were recognised by the immediate award of the D.S.O. – an event which was hailed with universal satisfaction by the Squadron.*'[6]

The understatement of '*splendid*' and '*satisfaction*' typified the era – putting to shame our modern use of words such as 'heroic' or 'legendary'.

Hayter would have soon learnt of the incident. Losing a foot to flak might once have shaken the 20-year-old, but months of relentless sorties and constant danger had blunted such shocks. Perhaps there was a flash of horror, a pang of admiration, or a flicker of sorrow – yet in the furnace of war, such feelings were quickly buried beneath the armour he had forged from witnessing too much death. War had a way of dulling even the most harrowing news, and Hayter, like many, was learning how to keep moving forward as the losses mounted.

There was little time to dwell. The arrival of the Bostons shifted focus to intensive daytime formation training. Crews flew six-aircraft box formations at 7,000–8,500ft (2,100–2,600m), the lead setting the aim point. As Phillips' recent sortie had shown, the tactic concentrated firepower but made the entire formation hostage to the lead's accuracy. It also offered mutual defence – though daylight invited heavy fighter and flak opposition.

Plans for the Bisleys of Nos. 13 and 614 Squadrons changed too. In the final push against Axis forces in Tunisia, they were now to fly close-support daylight attacks in formations of six or more. Like the Bostons, they would operate under fighter escort.

On the evening of 13 April 1943, No. 114 Squadron received orders to proceed at once to the new aerodrome 'King's Cross' near Souk el Khemis, Tunisia, which they would again share with No. 18 Squadron RAF. Next morning, most ground crew and equipment left Canrobert. On arrival, they set up camp and established fuel and bomb dumps.

By mid-April, the Tunisian front was unravelling quickly. The Eighth Army, having smashed through the Mareth Line, joined the Americans advancing from Gafsa. Together they swept north, taking Sfax and Sousse before moving past Enfidaville. The Germans, already stretched, were losing ground. After his tactical triumph at Kasserine Pass the previous month, Rommel had been recalled to Germany for health reasons and inevitable disputes with high command. Arnim now led the remaining Axis forces in Tunisia. The stage was set for a decisive Allied assault – British First and Eighth Armies with American and French forces – aimed squarely at Tunis. Outnumbered and cornered, Axis troops braced for the final blow.

In this struggle, Allied air power was critical. By 17 April 1943, the reorganisation was complete, but No. 114 Squadron waited until the 21st for its first assignment. That day, Bill Hayter flew Boston Mk III Z2284, taking off from King's Cross at 1315 hrs and joining a six-aircraft box formation. His crew comprised P/O R. Almond, W/T operator and dorsal gunner, and Sgt Robinson, ventral gunner. The mission targeted Longstop

Hill.[7] Despite poor weather, the formation bombed from 6,800ft (2,000m) and returned safely, Hayter landing at 1420 hrs.

Many operations followed, the close proximity of No. 144 Squadron's forward base allowing short turnarounds and often two sorties a day. Hayter and his crew flew repeated attacks in Boston Z2284, sometimes forced to abort by clouds, fog, or the absence of fighter escort. On one occasion, brake failure caused an aircraft to overshoot the runway, '*breaking the nose*'[8] after crashing into a hut – the crew emerged unscathed. Yet there were successes too: strikes against well-defended positions saw bombs fall '*right along the Wadi,*[9] *making an excellent pattern*', leaving crews '*highly satisfied with the attack*'.[10]

Given the RAF's propensity for flying around and dropping things on people, that particular outcome would have put smiles on all concerned.

Just when the sorties seemed to settle into routine, 25 April 1943 delivered a sharp reminder that the front rarely allowed for monotony. Bill Hayter, his crew, and their trusty Boston Z2284 took off at 1640 hrs to join a two-box formation. Their target was an enemy strongpoint in a wadi, west-south-west of Bir Mecherga, with six aircraft led by six from No. 18 Squadron RAF.

As they neared the target, the skies erupted. Five Messerschmitt Bf 109 fighters appeared about 5 miles (8km) out, only to be engaged immediately by six escorting Spitfires. In the ensuing chaos, three Bostons were hit by cannon and machine-gun fire, one critically. Two bombers retaliated, scoring hits on a Bf 109. The confrontation split the formation; Hayter's box regrouped and made a second pass at the target.

The bombing run was abortive. The lead aircraft's bomb doors failed to open, and the following aircraft had no opportunity to release their bombs before passing the target and friendly lines. With ordnance still on board, they were forced to return to base, frustration mounting. Meanwhile, the other No. 18 Squadron box bombed a secondary target 5 miles (8km) east of Bir Mecherga before also returning to King's Cross.

This left the critically hit Boston AL296, designated 'D', flown by Sgt C. Baker with Sgt B. Roblin as navigator, Sgt H.F. Palmer as W/T operator and dorsal gunner, and Sgt W.F. Enman as ventral gunner. The aircraft had been struck in the starboard engine, fuselage, and rudder.

If there is any doubt about what happened next, in a rare instance of detail, the No. 18 Squadron RAF record speaks for itself verbatim:

> Sgt. Baker, who was flying No. 3 in the formation, saw one Me 109F approaching from astern and below and directing its attack, apparently to No. 6 in the box. A moment later, incendiary tracer entered his aircraft and there was an immediate rev drop in the starboard engine. Sgt. Baker attempted to keep up with the formation, but was unable to do so. He broke formation to port and aimed his bombs at the primary target, which other crews confirm he hit. The W.Op/AG [W/T operator/air gunner] then reported a fire in the starboard engine outboard, whereupon Sgt. Baker turned and set course for home.
>
> As the fire increased, he dived to the deck, but it became so intense that he decided to crash land. A belly landing was made at 1715 hrs eight miles east of MEDJEZ-EL-BAB (J.7033), and although the fire was burning fiercely, the crew got out without injury.
>
> Realising they were in 'No Man's Land', they concealed themselves in the corn about 400 yards [360m] from the aircraft. On the other side of the aircraft they saw two German soldiers appear and stand watching the machine burn. Shellfire passed over them from both the East and the West. The crew crawled on their hands and knees through the corn westwards for about a quarter of a mile. They came to barbed wire entanglements, which they surmounted, and then to the wadi, six miles East of MEDJEZ-EL-BAB (J.6834), which was fraught with mines and wire booby traps. They got safely through, however, and three to four miles out of MEDJEZ-EL-BAB were met by a British patrol, who was standing by to go on a night raid. Another patrol took them to a Lieutenant-Colonel, who informed them that a raid was to take place at 2300 hrs that night in the very area where they had crashed and the information they had supplied about the area would be

> of much value to the raiding party. At Brigade H.Q. they were fed and wined.
>
> They were being driven back to base in a captured German car, wrapped up in blankets, when the car went off the road and rolled about twenty to thirty yards down an embankment, but fortunately landed on its wheels. Everyone escaped injury except Sgt. Palmer, who sprained his wrist, and Sgt. Roblin, whose forehead was bruised. This was half an hour after midnight.
>
> While the salvage wagon was pulling the car up the embankment an enemy aircraft dropped the stick of bombs 50 to 100 yards [45–90m] away. The crew walked for about half an hour before getting a lift into MEDJEZ-EL-BABRAF R.A.F. Hospital, where they were given tea and provided with transport back to base, arriving at 0800 hrs, 15 hrs and 20 minutes after setting out on the mission.[11]

Apart from the obvious revitalising powers of tea, this extraordinary sequence of events puts anyone complaining about 'a hard day at the office' to shame. It is certainly a tale worthy of an acronym of recognition – or at the very least, a well-placed expletive of amazement.

Remarkably, just two days later, on 27 April 1943, Sgts Baker, Roblin, and Enman were back in the air. Sgt Palmer rejoined them on 29 April, along with war correspondent R.K. Macdonald, who – one imagines – could scarcely have been bored by the story the crew now had to tell.

Between 26 April and 10 May 1943, Bill Hayter and his aircrew flew 13 more sorties, most in Boston Z2284. While many missions were routine, a few brought moments of drama: Sgt Scott, an observer in another aircraft, was struck by flak in the cheek, and Boston W8365, piloted by F/O Gellatly, was badly mauled but limped back to base. Two anti-shipping missions also tested the crews: the first failed to locate any vessels and bombed a secondary target, while the second found a ship off Bizerte '*already low in the water and derelict*'.[12] Despite dropping a full stick of bombs each, all missed – a slightly embarrassing, if not futile, effort.

On 10 May, Hayter and his crew flew their second sortie of the day against the aerodrome at Menzel Temimi, one of the last enemy-controlled airfields in Tunisia. This time, the operation succeeded. According to squadron records, '*All the crews were highly satisfied with the results of this operation, which they considered to be one of the most successful of the campaign. All but three or four bombs fell across the aerodrome, with one of these landing on the main road.*'[13] The mission marked No. 114 Squadron's final sortie in the Tunisia campaign.

Between 21 April and 10 May 1943, the squadron had flown 35 operations without losing a single aircraft to enemy action, and with only two injuries among crews. As the records noted, '*All organised resistance in Tunisia was over, and apart from mopping up, the great objective had been achieved – the Axis had at last been driven right out of Africa.*'[14] This success opened the door for Allied dominance in the Mediterranean and a foothold on the European continent from the south.

However, the campaign had been costly. Allied forces suffered roughly 76,000 casualties, while Axis losses in Tunisia alone included some 40,000 casualties and over 230,000 prisoners. Comparable in scale to Stalingrad, the defeat in Tunisia left the Axis in tatters, and the total North African campaign cost them roughly 620,000 personnel. Whether such staggering losses rattled Hitler's moustache – or merely hardened his delusions – remained uncertain.

What did remain clear was that the war was far from over.

Chapter 6

THE BRISTOL BEAUFIGHTER

Indigna arma militi datis: et virtus cum ferro degenerat.
'You give the soldier unworthy arms: and with poor steel, his courage decays.'

Vegetius, *Epitoma Rei Militaris*
(c. fourth to fifth century CE)

On 13 May 1943, orders arrived signalling imminent changes. Three days later, Bill Hayter and his aircrew were transferred from No. 114 Squadron to No. 13 Squadron at Oulmene, alongside eight other pilots and their crews. Their wing commanders (W/Cdr), J.R.K. Thompson DFC and P.W.L. Thomas, were included in the exchange. Nos. 18 and 614 Squadrons also swapped crews as part of a wider reorganisation of No. 326 Wing. No. 114 Squadron records noted it was '*an announcement which was received with great disappointment by the crews concerned, who deeply regretted being parted from their Bostons*'.[1] For Hayter, it carried a personal sting, parting from his close friend F/Sgt Jim Redman, who he had known since Canada.

Nos. 13 and 614 Squadrons RAF were now reassigned to the Northwest African Coastal Air Force (NWACAF) under Air Vice-Marshal (AVM) Hugh P. Lloyd. No. 13 Squadron returned to Algeria, arriving at Blida aerodrome by 24 May 1943, and promptly attended lectures on general reconnaissance.

Discontent was evident, peaking when crews voiced concerns during an address by the acting A/Cdre Kenneth 'Bing' Cross[2] on 25 May 1943. No. 13 Squadron records note: '*The main points raised by the aircrews were the fact that they were being taken off Bostons, which they had flown with so much success, and put back onto Bisleys, and that some of them were on their second tour of operations and now had to complete a further 500 hours of GR [general reconnaissance].*'[3]

Hayter had yet to contribute to any GR effort, but the collective anxiety was palpable. The Bostons were fast, reliable, and battle-tested – a rare mix of security and effectiveness, proven in the Tunisia campaign. By contrast, the Bristol Blenheim Mk V 'Bisley' was a tangible step backwards: slow, under-armed, obsolete, and prone to failure. This relegation deepened the weariness of crews already hardened by long and hazardous service.

However, in the military hierarchy, there was little – indeed, no – recourse for such grievances.

Beyond its cumbersome acronym, the NWACAF undertook vital Mediterranean operations: coastal air defence, sea and air reconnaissance, rescue missions, anti-submarine warfare, protection of Allied shipping, and interdiction of enemy vessels. For No. 13 Squadron, much of the immediate work involved convoy escort and U-boat hunting.

Despite the drama often linked with German U-boats, patrolling for them mixed monotonous flying with intense observation – a taxing combination given their contradictory nature.

Submarines on both sides typically remained submerged by day and surfaced at night to run diesel engines, recharge batteries, and refresh stale air – essential to prevent carbon dioxide build-up and asphyxiation – and, if conditions allowed, to bake bread and cook meals. Aircraft patrols were limited to daylight, forcing crews to scan vast seas for the oblique, often fleeting view of a tiny periscope, almost always the only visible sign of a submerged submarine.

A Type VII U-boat could manage only 5 knots submerged, compared with 17 knots on the surface. Attacks from the surface were easier, offering better manoeuvrability, more effective weapon deployment – including the deck gun – and improved target visibility. Submerged operations limited all these advantages. Consequently, many U-boats had to surface, leaving them vulnerable if aircraft spotted them before a crash dive.

The relatively calm, clear Mediterranean waters aided spotting, while countermeasures were few. One exception was the British submarines of the 'Fighting 10th' Flotilla, under Lieutenant Commander (Lt Cdr) A.H.M. Simpson in Malta, which stayed submerged in the harbour by day, cobalt-blue camouflage foiling Axis aircraft – a detail often lost in black-and-white photographs.

German U-boats were few, despite bases at Salamis, Greece, and La Spezia, Italy;[4] no more than 63 ever entered the Mediterranean. The region was dominated by other nations' submarines: Italy had over 100 when they entered the war (although not all operational), France around 40, and Britain roughly 60. Attrition was high, further reducing the chance of spotting a submarine: the Italians lost most of their fleet, many French submarines were scuttled, neutralised, or switched allegiance under Vichy France, the British lost around 40, and not a single German U-boat survived the theatre.

Spotting an enemy submarine was a true 'needle in a haystack' undertaking.

No. 13 Squadron resumed operational flights on 6 June 1943. Hayter took off at 1357 hrs in Bisley 'L', BB163, with F/Sgt D.L. Jeffery and P/O R. Almond on a U-boat hunt, returning at 1745 hrs, described – unsurprisingly – as '*Uneventful*'.[5] Six similar sorties followed through the end of June, all without result.

This emerging pattern was disrupted when Almond unexpectedly fell ill. Throughout his service with No. 114 and later No. 13 Squadron, Hayter's regular crew had comprised Jeffery as navigator and Almond as W/T operator/air gunner.[6] On 18 June, Almond was temporarily replaced by W/O R.H. Hooker on a reconnaissance sortie. Almond was admitted to the 96th General Hospital on 26 June and later reposted to Blida as '*non-effective*', removing a key, trusted member from the tightly knit trio.

In July 1943, No. 13 Squadron recorded 218 operational sorties, totalling 911 hours 40 minutes, none involving Hayter. The squadron also logged 203 non-operational sorties (152 hours 50 minutes) for training, orientation, aircraft/equipment testing, ferrying, and weapons exercises. Hayter was likely engaged in these non-operational tasks, effectively taken off the line due to Almond's absence. As a result, he did not participate directly in Operation Husky, the invasion of Sicily beginning on 9–10 July 1943.

Although the Axis defeat in Tunisia provided the Americans with valuable experience, Allied leadership opted against a premature cross-Channel assault into northern France, instead targeting Sicily as the gateway to mainland Italy. This operation aimed to strike at '*the soft underbelly of*

Europe' – a phrase often attributed to Churchill, though its precise origin is debated.

To support this strategy, the Allies relied not only on air cover from North Africa and Malta, but also on a clever, if somewhat macabre, deception known as Operation Mincemeat. The scheme was masterminded by Lt Cdr Fleming, a personal assistant to Admiral (Adm.) John Godfrey, Director of British Naval Intelligence. Mincemeat involved planting a corpse with fake documents to mislead German defences. The deception worked brilliantly, helping to divert German resources to Greece and Sardinia, and thus clearing the way for the invasion of Sicily.

If proof of the man's creativity were still needed, Ian Fleming went on to create James Bond – licence to kill, thrill, and make unstirred Martinis eternally fashionable. He also wrote *Chitty-Chitty-Bang-Bang*, which 'Q' would surely have dismissed as '*adorable, but unspyworthy – not to be returned in pristine condition, if at all*'.

Powered by materiel superiority, Operation Husky struck Sicily's southern coast. A storm delayed the landings but proved fortuitous, hiding Allied intentions and catching Axis forces off guard – a scenario later repeated on 6 June 1944 at Normandy. Over 150,000 troops landed from 3,000 ships, supported by 4,000 aircraft. The Axis, having vastly underestimated the attack, were further hampered by largely ineffective Italian units.

Operation Husky was not only vast in scope but also revealed a rivalry first noted during the Tunisia campaign. Flamboyant 'Blood and Guts' Patton led the US Seventh Army ashore at Gela, while Montgomery, famed for meticulous planning and caution, commanded the Eighth Army up the eastern front towards Messina. Patton's task was to protect Montgomery's flank and secure the island's north-west, enabling a coordinated push north. Their clashing egos – Patton's hard steel helmet versus Montgomery's softer, more comfortable beret – threatened coordination and sparked a near-childish contest to outshine one another.

Meanwhile, *Generalfeldmarschall* Albert Kesselring managed to evacuate most of his troops to mainland Italy. Still, Operation Husky delivered decisive results, shifting the strategic balance in the Mediterranean and critically weakening the Axis from within, as we shall later see.

Just days before Sicily was fully liberated, Bill Hayter resumed operational sorties in Bisley 'O', aircraft BB149, taking off at 1345 hrs on 14 August 1943. Accompanying him were F/Sgt D.L. Jeffery and Sgt S.W. Knight. Tasked with convoy escort, they returned safely to Blida at 1815 hrs.

Numbed by boredom, Hayter felt considerable relief knowing this would be his last sortie of any type with No. 13 Squadron. Records from the previous day list his marching orders: '*The following officers were detailed to No. 47 Squadron: F/O's HAYTER, EDWARDS, DIXON, ROSSNER, GRAHAM, BOND, UNWIN, HAYDEN and SMART.*'[7] An entry from just a few days earlier, on the 9th, shows that Unwin, Hayden, Smart, and two others had only just joined No. 13 Squadron – too recently, in fact, to have completed even a single orientation flight before being moved on.

No. 47 Squadron carried out dramatic 'hit-and-run' operations from Protville II aerodrome in northern Tunisia, built by US Army engineers during the Tunisia campaign. By July 1943, the squadron had upgraded from ageing Beauforts to the advanced Bristol Beaufighter Mk X, twin-engine heavy fighters famed for long range, high speed, and formidable armament: four .79in (20mm) Hispano Mk III cannon, six .303in (7.7mm) wing-mounted Brownings, and, if fitted, a .303in (7.7mm) Browning or Vickers K gun for the navigator/observer. It was arguably the most powerful fighter of its time. The TF variant – nicknamed 'Torbeau' – could even carry a 1,650lb (759kg) torpedo, greatly enhancing its maritime strike capability.

Impressive as that may sound, carrying a torpedo imposed serious drawbacks. Mounted beneath the fuselage, it slowed the aircraft, reduced manoeuvrability, and blocked the pilot's ventral escape hatch – limiting emergency egress to the hinged canopy. Torpedoes were effective only against large ships and useless against the smaller vessels that came to characterise Axis shipping as a result of attrition, particularly in the Aegean. Launching one required a straight, steady approach, leaving the Beaufighter highly vulnerable to flak and enemy aircraft. To mitigate this, strike formations had to include 'anti-flak' Beaufighters, which suppressed enemy defences and/or drew fire from the torpedo-armed aircraft.

Nonetheless, the transition to the Beaufighter must have been transformative for Bill Hayter. Its fighter-like cockpit, powerful performance, and heavy weaponry marked a dramatic upgrade from his experience in the Bisley and even the Boston. The Beaufighter's agility and firepower offered a completely different piloting experience – likely instilling Hayter with new confidence and effectiveness during operational sorties – a game-changer in ways that were not immediately obvious.

It did not take long for one of the new transfers to land himself in hot water – if that's the right kind of analogy for this kind of story.

Pilots F/O L. Rossner and P/O J.S. Hayden, already Bill Hayter's fast friends, were assigned to a ten-Beaufighter sweep along the Italian coast from Fiumara Grande to Porto Santo Stefano, then across Corsica from Bastia to south of Alistro. They took off from Protville II at 1105 hrs on 24 August 1943. One plane turned back with an oil leak; ten minutes later another fell out with engine trouble. The remaining eight pressed on. At 42º08'N, 11º36'E, two barges and a tugboat were spotted 5 miles offshore, heading south, with a schooner nearby and two probable destroyers hugging the coastline northbound.

Rossner and a wingman tore into the barges, their cannon blazing; one vessel's hatch blew open, '*flames shooting up*'. Hayden and two others strafed the schooner, their rounds ripping through the wooden deck, splinters flying and smoke billowing, leaving it '*sinking*'. Shore batteries erupted in response, forcing the pilots to weave, dive, and dodge the deadly bursts.

Then, out of nowhere, the last Beaufighter in the scattered formation encountered an Italian Reggiane Re.2001 Falco II head-on. The nimble fighter swung around and attacked, unleashing a torrent of machine gun fire from successive stern passes as the Beaufighter plummeted from 3,000ft (915m) in a desperate evasive dive. The trailing rounds spattered into the water as the Beaufighter pulled up at wave-top height. Splashes were '*observed under both wings*' as the aircraft jettisoned its torpedo to regain speed and agility, narrowly evading the final enemy burst before escaping.

Unknown to the others, Hayden had clipped the schooner's mast during his attack, damaging the wing and leaving him struggling to maintain control. He broke off toward North Africa, but safety would not come easily. As he and his navigator/observer, Sgt A.R. Cottle, limped home, two German Focke-Wulf Fw 190s appeared. Hayden pushed his battered Beaufighter to the limit, barely shaking off the fighters. With the aircraft failing, he was forced to ditch '*7 miles [11km] off Tunisian coast*'. Both men survived and were later rescued by a high-speed launch and taken to Bizerte.

However, the show was not quite over. At 1405 hrs, the remaining seven Beaufighters spotted another convoy at 42°10'N, 09°40'E – a medium-sized coastal freighter of 1,500–2,000 tons, accompanied by two small escort vessels heading north. They launched three torpedoes, '*one wake seen to run amidships, and one just astern*'. While no torpedo hits were confirmed, one Beaufighter struck the freighter's bridge with a five-second burst of cannon fire, '*resulting in numerous pieces of superstructure flying off followed by a large flash*'. Meanwhile, the other aircraft tore into the smaller ships with relentless cannon fire, leaving them '*in a sinking condition*'. With torpedoes and ammunition spent, and fuel running low, it was finally time to head home.[8]

On 25 August, No. 13 Squadron records proudly note: '*F/O HAYDEN, recently detached from No. 13 to No. 47 Squadron, was the subject of a lengthy paragraph in Stars and Stripes, describing a brilliant sortie carried out in a Beaufighter of No. 47 Squadron.*'[9] That Hayden had never actually flown for No. 13 Squadron seemed beside the point.

The article did, indeed, make front-page news in the American newspaper *Stars and Stripes*, *Algiers Daily*, on 26 August 1943:

> *Beaufighter Pilot Has Some Difficulty With A Schooner*
>
> ALLIED FORCE HEADQUARTERS, Aug 25 – Back safe in North Africa today after at least three close brushes with death were Flying Officer J.S. Hayden, of Townsill, Plymouth, and Sgt. A.R. Cottle, of Harrow, Middlesex, the pilot and navigator of an RAF Beaufighter which attacked an enemy schooner off the east coast of Italy near Rome yesterday.
>
> In pressing home a cannon attack on the enemy vessel, Hayden dived so low that his Beaufighter hit one of the ship's masts, which broke up and crashed on the deck. Immediately after, the schooner blew up and sank.
>
> Contact with the vessel's mast had damaged the RAF plane's starboard engine and undercarriage, so the pilot turned

> for home. During its limping return journey, the aircraft was jumped by two FW-109's [sic] which opened up fire but broke off the attack without doing any damage.
>
> Soon afterward, however, the Beaufighter conked out completely and Hayden and Cottle scrambled off it and onto their dinghy just as the plane sank beneath the waves. An American destroyer which had seen the British fighter in trouble sent out a boat to pick up the two airmen. Right now they are resting up, thankful to have been spared to fight another day.

There is no doubt that the Beaufighter's power and capabilities were considerable – and therein lay the problem, especially for less experienced pilots on the type. Its potential tempted them to push harder, but in the close quarters of shipping attacks, such daring often invited trouble. It had taken Hayden no more than ten days in his new squadron to learn this fact – the hard way.

Would his friend, Bill Hayter, also take heed?

Chapter 7

TARGETS OF OPPORTUNITY

Καιρὸς ἄφαντος εἰσέρχεται.
'Opportunity enters unseen.'
Heraclitus (c. 535–475 BCE)

At 1432 hrs on 2 September 1943, a formation of ten No. 47 Squadron Beaufighter Mk Xs took to the skies from Protville II in northern Tunisia, led by S/Ldr G.F. Powell, with P/O G. Terry as his navigator/observer. Among them was Bill Hayter, piloting Beaufighter 'Q', with F/Sgt D.L. Jeffery. Their mission brief was simple: strike any enemy vessels in their Mediterranean patrol area.

By late afternoon, reports came in of enemy destroyers and merchant ships near the Italian coast. At 1751 hrs, the squadron spotted a convoy – four vessels, including two unusually large landing craft – ploughing along at 5 knots on a bearing of 135°. From the cockpit of lead aircraft 'J', S/Ldr Powell took them for slow, vulnerable tankers.

As they closed in for the kill, Powell realised his mistake: shallow-draft landing craft, useless targets for torpedoes. He radioed to abort, but the message never reached the others.

Skimming the waves at just 50ft (15m) – referred to 'on the deck' or 'at naught feet' in RAF parlance – Hayter and the other aircrews struck hard, cannon blazing as they tore into the port beams, flames and smoke erupting from the vessels. But the assault quickly descended into chaos as the enemy unleashed a storm of defensive fire.

F/L J.R. Hastings and F/Sgt F.P. Hill in aircraft 'D' were hit – flames engulfed the plane as it spiralled like a fiery comet into the sea, a towering splash throwing water skyward. Moments later, Sgt R.A. Forbes in aircraft

'G' fought his burning starboard engine, black smoke trailing ominously. On the brink of disaster, he managed to ditch safely. Both he and his navigator, Sgt A. Dingwall, were soon bobbing on the surface in their Mae West life jackets,[1] but no self-deploying inflatable dinghy was in sight.

Under relentless fire, the remaining eight Beaufighters broke off and returned to base, leaving the fate of their comrades uncertain. Hayter touched down at around 2030 hrs, like the others. However, two men (possibly four) and two aircraft had been lost – a heavy price.

On 18 September at 1440 hrs, ten No. 47 Squadron Beaufighters took off for an anti-shipping mission east of Sardinia, led by W/Cdr J. Lee-Evans DFC. Soon afterwards, Sgt N. Hoiles and his navigator/observer, Sgt P.B. Cameron, ran into trouble: port engine failure forced them to turn back. Flying at just 75ft (23m) and struggling to maintain 135 knots (250km/h) on one engine, Hoiles wrestled with the controls, utterly exposed.

As if fate were mocking them, a Junkers Ju 88 appeared, passing directly in front and then alongside. Hoiles and Cameron watched in disbelief as the German aircraft waggled its wings and carried on east. The encounter only stiffened their resolve to get back. After all, it was a tale the boys back at base would never believe – even after a few drinks.

At 1630 hrs, disaster struck. Hoiles' remaining engine seized – suddenly upsetting the delicate balance he had fought so hard to maintain. The Beaufighter's wing dipped into the sea, and the aircraft cartwheeled violently and mercilessly across the surface. His next memories were confused. '*Pilot remembers nothing until he recovered consciousness amid debris. The dinghy was beside him, but his observer was missing.*'[2] Hoiles was rescued the next day drifting 50 miles (80km) north of Bizerte; Cameron was lost.

At 1700 hrs, the remaining Beaufighters spotted their targets – a merchant vessel and a supply ship – moving steadily through the water. With the sun behind them, they struck with full force. Pieces were seen '*flying off the bridge*', and '*two very large red flashes*'[3] erupted just below the funnel, followed by thick black smoke. The full results of the torpedo attack went unobserved amid the chaos.

Just three minutes after breaking off, calamity struck again. S/Ldr K. Painter reported engine trouble over the radio. He and F/O Glen-Davison had no choice but to ditch. The crew of another Beaufighter saw them climb into their dinghy, awaiting rescue, while the remaining aircraft turned for home.

Not all combat was 'equal', for want of a better word. On 23 September, four No. 39 Squadron Beaufighters, also based at Protville II, were sent to intercept ponderous transports ferrying men and equipment between Corsica and Italy. Two were flown by No. 47 Squadron crews. One No. 39 aircrew turned back with magneto trouble, leaving three Beaufighters to engage two Savoia-Marchetti SM.82 Marsupiales and four Junkers Ju 52s flying at 100ft (30m) above the water. The SM.82s carried a dorsal .51in (13mm) MG 131, but the Ju 52s were typically defenceless.

F/O J. Hayden of *Stars and Stripes* fame, with Sgt J. MacMaster as navigator/observer, attacked an SM.82 head-on; it '*burst into flames and crashed into the sea*'.[4] The remaining No. 39 crew, F/Sgt D.R. Jolly and F/Sgt P. Cordy, had their cannon jam on the first pass. They made no further attacks, suggesting their six wing-mounted .303in (7.7mm) Brownings had been previously removed to save weight and extend range.

Cannon fire from No. 47 Squadron's F/Sgt A. Woodfield, with P/O T. Miles, tore chunks from a Ju 52's tail and holed another's starboard wing. But it was not all one way: from hatches and fuselage windows of the lumbering transports, hand-held sub-machine guns rattled as desperate troops fired wildly as the Beaufighters slashed past like angry hornets.

No frequent flyer mileage points for them!

Soon afterwards, two Arado 196s were seen circling the wreck of Hayden's kill. The Beaufighters gave chase, firing bursts, but scored no hits. At 1640 hrs, six more Ju 52s appeared, flying even lower. Attacking head-on, the Beaufighters drew '*much return fire from all e/a [enemy aircraft]*'.[5] Woodfield struck again, setting a Ju 52's port engine ablaze and forcing a ditching. Ten minutes later another SM.82 was engaged, but it escaped.

The next day, another similar encounter by three No. 47 Squadron Beaufighters against twelve Ju 52s was complicated when they were intercepted by two Italian Re.2001 fighters, but no hits or losses on either side were recorded.

Bill Hayter did not take part in these particular combat operations. However, on 10 September he led the first of three No. 47 search-and-rescue missions – a task demanding a different set of skills. At 1600 hrs, he and F/Sgt D.L. Jeffery lifted off from Protville II in Beaufighter 'W'. Flying alongside was Hayter's close friend, F/O L. 'Ross' Rossner, with F/Sgt E. Levy in the rear seat. Their assignment: to escort a Catalina flying boat on an air-sea rescue west of the Straits of Bonifacio.

At 1700 hrs they rendezvoused with the Catalina from Sidi Ahmed and began the slow, tense search. Hours of scanning the endless sea yielded nothing – until, at 1950 hrs, a grim scene appeared: two rowing boats, four dinghies roped together, and three men clinging desperately to a block of wood. Oil fires burned on the waves, flickering like tiny beacons in the dusk.

The Catalina descended onto the rough waters as the Beaufighters wheeled overhead, keeping watch. One by one, the men were pulled from the block of wood, their faces drawn with exhaustion and relief. With survivors secured and fuel running low, Hayter and Rossner finally broke off and headed for base. Both Beaufighters touched down at 2135 hrs. Another mission would return for those still adrift – but for now, it was a quiet, meaningful victory.

Although Hayter and his squadron had only a broad, propaganda-tinged sense of events, they were about to be caught up in a rapidly shifting strategic drama.

Defeats in North Africa and the Soviet Union, and the bombing of mainland cities – Rome itself on 19 July – broke Italian morale. Strikes and protests over food shortages and war weariness swelled into a nationwide uprising that made Mussolini's downfall inevitable. On 25 July, after a secret Grand Council vote, King Victor Emmanuel III dismissed and arrested him, appointing Marshal Pietro Badoglio as prime minister. Though Italy remained nominally in the Axis camp, Badoglio opened clandestine talks with the Allies. The Battle of Sicily ended on 17 August with Allied victory. On 3 September Italy signed the Armistice of Cassibile, announced by Eisenhower on 8 September.

On 9 September 1943, shortly after returning from a stay at the White House, Churchill cabled General Wilson, Commander-in-Chief (C-in-C) of the Middle East (ME), with the often-quoted words: '*This is the time to play high. Improvise and dare!*', thus setting in motion Operation Accolade.[6]

First conceived earlier in the war and revived as Italy's surrender neared, Accolade aimed to seize *Rodos* (Rhodes) and the *Dodekanisa*

(Dodecanese). Churchill pushed it as a bold sequel to Sicily – securing the Eastern Mediterranean, strengthening British influence, and possibly drawing neutral Turkey into the war. He wrote: '*It seemed to me a rebuff to fortune not to pick up these treasures*,'[7] adding that controlling the Aegean and Dardanelles would create a naval shortcut to the Soviets and spare the perilous Arctic convoys.

Indeed, Italy's switch to the Allies made the islands briefly attainable – offering a Balkan springboard and disrupting Axis supply lines. But Washington had other priorities. Despite Churchill's repeated telegrams to President Franklin D. Roosevelt, the Americans were focused on Italy and Normandy, dismissing the Aegean as a sideshow. With the 'Rome or Rhodes?' question thus answered, Accolade was pared back, left to British dogged determination alone.

On 8 September, the Italian garrison on Megisti (Kastelorizo) surrendered to a British detachment and was soon reinforced by Allied ships and equipment. The next day, a covert British delegation led by Major (Maj.) George Jellicoe[8] parachuted into Rhodes to sway *Ammiraglio* (Adm.) Inigo Campioni and his 40,000-man garrison. But he was outfoxed by *Generalleutnant* (Lt Gen.) Ulrich Kleemann, whose 7,000-strong *Sturm-Division Rhodos* (Assault Division Rhodes) were already deployed in key positions around the island. They struck on 9 September, and by the 11th, Rhodes was in German hands; Jellicoe's desperate mission had failed.

Rhodes, keystone of the archipelago, had three airfields – giving the *Luftwaffe* local air superiority. Some 10,000 Italian Fascist loyalists still fought alongside the Germans, and Hitler, determined to protect his flank, rapidly reinforced the Aegean with aircraft and resources from other fronts. Undeterred, the British occupied several islands – including Kos, Samos, and Leros – and the pressing question soon became whether they could hold their fragile grip.

An answer was not long in coming. Kos, with its strategically vital airstrip, fell to German forces on 4 October 1943, after a swift amphibious and airborne assault code-named *Unternehmen Eisbär* (Operation Polar Bear), commanded by *Generalleutnant* Friedrich-Wilhelm Müller. Some 1,400 British personnel and roughly 3,500 Italians surrendered. Müller promptly executed 100 Italian officers for their betrayal of the Axis.

The repossession dealt a decisive blow to British ambitions, leaving Leros – the last major defensive outpost in the Aegean – seriously exposed. A desperate race ensued to hold off the German attack and maintain supply lines to the islands still in British hands. With the Royal Navy and RAF based in faraway North Africa and *Kypros* (Cyprus), success was far from certain.

Into this perilous situation was thrust No. 47 Squadron, ordered to redeploy from Tunisia to Gambut III, Cyrenaica, though temporarily operating from El Adem. The squadron's new Aegean hunting ground would prove deadly, with crews facing both enemy aircraft and intense anti-aircraft fire from heavily defended targets. Bold new tactics followed: Beaufighters now escorted American Mitchell B-25G gunships, each armed with a weapon of unprecedented size – a modified 2.94in (75mm) M4 tank cannon.

Sorties from Cyrenaica to the Cyclades[9] spanned some 350 nautical miles (650km), roughly two hours each way, under constant *Luftwaffe* threat from Rhodes, Crete, and airfields near *Athina* (Athens). German radar systems – Freya and Würzburg-Riese, remnants of which still exist on Milos – enabled early detection at 100 miles (160km) and precise fire control at 37 miles (60km), forcing RAF pilots to fly 'on the deck' for hours. Even a brief lapse in concentration could prove catastrophic.

Nonetheless, at such low altitudes, Beaufighters excelled as stealthy strike aircraft. Their air-cooled Hercules radial engines employed quieter sleeve valves instead of conventional poppet equivalents, reducing forward noise and providing a tactical edge. Widely used in the Pacific, they were reportedly dubbed 'Whispering Death' by the Japanese – though this name likely reflects Western press sensationalism, with no corroborating Japanese accounts.

No. 47 Squadron's first baptism of fire using the new tactics on 26 October 1943 proved intense. A pair of Beaufighters, piloted by Bill Hayter's close friends F/O J. Fletcher and F/O J.S. Hayden, with F/O T.E. Jones and Sgt L. Grimshaw as their respective navigators/observers, escorted three B-25Gs from the American 321st BG on an offensive sweep in the Aegean.[10]

Approaching the western tip of Amorgos, the B-25Gs prepared to strike a small enemy vessel but met fierce resistance from two Arado 196s and heavy flak, forcing them to break off. Later, the formation encountered three rare Ju 52 floatplanes, flanked by three more Arado 196s. Fletcher, in Beaufighter 'J', scored a hit on a Ju 52 at long range, but drew retaliatory fire that damaged his aircraft. A B-25G crewman later witnessed the Ju 52 crash spectacularly into the sea.

Hayden, piloting Beaufighter *'S' for Sugar*, also engaged but struggled with jammed cannon. The formation withdrew, heading for home. Remarkably, Fletcher set down his battered Beaufighter despite a burst tyre from the Arado's onslaught. While the aircraft was damaged on landing, both he and Jones suffered only minor injuries from splinter fragments.

The next two missions were flown without B-25Gs, including a notable encounter whose significance runs deeper than it first appears.

In the pre-dawn darkness of 29 October 1943, the British submarine HMS *Unsparing* (P55), commanded by Lt A.D. Piper DSC and two bars, RN, cruised on the surface west of Astypalaia (Stampalia). A slender crescent moon cast only a faint silver glow across the Aegean, leaving the waters cloaked in shadow – ideal for stealth. At 0227 hrs a darkened vessel appeared on bearing 220°, steaming east. As Piper closed the range, it became clear he had found a promising target.

Unsparing stalked to within 5,000–6,000 yards (4,500–5,500m). The target proved to be the *Ingeborg*, a 1,160-ton former French ship (*Sainte Martine*), escorted by the *Nioi*, a commandeered 60-ton Italian MS-class torpedo boat, and *KFK-3*, an armed fishing vessel. Several landing barges, laden with men and supplies were also in the convoy.

At 0447 hrs Piper commenced his attack. Four torpedoes surged from the tubes before *Unsparing* dived. Moments later a violent explosion shook the surface. Piper's log is laconic: '*One torpedo is thought to have hit the target. No counterattack followed.*'[11] In fact, *Ingeborg* sank with troops and materiel aboard, survivors left floundering at 36°33'N, 25°48'E.

Two vessels of *Küstenwachflottille Attika* (Coast Patrol Flotilla Attica), *GA-01* and *GA-54* under *Korvettenkapitän* (Lt Cdr) Brune, had just landed 77 men of the *SS-Polizeigebirgsjäger-Regiment 18* (SS Police Mountain Infantry Regiment 18) on Amorgos. Ordered to respond, they raced toward the wreck site to rescue survivors and hunt down the submarine. By dawn, *KFK-3* had reached Astypalaia with 111 rescued, though many remained adrift.

But Piper was not finished. At 1011 hrs *Unsparing* torpedoed *Nioi* as it was recovering further survivors. His log notes with brutal clarity: '*Fired one torpedo at an R-boat stopped to pick up survivors. It hit and disintegrated.*'[12] Almost at once four depth charges thundered, followed by two closer explosions – a landing craft's blind attempt at vengeance.

Then, at 1025 hrs, the drama intensified. Nine No. 47 Squadron Beaufighters swept in at wave-top height from the south-east – four carrying torpedoes, the rest in anti-flak roles – only to be met by three Arado 196 floatplanes.

F/O J. Dixon in Beaufighter 'W', with P/O G. Terry in the back seat, was the first to be hit. An Arado came head-on from below, its cannon shells smashing into their starboard engine. Flames engulfed the wing; the Beaufighter spiralled out of control and plunged into the sea in a towering plume, vanishing just 300 yards (270m) from the enemy ships.

The Torbeaus pressed on, skimming the surface and releasing their weapons. White trails knifed toward the convoy, but no immediate results followed. An explosion did erupt near the ships – whether a torpedo or Dixon's crash was unclear.

Beaufighter 'F', flown by F/O J.A. Unwin, with Sgt K. Farmer, was then attacked by another Arado. Unwin fired back, riddling it with machine gun rounds and forcing it down. Other Beaufighters strafed the escorts with cannon fire before breaking off under a storm of flak.

The relevant entry in the *Kriegstagebuch (KTB) der Seekriegsleitung, Operationsabteilung* (German Naval Staff War Diary, Operations Division) recorded: '*Eight [sic] torpedo bombers attacked a submarine-chaser group south of Amorgos with bombs, torpedoes and machine-guns. At the same time, torpedoes fired by the submarine were evaded. Two [sic] of the attacking planes were shot down.*'[13] The *KTB Kriegsmarine* (German Navy War Diary) reported, '*Five personnel seriously wounded by strafing fire.*'[14] Depth charges continued until 1034 hrs as the hunt raged.

But by then *Unsparing* was gone – silent and deep – leaving only wreckage, death, and confusion behind.

The near-simultaneous attack from sea and air was extraordinary. Allied submarines and aircraft seldom converged so closely, even by chance. Unaware of Piper below, the Beaufighter crews almost certainly distracted the Germans just long enough for *Unsparing* to slip away.

This mission proved a turning point for Bill Hayter and the other pilots in his close-knit circle, stirring realisations that weighed heavily that evening. For Hayter – already battle hardened despite his youth – it marked a profound shift. He now saw not only the immediate dangers of combat, but also the creeping emotional strain pressing on his friends. The camaraderie that once sustained them carried a darker burden – the knowledge that each mission might be their last. The illusion of invincibility, long upheld by deliberate denial, had cracked.

Worse still, they felt the pull of two irreconcilable forces: duty to the squadron and the primal instinct to survive. The urge to protect one another and complete the mission clashed with the creeping fear that any sortie could end in disaster. This inner conflict only deepened the strain, as each man wrestled with the tension between obligation and self-preservation.

Barely 24 hours after the loss of Dixon[15] and Terry,[16] Fletcher and Hayter stepped forward to volunteer once more. On 30 October 1943 they were tasked with escorting a pair of B-25G gunships on a strike against Naxos harbour.

But rather than hearing it through us, let Bill Hayter himself recount the events of that fateful day …

F/LT W.E.J. 'BILL' HAYTER WWII RAF PILOT

Preface

If Valour's best be gallantly to die,
Fortune to us of all men grant it now.
We set Freedom's crown on Hellas' brow,
Laboured, and here in ageless honour lie.

Simonidas, the Athenian Monument.[1]
Trans. W.C. Lawton

Chapter 8

PRELUDE

There is evil in the desert at night. In England, all things tell of a land at rest, but of a kind which lives and feels – for a little while everything is subdued and perfect, and it is then that one is most aware of the dreams and visions which make up the deep unravelled truths of existence. The dim outline of a tree against running clouds, the road that disappears before reaching the bend, and beyond it the distant lights of a town going out one by one until only a few are left as scattered sentinels against the dark; all these are comforting witnesses of a sleeping world. Even if one closes one's eyes, one can still be very conscious of life. All nature murmurs, occasionally to be interrupted by the hoot of an owl, the whistle of a train, or accompanied by the dismal moaning of the wind in the telephone wires. In the desert it is not so, for the desert is dead. Dead and vast and evil, and in that evil has madness. For all her brightness, men will turn away from the desert moon, subconsciously aware of the fact that she is staring down greedily on the land which is as dead as her own. Suddenly realizing the terrifying immensity of the loneliness, they will seek the company of their fellows, but should a dog be out when the light of the moon lies like a shroud across the sands, it will throw back its head to howl desperately at the eternal silence, and then will slink away dismayed at its sacrilege in the Garden of Death. No answer comes back from the desert, no echo, nothing.[2]

My bed faced the door, and above the door was a round window open to the sky. Through it the stars shone, and at first they seemed to bring a certain relief. 'Concentrate on them hard,' I thought, 'and maybe you will think less of other things.' They gave no comfort, no hope. They too were cold and dead and suddenly hateful, for everything within me cried out for warmth and life. Turning my face to the pillows I tried to force myself to sleep like the others. All I asked for now was forgetfulness. Somehow it seemed wrong that they could sleep now, even though hours had passed since we had blown out the light; but then they must be very tired, and also this awful thing had been going on for a long time, making it perhaps even worse for them, as they had seen the change gradual but inexorable, than for me, who that very day had been confronted with the fact in its entirety.

In the corner a match was struck, in a momentary dazzling, its flame casting uncouth swaying shadows as someone lit a cigarette. By the light I saw the others, and I saw too that they were not asleep. Not one of them was.

The man[3] who was in the bed next to mine passed me a cigarette without speaking a word, and I lit it without a thank you. The tension was almost unbearable, and I wanted to shout out to break it, like a dog or a madman, anything to break that awful mood. The night had no peace in it, it seemed to be hiding evil spirits, and outside the desert, bleak and cold and bare closed us in, stifling the mind. How hateful the desert was. Hateful for its immensity, for its passivity which could know no change and give us no comfort, but above all, hateful for its falseness: its very vastness, its never changing quiet undisturbed by man, even its overpowering listlessness seemed to promise rest, if not peace, but the sands had some power to change their own gifts, peace and rest, into the great mystery which they understand and which we call death.

Thus we lay that night, and none spoke, though the same thoughts were running through our minds. What could any of us say? We had all known them and loved them and we all knew that now they were dead. There was nothing to say about that. The world had become very unimportant without them, and I would not have minded being dead. If death were the only release from this, how welcome it would be. Only a sleep eternal in our eternal night. They had died far from here, out in the sunshine in one of Earth's loneliest places, and that at least made some difference. Out of the past came the memory of that place, of the island and the little bay with the mountains rising behind it, and of the happiness I had found there. Memories: of standing naked at the stern of the boat, the salt water running down my body, saying to myself 'I am really happy now, this moment will never be forgotten.' Closing the eyes, I had thanked God for life. Only a week had elapsed since then.

Sleep is impossible, but the numbness of the first shock was passing from my brain, and thoughts came more easily. There was even a certain comfort in looking back and wondering how it had all happened, where the beginning was and if this were the end. Wondering if there was a plan which had ordered it, or a reason for the selection of those who should live and of those who must die. Lew so boisterously alive, and Titch, who had feared death but had faced it. Fletch, who [was] glorified in fighting, and Dicky, who could not keep out of trouble, Tony and many others were all dead and three weeks previously they had been alive. It was just three weeks since we had come to the desert. I could remember my arrival well, and it almost made me smile.

Chapter 9

THE ROAD TO THE ISLES

The hood was open and it was cool where I was, with the air rushing by at over two hundred M.P.H., but below I could actually see the heat on the parched desert. I could see it in the thick haze, which lower down would throw images, tantalizing men dying of thirst with visions of cool pools of water surrounded with palm trees, where no water was, and where nothing grew. I could see it in the sunshine, pulsing in waves from its source, scorching with fingers of fire a wilderness which it had killed countless years before, angry to see life where it had decreed death. It was a heat almost liquid, thick, stifling, and irresistible.

Mercilessly, the sun beat down on the two seas beneath me, the sea of water and the sea of sand, water which could quench no thirst and land which could yield no food; and, overall and through all, was this menacing, destructive heat. Not a cloud nor a bird broke the endless monotony of blue sky.

Far away to my left, the line which divided sea from land curved like a snake to form a bay of sapphire blue, and in this bay, white as the scarcely moving surf which crept up to its seafront, lay the town of Tobruk. In its harbour, I could see a few motionless ships. Nothing stirred. No smoke rose from the chimneys of the little town to indicate that in those houses people lived, and none came from the funnels of the ships which linked it to the outside world. Both the town and the ships were dead. Had I gone nearer, I would have seen roofless houses and bomb-pitted streets, great craters which had once been homes, and piles of rubble slightly higher than the surrounding desolation where churches and mosques had stood and fallen side by side. There were no inhabitants left because there was nothing to inhabit.

The war had been very real for Tobruk. Once the scene of motor racing, it had become the trophy of a far grimmer race, changing hands many times as [the] Eighth Army and Afrika Korps fought for the honour of its possession.[1] In the contest, it had ceased to exist as a town, and in exchange for its destruction, it could show nothing within its limits but the graves of many of those who had fought over its battered remains. Completely destroyed it lay, a perfect symbol of war.

There was no glory in the ruins of Tobruk, and its wooden crosses had neither beauty nor the power to recall tales of heroism fast fading into oblivion. Already the desert had begun to cover them over. Blood and sweat, toil and tears there had been in plenty here, and for many, death too, coming in some cases like a release from a life which was no longer worth living.

Let people see Tobruk and they will need neither war nor war memorials.

To me that day, though, it looked like a town, and there was nothing to show that the town was no more real than the ships which seemed to float in its harbour, but which were actually submerged under water so clear that their every detail was visible, every detail except for the one that life had departed, leaving them as submerged wrecks in a pool of crystal, like flies enclosed forever in a piece of amber. It held a particular significance for me, because I had reached journey's end, and I was thinking more about rejoining my squadron than anything else.

They had left ahead, and I had followed them leisurely down from Tunis in the squadron Hurricane, a sweet aircraft to which we had absolutely no right and which the C.O.[2] was rumoured to have won at cards. Should anyone be so bold as to ask why we had it, he would be told that we needed an aircraft to practice fighter attacks with, which was true, but as it was completely incapable of keeping up with the Beaus, the excuse was not altogether valid. Personally, I would have classed it with dartboards and beer as 'comforts'.

I had flown over the mountains, petrol shortage forcing me to land at Gabes.[3] And from there on down the road, Montgomery's Road, on to Tripoli, and thence to Misurata,[4] where I had stopped the night. The squadron had once been stationed there and the Wing Officers invited me to a party. The food was good, the company congenial, and the drink somewhat excessive. In consequence, it was no surprise after leaving the table when someone suggested a song.

Now, in the desert, there were two very definite – I might say traditional – approaches to this matter, the one controlled by alcoholic refreshment, and the other by its lack. The officers and sergeants messes had drink, the airmen did not, which gave the last named a rather lugubrious outlook on life which, when translated into song, would invariably produce 'The End of a Perfect Day' and 'Nellie Dean' both sung as if at a funeral. The officers and sergeants, on the other hand, had a most colourful and varied assortment of doubtful ditties, and it was from there that we drew on this occasion. It was unfortunate, and we should have stuck to lemonade and Nellie Dean.

It had been quite gay until a devil-dodging M.O.[5] began to object to the songs we were singing on religious grounds. He objected strongly, feeling his soul enraged. The C.O. suggested that he should take his soul to the comparative safety of his tent, which seemed the best thing to do, but he preferred objecting.

After that, it became even more hilarious, but I felt annoyed with the man because it was so ridiculous. If he objected, nobody asked him to stay. But [by] staying, he was certainly responsible for any anti-religious feeling there was that night, and there was quite a lot of it.

{It is sanctimonious that devil dodgers like he who are largely responsible for the complete failure that the church has had in this war to give a popular lead.}

Leaving next morning from Misurata, I had gone to Marble Arch,[6] where I had signed my name in the book under George Formby's.[7] The desert seemed to be looking up! The great arch through which Mussolini was supposed to ride in triumph looms ugly and modern looking at the edge of the 'drome and [undecipherable] its great age, I enquired into its history. Hundreds of years ago, there was no official boundary between the Carthaginians and the Libyans,[8] so it was decided that each nation should send out a man walking from the two capital cities along the coast, and where they met the frontier would be placed. This was done, but the Carthaginian emissary was accused of cheating by his rival, and in his vehement protest of his innocence he said that if the Libyans believed that, they could bury him there alive. They did, and the arch was erected to commemorate him. Being a Carthaginian he had probably run all the way, and deserved everything he got, including the arch.

The next stage in my journey had taken me high up out of the desert to Cyrene,[9] 2,000 feet up behind the beautiful but precipitous Derna passes. A profusion of wild flowers grew in there amongst wild rocky hills, and an old Italian settlement had been taken over to lodge members of a Hurricane squadron. I had spent another night there, setting out early in the morning for El Adem,[10] where I believed the squadron to be. There I made a very bad mistake, because I shot the place up[11] (NAAFI gap),[12] and on landing found that 47 Squadron[13] was not there at all, but at Gambut[14] and, moreover, that the C.O. took a very poor view of pilots shooting up his 'drome. Without waiting to be asked, I jumped back into the Hurricane, and headed for Gambut, 30 miles away, and thus it was that I could see Tobruk slipping slowly behind me to my left.

There were two daylight torpedo squadrons operating over the Mediterranean and we had been moved down from Tunisia in a somewhat belated endeavour to restore a situation in the Aegean, which, with the fall of our last fighter base at Kos,[15] had become desperate. Just how hopeless it was, we were soon to find out.

The original idea of bypassing Crete, which was strongly garrisoned, and establishing a strong foothold amongst the lesser islands was sound enough; indeed it appeared easy for the garrisons were mostly Italian, and Italy had just surrendered. Germany, seeing the danger to the back door of Europe, reacted fast. A spineless garrison of Italians had surrendered Rhodes to them, and on Rhodes, as a fighter base, our whole strategy depended. The side which held Rhodes would have a superiority; having lost it, we should have withdrawn.

Instead, we went in to be massacred.

I had only been on the squadron for two months, but there were nine crews of us who had joined it together from Algiers, where we were on rest [from] searching [for] submarines, although we were all close support for bomber crews. We had jumped at the chance when volunteers had been called for, because we were fed up with the luxurious life at Algiers, devoid as it was of any excitement, and we also thought that our chance of getting home would be improved.

The squadron had had some losses since then, but our nine crews had remained intact and amongst us a very close friendship had sprung up. So that whenever possible, we would stay together. Our tents were grouped together, and if there was an expedition anywhere, together we would go. We even used to operate together whenever possible, and although our number prevents this completely, we used to split up into pairs. When one of us was in trouble, which happened not infrequently, like the time we pursued an Air Commodore down the Tunis road, making rude gestures at him from our '*gharri*',[16] then we were all in it. It was important in this particular instance that having realized that we had overstepped the mark, we attempted to use speed to escape the wrath to come, but were caught up.

This gave rise to the following:

> The name Sir Harold in dispatches for the speedsters that he catches!
>
> But blood is blood, and race is race, and so to save the squadron's face,
>
> We drew from stores some flashy gharris, that went faster than Sir Harry's.

{Such impromptu rhymes, though amusing enough in the course of conversation, fall rather flat in written narrative.}

When we were reported, but no further action came, this was added:

> We fear Sir Harold's time is passed, he's had a case dismissed at last!
>
> But blood is blood, and race is race, and so to save the S.P.s face,
>
> He's volunteered to form a flight, to track down bikes with no red light.

Morale was excellent, and we all took an intense and very sincere pride in being 47. It was not that we thought that 47 was the best squadron in the Middle East – from the C.O. to the last erk[17] – we knew it. We even had the best cat in the desert, a wild one which we had caught as a kitten, but that is another story.

The Beaufighter carries a crew of two and whereas all the pilots except for one were officers, most of our navigators were N.C.O.s.[18] Probably the most brilliant and certainly the most erratic of the pilots was the one N.C.O., Trevor Woodfield,[19] a very good friend of mine who had shot down four enemy aircraft. He and Lew Rossner[20] were, I think, the only two completely fearless men I have ever fought with.

The road beneath me curved somewhat, the land to its left tortured with the innumerable cuts of wadis, and to its right rose the ridge of Gambut. Beside the road was the single white blockhouse which was the only justification the place had for a name. There was not even a well there, and all water had to be brought in. Over to my right, a dense pall of dust hung motionless in the air, and towards this I headed. This dust was always present because a solitary aircraft taking off would render the 'drome practically invisible for half an hour. A solid row of Beaufighters marked the edge of the field, and beyond them were tents laid out in rows like a miniature town, the various messes indicated by the larger ones.

Without much difficulty I picked out the officers' mess and headed for it in a diving turn. When right down, I pushed the throttle forward, and went flashing down the alley between the two rows of tents towards it. I pulled back on the stick and shot over the flipping roof, rolled and turned back. A crowd gathered outside, and I repeated it, enjoying the exhibitionism.

Suddenly and completely without warning, a sand storm sprang up, cutting visibility down to about 150 yards. I had seen that the 'drome was clear, and so I came in to land, and settled down in a very reasonable landing. When the machine had reached the end of its run, I turned it back towards the dispersal. When I got over to that part of the field, it was free of sand, and one of the ground crew stood with his arms up, waving me in. About 50 yards away from where I was to leave the aircraft, its tail rose slowly into the air, and its propeller nosed over into the earth and broke. By a piece of rotten luck, both wheels had sunk into a soft spot at a time when there was a strong following wind. I switched off the engine and petrol, and climbed out, feeling shamefaced.

2,000 miles without incident followed by breaking the aircraft within 20 yards of dispersal.

I took my kit out, gave the Hurricane to the ground crew and walked up to the mess.

I was met there by F/O Rossner with the following remark: '*I hate your guts, Hayter!*'

His face was as stern as a judge's announcing a death sentence, but his eyes were full of merriment, and I could hardly restrain my laughter.

'*What's the matter, Ross?*' I said.

He looked me up and down with ferocity and contempt.

'*You have the nerve to stand there and say "What's the trouble?", you clueless clot. Observe my hollow laugh! I hate your guts because you've let me down. When you did that damn fool shoot up, everyone in 603 Squadron said you were mad, but I defended you, purely for the squadron's sake, and said that you could fly pretty-well everything, and now you do that? I've never been so mortified in my life*!' (Ross was like that, a born mimic, every time he spoke, one had to laugh.)

Together we went into the mess tent, where he had ordered me a meal, for it was well after lunchtime, and as I ate he told me of the few things which had happened to the squadron since they had left Tunisia. Our own ground party were coming up by road and were not expected to arrive for at least ten days, so we were living with 603 Squadron.

'*This place doesn't look so hot*,' I said untruthfully.

'*Well, actually, it's not so bad.*'

Ross was an optimist. '*We don't have grasshoppers to chew out our socks down here, nor spiders, nor beetles in the tents, and there's sport.*'

I was interested and slightly perturbed. '*Not chasing Air Commodores and making rude gestures at them again?*' Ross had his own ideas as to what constituted sport, and there had been that recent incident.

'*No, this is different. First you get a tin, then you look around your tent for a scorpion, put it inside, add seven or eight of the local man-eating ants of which you will find a superabundance here, and lay your bets.*'

I did not like this nonchalant attitude towards scorpions, even sporting ones, in the tent.

'*To turn from your sordid blood sports*,' I said, '*to a more elevated plane, I don't suppose that any of your lazy blighters have bothered to reserve me a tent?*'

Lew chuckled and told me to come and look. There was one old sickbay tent, and all my kit which I had been unable to get into the Hurricane was inside.

'There you are, complete with the red crosses. They're a bit small to protect you from your attack, but they may be of some use when Jimmy finds out what you've done to his Hurrybox.'

'Jimmy' was the C.O. behind his back.

'He's away now, but he'll be back. I'm in the next tent with Dicky,[21] *and the silly twerp is inventing a system of cooking breakfast without getting out of bed, so I'd better go and see if the tent has burned down.'*

The next two days were spent arranging our tents. The battle had swayed back and forth over Gambut, and debris from the fighting littered the desert as far as [the] eye could see. There were burned out tanks, and unused ammunition, either abandoned in haste, or left when no one remained alive to feed the guns. British and German helmets lay together in reeking slit trenches. Everything was confusion and waste. The remains of two armies where death had passed, and left to the abomination of desolation. By careful selection, we found much which we could put to good use as furniture: chairs from the seats of smashed vehicles, and tables from German telephone wire drums laid on their sides.

The squadron went up once into the Aegean on offensive patrol, bringing back some very beautiful photographs of the islands, but little else. They had met with very little of note, either in the way of opposition or of shipping to attack.

Then the weather broke. It began with a breath of air like a car's exhaust, and soon the sandstorm followed. From the mess we could see it coming. A cloud of sand obscuring the limitless horizon, and rushing towards us. As in the Bible, it grew from a cloud the size of a man's hand, but we could not run before it, nor was it to bring us needed rain. Behind us the haze and the endless sands stretched far away, and before us a wall of sand was steadily advancing, raised up by this parching hot wind from the desert, twisted into fantastic shades of black and brown, blown into ever changing shapes, as it eddied and twisted upwards, and came on towards the camp.

As a wave it hit the outlying tents, and swallowed them up, and then suddenly we were no longer looking at something about to happen. The cloud swept over us, and cut out the day. It came on us like night, but it was too sudden and too close for that. It was more like blindness, dark amidst the blaze of noon. For a short while, we could see the sun, a pale luminous disc, almost cut off, and then it too disappeared.

I have known sandstorms raised by strong winds which cut through everything. One can feel the grains of sand cutting into one's face, and one can see them rushing on. But in this case, the sand was so fine that it was part of the air, like smoke. We could not see from one end of the mess to the other, and slowly the sand began to cover everything. It was enveloping and all-penetrating, and anything which could not keep out the air, could neither keep out the sand.

Objects on the tables became mounds of sand, and as it got into one's hair it gave the curious illusion of a powdered wig, but the worst was the way it got into the eyes and the throat. If only we could have looked on as mere spectators, it would have been amusing seeing everyone being transformed into a sandman in a tent where everything would quickly lose shape in graves of different size.

Most of the jokes which are considered funny are about unpleasant things happening, but to others, and this was happening to us.

Towards evening, the wind dropped, and as suddenly as it had risen, the sand fell back to the ground, and it was light, and we could breathe once more. As much sand as possible we removed from our beds, but it was a pretty miserable night because we had no means of cleaning ourselves, and the sand had entered well and truly into our systems. It would not have been much use if we had been able to get rid of it, because next morning, and all through the next day, the sand blew up in undiminished clouds, stifling and choking, and we spluttered and cursed and ate our food as best we could.

Next day was clear, and it was spent in trying to clear up, the aircraft in particular. That was no easy job – the aircraft needing much attention, but they were ready for a sortie the following day.

The squadron went out in the morning, and when they came back, there were two crews missing, and Fletch[22] had shot down two enemy aircraft. The missing crews were 'Dicky' Dixon, the man who shared Ross' tent and cooked his breakfast in bed, and Arthur Unwin.[23] The reports on the attack were many and varied. '*Quot homines tot sententiae*,'[24] but it seemed that a ship had been attacked, and one aircraft had been seen to disappear around an island in flames, though which of the two it was, or what had become of it afterwards was not known.

Later on, we found out it was Dicky, with George Terry,[25] his observer.

For a full half hour after the others had landed, the sound of an engine in the distance had us all running out into the field, and soon after Arthur landed. We knew it was he before he touched down by the letter on his Beau. We went out to meet him and to hear his story, and I can remember the feeling of relief when I knew he was alright. Only it made it worse about Dicky, knowing that he had gone in a 'flamer'.

We would never have all lives in danger again by his mad inventions, or blush for his lack of tact.

There are two things which I will always remember about Dicky. The first of these is the system he had for outwitting the petrol commissioners in England by making a tank which fitted exactly into his gas mask bag with an auxiliary lead to his motor bike engine. This, in the days of coloured petrol, when one's tank was always liable to be examined, was brilliant.

The second incident made me furious at the time, but I couldn't help laughing. One day, we had gone out to see the remains of Carthage, and were having tea afterwards in the offices and sisters' club in Tunis, when Dicky walked in looking completely lost. He was wearing some strange uniform of his own design, and was rendered even more curious by the fact that he had no hair owing to an unfortunate misunderstanding with a barber.

Titch Hayden[26] shouted over to him: '*Why didn't you come out to Carthage with us, Dicky?*'

Everyone in the club was looking at him when he answered.

'*Why go out to Carthage to see the ruins when they come in here to tea every day?*'

Poor Arthur [Unwin],[27] he had the long loose limbs and slightly awkward gait of one who has outgrown his strength, coupled with one of the mildest and most generous natures I have ever met. He was always very meditating and quiet where the rest were gay and exuberant, but when he spoke it was always to say something pleasant. There was something about him which suggested books and playing fields as his right medium, not war, although he was as good as anyone at it. I think that Arthur would have looked just right at Cambridge.

When Death dealt so cruelly with the squadron, it had passed Arthur by, for a little while, and during that little while, something was born in him which had never been there before, he became an avenging Angel.

He said nothing to me about it, nor, for that matter, do I think that he confided in anyone, but the change in him was so noticeable in his actions and in his whole personality that I think everyone must have seen it.

Before, he had always been calculating, introspective, and completely undemonstrative, but afterwards, he became a man of incalculable and ever changing moods.

Although only a Flying Officer, he was also a Flight Commander, and at one time he and I used to lead the squadron on alternative sweeps, and if he saw nothing, he was very sullen, whereas if anything good happened, he would be a picture of exhilaration.

Arthur got us even with the Arados, and came back with a brief and memorable account of the action: '*Met 4 Arados. 2 shot down, two shot off.*'

It was obvious that he would not be able to continue at the pace at which he was going for long and live, and I think that he knew it too. I was not on the squadron when he died but I got news of it, and I think that V.C.s[28] have been won for less. Three times running, he led the squadron in to an attack on a harbour before turning for home, just in time to escape from the enemy fighters which had been signalled for. He would have got away with it, but a new crew on the squadron unfortunately lagged behind the rest, and the MEs jumped him. His position was desperate, even for an experienced pilot, and he called for help over the wireless, whereupon Arthur gave orders to the others to go home and turned to fight, and by doing so saved the other aircraft, and Arthur joined those whom he had given his life to Avenge.[29]

Greater love has no man than this.

That night, Ross came into my tent.

'*You'll have to take care of my things, Bill, now Dicky's gone.*'

Thus, we prepared for our own deaths.

It was the beginning of the end for most of us. Together, we walked over to the other side of the camp, where there was an ENSA[30] show. Ross was very cut up about Dicky. They had been together for a long time and he kept on reproaching himself for not having turned back to look for him.

'*He was such a helpless little blighter when I wasn't around to keep him out of trouble.*'

Keeping Dicky out of trouble had been a full-time job, which Ross had taken upon himself. The ENSA show was full up, and we walked back across the camp. We did not talk very much, for he was obviously very full of his own thoughts, and thinking that he would rather be alone, I left him at his tent, and continued to the mess.

He was a very great friend of mine, and I never saw him again.

Round a table in a corner of the tent a small group sat talking. Fletch, who was at the bar, asked me what I wanted, and I chose a Green Mamba, which consists of rum and crème de menthe.[31] I helped him to carry the glasses, and we sat down with the others. Titch Hayden, boyish and good looking, was serious for once, sipping his drink moodily, and deep in discussion with Duggy Smart,[32] his best friend. Tony Bond[33] and Nobby Greentree,[34] a New Zealander, were listening attentively.

'*You know that Dicky has nothing to do with it*,' said Titch. '*I've told you about it before, only it gets worse every day, and nothing can be done about it. If only there were just me, I'd resign my commission tomorrow and get out and be a coward, but I can't. If I did, I'd be yellow all my life, and someday I'd meet one of you chaps, and I couldn't face it. If I had a rest I'd get over it, but that's impossible now, in the middle of a campaign. I want to live, but I'm going to die, I know it. That's not a premonition or anything stupid, it's just that I can't pilot anymore. When I land it's just gravity and the grace of God.*

That's why I'm afraid. I no longer seem to be in control of the machine. Concentrating as I never did before I do things for which I would have been grounded before going solo. If I could control my hands, I might control my fear, and I can't sleep at night thinking about it!'[35]

They were the words of a brave man, and suddenly I felt deeply sorry for him. He had laid his soul open before us, as if for our judgement, and in so doing, he had torn aside the veil to let us gaze into a world which I, at least, could scarcely understand. Like all pilots I had been afraid, more often than many, but that was a passing fear in the presence of danger. I had scarcely fringed the terror of flight fantastic[36] and ever-present, as Titch knew it.

I, too, thought that he was going to die.

He went on; it seemed like a plea to justify himself in our eyes, as if our approval were terribly necessary and important to him.

'*I was no more frightened than any of you before, you know that. It was that awful attack. You know what happened, I went on firing far too long, right in to point blank range. It didn't frighten me, and then I hit the mast and crashed into the sea. Nothing has been the same since.*'[37]

Our impotence to help him struck us all, so whilst I brought another round of drinks, the others tried to distract his mind by talking of other things.

As it invariably happened in all discussions in the desert, when the hour draws on and the lights are low, conversation turned homewards and of what we would go back to. One talked longingly and fervently at these times, because home had become a religion, and it was good that it should be so: that the soul should look upwards towards the light, rather than forget and be enclosed in darkness. It did not matter that the light was a star of idealisation, from which the lies and truths, and pains had all equally been removed by separation whensoever they had been unpleasant, all making place for the one thing, the idea, the dream of perfection, built from the distorted memories of reality.

It was a pretty bedtime story which we pretended to ourselves to believe. That once we were home, we would always be happy, and never complain about anything again. Then people would begin to pass round photographs of their families which the others would effect a vast interest in, and someone would tell the latest saying of his little Pam, which no one but the teller was interested in either, and so it went on whenever a few drinks had made the heart expansive and the gregarious instinct of man had made him wish to confide in his friends.

The whole thing was ridiculous, sentimental and annoying, but it was strangely moving.

Home was so far, and the desert was very bare, so bare that it was only thus that echoes of things which we had loved long since and lost awhile could return in the cool of night to comfort and refresh.

Well we knew that our presence in the desert, that we hated so much, was necessary, and that someday, some happy day, when the bells of victory would sound, we would in some small measure have brought them nearer, but what we could not know, for we were not prophets, was which of us would ever hear them.

> Ah, I may not look back now, neither he turned nor stayed.
> But should I live, I'll seek her once that my vows are paid,
> And should I die, I'll haunt her, I being that God made.[38]

That is what England meant to us then. I have seen her since, in all the green loveliness of Spring, but of those eight crews which joined the squadron with me that August [1943], seven had been shot down within a few weeks.

Almost everybody went to bed fairly early, but Fletch and I sat up late, talking of life while we thought of death. Fletch was, of course, much pleased with his two kills, which had been confirmed by the other aircraft, and we had a drink to celebrate it.

Suddenly he said, '*Titch won't last long.*'

It was a plain statement of fact which required no answer. Fletch had been on the squadron longer than we. I liked him, but could not pretend to understand him, he was always a mystery man to us. He seemed to have no background. No one knew anything about his life prior to the arrival on the squadron, except that he was an exceptional shot, which we would have found out anyhow. There was something in his past which he never spoke. I wondered what it was.

Looking at him I tried to read something in his face, it was not the face of a boy just out of his teens as I knew him to be. His features were mobile, and his expression commanding, arched eyebrows and strong chin, the face of an aristocrat, but behind that air of authority, in his cold grey eyes lurked a hint of sadness, of suffering, almost of fear.

It seems ridiculous to mention fear in this connection with Fletch, for he loved fighting more than any pilot I have ever known, at least I think he did. He always volunteered for every op, every fighter he saw he attacked. His black wavy hair was already streaked with grey – something had brought that about. His was not a face one would forget easily or mistake in a crowd, but it was his hands that one looked at most common, the long, fine and sensitive hands of an artist.

'*Yes*,' I said, conscious of the fact that I had been staring. '*I think that Titch is going to die. If only his spirit were weaker, he'd crack, and the swine at base would sling him out for lack of moral fibre, but it's as strong as steel. There's nothing else to keep him going.*'

Fletch went on very quietly, almost as if he were talking to himself. '*Something terrible is going on inside him. There should be a certain fulfilment in dying now, at a time when death seems so far more important than ever life would afterwards. Inside, we all see ourselves as little tin heroes to a certain extent, and the natural fulfilment of heroism is death.*

To die now would be the best thing which could happen to us, still dreaming our dreams and believing in our fairy tales, but it's different for Titch because he only sees the foulness of it.'

'*We are misfits really,*' he continued. '*The world doesn't want us, in fact will be a damn nuisance to it afterwards. We won't belong, and we won't be satisfied. You see we haven't the delightful simplicity and tolerance of the erk, and we have seen too much – people will talk about wasted years, the fools, but this has been concentrated life. The wasted years are yet to come, the boredom, the mediocrity, and the search for security. If we could die now, be killed suddenly and painlessly in action, then we would at least miss the awful delusion, the frustration, and bitterness which are what we shall get from this war.*'

For the second time that night I thought that I had been listening to someone who had not long to live. Whatever fear lay hidden in Fletch's eyes was not the fear of death. Silently, I wondered why he wanted to die. It was certainly not merely for the reasons he had given. There was something very frightening in what I had heard. What had brought about this talk of Death, this morbid introspection so alien to the squadron? It had never happened before. Death could not be driven entirely from the back of the mind, but there it would be left, a skeleton in the cupboard to which no reference was made. Was there some meaning in it, some prophetic glimmering of a calamity to come?

There was something revolting in such a thought. Whatever may be ahead, however disastrous it may be, it is given to us to remain in ignorance of it until the predetermined hour is come.

We said goodnight – it should have been 'goodbye'.

30 October 1943

The next day dawned, clear and sunny. It was the 30th of October. The squadron was standing by for a shipping strike. Down in the briefing room, the crews at readiness were waiting to go, smoking the eternal last cigarette, cracking jokes, and checking up on charts and photographs. The navigators, always more conscious of their own importance on these occasions than the pilots, also looked more serious as they placed their carefully folded maps into their bags, or stuck them into the top of their flying boots. The C.O.

had just finished speaking, and intelligence, met [meteorology], and signals officers were flitting around amongst the crews like bees buzzing from flower to flower, efficient but worried in case anything had been missed. It was a scene I knew well, unchanged and therefore reassuring.

Gone were the misgivings of the night before. Outside the aircraft were drawn up in a thick line, their torpedoes slung underneath. We had already put our parachutes and dinghies inside them, and we wore our Mae Wests.

There was much laughter as jokes broke the inevitable pre-takeoff tension. The heterogeneous assortment of dress was amusing. No two seem to be wearing the same mixture of tropical and flying clothing. Here a navigator with flying coat and gloves would be in earnest consultation with his pilot whose open necked shirt and rolled up sleeves would be adorned with a magnificently coloured silk scarf, their maps and bare knees would protrude from the same pair of heavy flying boots. Amongst us the C.O. moved from group to group, helping and giving advice.

The telephone rang, and we all moved towards the door, thinking that it was the signal to go. The C.O. answered it and then turned towards us.

'*Sorry chaps, you've had it. The recce kite hasn't made any sighting in the open sea, but we may want two crews later. Who wants to go?*'

Fletch was easily first, and several crews gathered behind him. As I had not yet operated in the Aegean, I was also chosen.

At about twelve, it was decided to send out a small force which consisted of two American Mitchells armed with 75mm cannon, and two Beaufighters. We did not take off until after lunch, but when we did, it was in a great hurry because of a last moment change of aircraft brought about by the fact that we were to make our attack in a harbour where the water was too shallow for the use of torpedoes, and as there was very little time, we just took the parachutes which were in them.

Personally, I never used to carry a parachute, because it seemed unnecessary, or rather futile when operating at a low level over water, and carried a cushion instead, but I had no time to go to look for it.

As navigator, I had a W/O from 603 Squadron called Tom Harper, because my own one, Jeff,[39] was in Hospital with jaundice at Benghazi. Tom had lost his own pilot, and he volunteered to come, although he had never done a shipping beat.

Wing Commander Lee-Evans, our C.O., drove us down to briefing with the American crews. It was rather a cursory affair, but we learned that our target was to be shipping in Naxos harbour, from a low level using cannon. The Americans were to lead, and Fletch was to be on the right, whereas Tom and I were to take the left. We went out to the aircraft as fast as possible, and the C.O. told me not to take any unnecessary risks, if it should look too 'sticky', because the previous day had shown us that conditions in the Aegean were not too easy.

It was about 2 o'clock when we jumped into the aircraft. Its letter was 'S' and it was about the oldest one in the squadron, without feathering props. My goggles, or rather Duggy Smart's ones, broke when I tried to put them on, and so I had to go without them, which very nearly cost us our lives. The straps I was not satisfied with, and so tightened them, and also strapped on the chute.

Already, the others were starting up. Methodical glance around the cockpit, petrol, brakes, flaps – everything as it should be and I pressed the starter. A cough, a preliminary splutter, and soon both engines were purring evenly. The ground crew had already done the running up, and after calling Tom and the other aircraft on the wireless, we were ready to go.

Waving away the chocks we started to taxi. The C.O. was waiting at the wingtip, he waved and then stood there watching, immobile. Unless he was leading, he always stood on the field, proudly watching his squadron taking off until the last machine had disappeared into the distance. He was a very fine C.O. a great leader and a friend to all.

A few days afterwards, he was shot down off Greece.[40]

As always happened at Gambut, a great cloud of dust rose behind the taxiing aircraft and lay still in the thick afternoon air.

We cleared our engines, and then the two Mitchells took off, and then Fletch, and then I, going fast in an endeavour to keep away from the ever growing sandstorm the others were throwing up behind them. In close formation, the Mitchells turned off to the left, heading out to sea, over the ridge and past the famous blockhouse. As soon as we had crossed the coast, the formation settled down, the two Americans very close to each other, and the Beaus at a comfortable distance on the wings. We began to lose altitude, levelling up at about 50 feet from the water, tested the guns, and set course northwards towards Crete and the Aegean isles.[41]

Chapter 10

THE ISLES OF GREECE

The day was warm and sunny, with a tendency towards unreality and drowsiness, and the water rushing by at great speed held some strange hypnotic fascination, as if the sky and the sea had conspired to drive us to sleep. Tom was doing check navigation for the Mitchells were leading, and occasionally he would take a drift, which is very easy over water when one is low.

At last, faintly as through a mist, the great mountains of Crete towered on the horizon, rising high out of the sea to our left, still at a great distance. The cannon sight, which was rather a cumbersome obstruction to normal flying, had to be fixed, and we tightened up the formation. Slowly, very slowly, we could see the enemy coast getting nearer, looking very beautiful as sunshine and cloud blended their soft tones about it, changing its substance from the delicate, almost diaphanous blue which had first greeted our eyes to the great immovable masses of greens and browns and purples that were fields, hills and mountains from close up. It was rather thrilling to know that those very hills and mountains gave refuge to hundreds of our men who still fought on years after the Germans had conquered the island.[1]

We turned parallel to the coast about five miles off shore in order to pass through the narrow straits between Crete and the isle of Kaso, the only low level route practical for us. Time dragged interminably now and we seemed to be in very close to Crete. From the air, if objects like houses cannot be clearly seen distances appear far smaller than they really are. We knew that the enemy would beware of our presence, for he had radio location posts[2] in the area, we knew, and he might send up fighters from Heraklion [Crete] to intercept us. The expectation of meeting fighters always acted as a brake on time. Should we meet none on the way in, then we could expect them on the way out. '*Facilis descensus Averno!*'[3]

As it happened, Tom and I were not worried by them on the way out, because when we left, we went by sea and we went by night.

Through the Straits, then we flew, and Crete was left behind, although for long its massive skyline of blue towered like a fortress wall protecting the little isles from the assaults of the open sea.

Once I stepped from the desert through a gate into a garden of enchantment and stood breathless, struck as much by the contrast as by the loveliness of the sight. It was as if I had taken the wrong turning off that long, glaring, dusty road, and it had led me to heaven. Indeed, the place was called the Garden of Allah. There was this same feeling when first we passed through the Kaso Straits into the isle-spangled waters of the Aegean. All around they lay, bathed in that inland sea, innumerable. Lovely in their gentleness, majestic for their antiquity.

> The Isles of Greece, the Isles of Greece, where burning Sappho
> loved and sung,
> Where grew the arts of war and peace, where Delos rose, and
> Phoebus sprung![4]

Some were just small bare rocks, uninhabited and gaunt, deserted now by the sinister sirens they had served so well, but still conjuring up pictures of the great days of Ulysses and shipwrecks of old. Others were white, like sails on an azure sea, while others still showed touches of green against their rugged backgrounds of dark rock. Happily, they had crept out of the sea, to lie still in the evening sun. From the water's edge, their slopes were almost sheer, except for where some mountain stream would find its estuary, after winding down in waterfalls from the high hills. Small villages would rest there, their white houses borrowed from the past. To their backs the hills climbed away in terraces, and before them were tiny harbours where lazy caïques slumbered, their white sails drooping, content that no breath disturbed their quiet repose.

The Mitchells altered course again, turning towards the left. To our right now lay the red volcanic island of Santorini. It was rather larger than the rest, and at its southernmost point was a great rock, perfectly white. In complete isolation, a monastery was perched upon it, far above us.

That narrow gap between Kaso and Crete might have been a gateway through which one could enter into the past. Everything looked as if it had come from an age long since lost in oblivion, a magic age of fantasy, half familiar and half mystery, an age of beauty and strange names belonging to a fairy tale which turns out to be true. It was as if the isles had slept for countless years whilst change went on around them, to awaken fresh and lovely in an era which was not their own. Nothing there belonged to the 20th century. It was too calm, too serene and, above all, too unhurried for that. No, to the past it belonged, and with it the past had remained. Here, if one bothered to measure them, the story of the years would surely be of what one could get out of them, not of what they can be made to contain.

Apollo's temple still crowns the isle of Delos, and Paros marble[5] still awaits the master touch of a new Praxiteles.[6] Nothing has changed. True, Demeter has now become the Virgin[7] and carousing Dionysius,[8] turned respectable is now known as St Dionysius, but he is a jovial saint inclined to be lenient if his feast day is celebrated as of old with Santorini wine.

This was my first trip into the Aegean, and it impressed strangely and very deeply. So deep was the feeling that it bore precedence in my mind over the attack which was due to take place in a bare ten minutes. I longed to be able to leave the formation and to have nothing to distract my admiration.

This had only happened to me once before, up in Tunisia, looking down at the mountains growing out of the green plain with the sea behind, and it has never happened since. It is a very wonderful feeling, as if some deep exaltation rushed through the veins, a feeling of almost mystic elation. It is a great and very wonderful thing when in danger of Death to realize the wonder and the beauty of Life; to see the eternal greatness of nature dwarfing man and all mortality to their true perspective, and yet being a man, to feel unconquerable and unafraid:

> And life is colour, and warmth, and light, and a striving evermore for these,
>
> And he is dead who will not fight, and who dies fighting has increase.[9]

Death there would not have mattered, for the place is eternal, and to die there would mean being absorbed into eternity.

I looked out beyond the wing tip, past the two Mitchells, to where the other Beau lagged slightly behind, as if reluctant to hurry. Fletch understood this feeling, it was with him every time he went out to fight. He had even tried to explain it to me the night before, but I had looked for some other underlying reason for his words. How had he expressed it? '*Concentrated life ... a certain fulfilment in death now.*' There had been an emphasis on the 'now' which had eluded me. Yes, Fletch understood, and he also understood that the mood must pass. There had been a note of urgency in his voice as insistent as the old message of the sundial: 'It is later than you think'. His argument had not been that he wanted to die, but that he wanted to choose his own death, climbing upwards at the zenith of his endeavour, or as he had said, '*dreaming our dreams and believing in fairy tales*'. Time was short for that, and soon the chance would be gone, leaving the frustration and the mediocrity of a life which must be lived to the end, a tedious soul-destroying existence holding nothing to fight for, no great obstacles to overcome, a long, weary, admission of defeat for a tin hero who had seen too much.

And I now agree. If only one could choose one's own death, how successful one's existence would have been! Our stay on earth is so short, and greatness only appears in man when he has much to strive for, and great obstacles to overcome, and so surely if he can die at the zenith of his endeavour, his is the greatest merit in whatever comes after. How incomparably preferable is such a Death to a life of mediocrity with nothing to fight for, or to the horrible frustration of having nothing to fight with. Herein lies true defeat.

Our little force was now approaching the Cyclades, so called because the isles form a circle around Delos, the sacred isle of Apollo. It was in this group of islands which Naxos, our target, lay. Shortly afterwards, we were running up its westerly coastline, and we closed in to prepare for the attack. My own position on the left wing was very unfavourable, as the land was to the right and there is very little latitude for manoeuvre in a harbour. In consequence, I changed position to the extreme starboard, about 200 yards behind Fletch. This move put us in echelon starboard, allowing the two Mitchells to go in first with their 75mm cannon.

A small jetty stretched out to sea from a headland in front of us, and near it a few caïques lay at anchor. Judging that this must be the harbour, the order came to attack. The plan was obvious. From the headland we would have protection until we were right inside the harbour, and after that, each for himself, we would endeavour to do the maximum of damage, counting on surprise. As we would be attacking at point blank range, surprise was the most important factor. One by one the noses of the other aircraft lifted for the headland and they disappeared from sight, like sheep jumping over a stile, and I followed, as I thought, into the harbour.

Alas for our calculations! The harbour was still about five miles off, and instead of water on the other side, there was land, little gardens in which men were working. So much then for our hopes of making a surprise attack.

Some of the Greeks stood up and waved their hats at us, great round Mexican looking things made of straw, whilst others threw themselves on the ground because we were so low. One of them, I can still see now, as he threw down his hoe and sprinted for a hedge which he leapt under, though what protection he expected from it would be hard to imagine. It all seemed rather amusing. The little gardens were so tiny and so beautifully kept that they looked absurdly fake, as if they had been taken directly from a Walt Disney film. I wagged my wing at the inhabitants by way of greetings, and wondered what they thought of this mad Englishman.

The land flashed by, and then the sea as we crossed another tiny bay with the ground rising around it and there was the harbour. That it was the harbour at last was evident before I actually saw it because streams of tracer were shooting up behind the hill. The others had already started to stir up trouble. The surroundings for the moment no longer looked beautiful nor did they in any way give a feeling of peace. Violently we started to weave, the aircraft giving perfect response to the controls as she was thrown from side to side, and down almost to the ground and up to about a hundred feet. We did not want to be caught like Paddy Finucane[10] by some chance bullet.

Hill and headland disappeared behind us as if they had never been, and we were in the harbour.

It looked very big, and over to the right in front of us was a small town. To the left a long jetty stretched out to sea. There were several ships in the port, and we were heading straight towards the largest one which lay in close to the town. There were also some Arado fighters, a motley array of caïques, schooners, and fishing smacks. The other ships were mostly moored near the jetty, and it was these that the Americans and Fletch were attacking, and the anti-aircraft defences were concentrating on them. Fletch's Beaufighter broke away hard to port, and the Mitchell immediately in front of him dived headlong into the sea at full speed. The pilot must have been killed or the controls irretrievably damaged, for no attempt was made to ditch, and it seemed almost impossible that anyone could have survived the awful impact. It transpired later that the whole crew were killed. All this I saw in a flash as I set my sights on the ship which lay before me, and then Tom and I had the harbour to ourselves.

I pressed the cannon button, noting with satisfaction the rhythmic thumping of the four guns beneath me. The ship looked like a destroyer, a menacing black shape outlining the flashes of its defences, and thin, hose like lines of deadly trace rushing from it towards us. Our position was almost perfect for an attack, because we were going straight down it from stern to bow, and judged that I could rake its decks without it being able to bring all its guns to bear on us. Having once assessed its range with accuracy, we stood a very fair chance of shooting it out with the gun crews. In consequence, I stopped waving and took no evasive action, nor did I fire in bursts but held my thumb hard down on the trigger so as not to waste a single second of shooting time. Straight towards her we went, all our cannon blazing continuously. The cabin filled with acrid fumes from the spent ammunition, but ahead could be seen flash after flash from the deck and superstructure of the ship, and no splashes in the water, which told that every shell was hitting the mark.

Slowly, slowly we seemed to move towards our target, and now, finally, I could see tracer coming towards us from the left and the right. We were hemmed in by fire, and there was no direction for a breakaway excepting straight ahead. The other ships and the shore batteries were all now shooting us alone. Slow lazy traces curled towards us, seeming suddenly to accelerate and flash by, red and deadly, but still we have a charmed life, and the return fire from the ship we were attaching had, I believe, been silenced. Tom had manned the machine gun in the back, but it was not very much use as an antidote to all the flak coming up from the sides. Then, at last, we saw some results from our fire, as explosions shook the ship, and flames leapt up from her decks. These explosions were reported by the other crews when they got back.

Suddenly, we were almost on top of the burning ship. For a split second I feared having waited too long to pull the nose up to avoid her mast. Violently, I heaved back the stick, opening the throttles fully, and we soared like a bird, and it was not until then that we were hit, not seriously at any rate. It must have been just at this moment that Fletch saw us for the last time, because he reported that the last he had seen us was in a steep climb, as if we were trying to make cloud.

Repeated jars made the whole aircraft shudder, and I feared that she might disintegrate. Whether it was some forward gun position on the ship we were attacking, which had been protected by the superstructure, the other ships, or the shore batteries that hit us, I don't know, nor did I very much care. At this time, I cared not at all. It was enough to know that we had been hit badly, perhaps too badly, for us to do anything towards saving our lives.

The aircraft itself was doomed. Tom called me up to say that we had been hit in the wing. Thank God the intercom was still working! I looked out and saw a jagged hole right through from bottom to top where the main petrol tank had been. Heavens knows why she had not caught fire. The petrol had already streamed out to form a great cloud behind us. A quick glance at the instruments showed the port oil pressure at zero. That meant an engine that would seize up and stop at any moment and we didn't even have feathering props. It would not have helped us if we had, for worst of all was the fact that all my strength, and one has a lot in an emergency, was needed to hold up the nose fighting its desire to plunge headlong into the sea. The trim, which was the only thing which could help me, I had already put on instinctively.

Such was our plight as we passed over a jetty and out of the harbour. One thing I know, and that was that the port engine would stop in a matter of seconds, with neither petrol nor oil, and that with one engine gone, no pilot could possibly control the stricken plane. *'S' for Sugar* had met her fate, an Aegean graveyard, and it was up to me to prevent Tom and me from going down with her.

I told Tom to prepare for an immediate ditching. We were far too low to bail out. Also, I apologised to him for having put him in such a mess, because even in a normal ditching with the aircraft under full control, it may easily happen that the whole crew will not get out. He was absolutely admirable about it, and appeared to be completely unperturbed. His only remark was that it had been a very good attack. Rather a remarkable thing to say under the circumstances, and I was very grateful to him for saying it. Our condition was my fault in a way, but the attack was my excuse.

We passed over a fishing boat, a medium-sized schooner used by the Germans for communication with a port that they held on the northern tip of the island. At the time, I thought that it was a Greek caique, which was a pity because it was right in our line of fire, and we would have had the almost certainly unique experience of sinking an enemy ship in the condition we were in. We turned to starboard, following the curving coast, and I told Tom to brace himself in preparation for the coming impact when we hit the water.[11]

All of this has taken some time to relate, but it could not have been more than a minute from the time that we entered the harbour to the time when we plunged into the sea. The place where we came down was only about two miles from the port.[12] The longest two miles that I have ever covered, as I used all my strength to pull back that stick on which our lives depended. Had I not adjusted the straps before takeoff, it would have now been too late. Apart from that, there was very little which could be done, except for turning the gun sight to one side, so that my head would be clear of it when the shock came. Also, I remembered Titch Hayden, who had made a good ditching,[13] saying that it was advisable to put one's head to the left, where there was a maximum amount of clearance. Then I did something which may have saved my life, for it gave me a clear passage out of the aircraft, but which also very nearly killed us both.

Just as I was levelling the aircraft above the water, with both engines throttled back, I opened the emergency release above my head. The result was wholly unexpected. As I have already mentioned, my goggles had broken and the sudden rush of wind over the open escape hatch lifted the sand which had been blown into the aircraft in the earlier storm, blinding me at the one crucial moment when life depended on the precise judgement of the eye. It was only with the greatest efforts that could I keep my eyes open at all, and I shouted to Tom to hang on, wondering if maybe the hatch could be closed. I looked up and saw the door still hanging on by its broken hinges and retaining wire, bent and twisted out of shape. Closing it would be a hopeless proposition, and any second we were going to hit the water.

'S' for Sugar lurched and fell, taking the final decision herself. The nose dipped violently, as all control departed from the now useless stick. After this, events were so rapid and unforeseeable that it would be very hard to describe them with exactitude.

As we hit the sea in a nose-down position the shock of impact was shattering. It was rendered even more so by the fact that we were travelling considerably above our stalling speed, probably somewhere in the region of 125 M.P.H. Had we been level, the aircraft would inevitably have bounced. One moment we were flying, and the next a violent crash faded away almost as quickly as it had come into stillness and silence, as if Death had already set it. Both engines had, of course, stopped, leaving an uncanny, eerie quiet, the sudden cessation of tumultuous fear laden clamour and strife, the quiet of eternal night.

For a brief instant I felt dazed, motionless. Glancing around the cockpit I could see the water creeping up fast over the instruments, then I was under water, and it was getting dark. Going under I cannot remember. The shock of impact should have stunned me, that it did not can only be attributed to the subconscious instinct of self-preservation, for the stimulus of fear was entirely lacking. This is quite unaccountable, for I have often been frightened, never for a better reason. As it was, I merely felt dazed. That it was the end I felt sure, and I accepted it calmly and dispassionately, without any great interest or regret. So intent had my mind been on the leading necessity of the moment, which had been the ditching, that it did not immediately switch over to focus itself onto the new essential of getting out. I had no doubt that I was going to die, but I did not react. Instead it relaxed as if a straining task were at last ended. It was like being under morphia.[14] I was about to die, and yet I could not think about it, for I was elsewhere, and though conscious hardly interested. Maybe in wonderful kindness nature can give detachment to the dying to soothe their last moments when comes the realization of Death.

Then, in a flash, came fear, overpowering the lethargy of resignation, and I was fighting, with all the force and energy of body and mind which I possessed, fighting for my life. One can fight hard when all must be gambled on a slender chance, and the idea of losing does not exist.

The brain's only thoughts are of means to an end, not of the consequences of failure. I looked back towards Tom's compartment, and there was air. I thrust my head eagerly towards it, but already the water had risen too high. I held my breath as all around me the cabin grew darker, it was almost black now. My last recollection within that sinking hull which had once been the gift of flight is of pulling the pin which held the straps around me, and getting up to go. That is all I can remember as, with bursting lungs, I left, and I cannot say which way I got out. On looking back on it afterwards, I thought it was through Tom's exit, which seems almost impossible, but I had the strength of ten men then.

One more memory sticks in my mind from those seconds under water when Death was so near, and that is of looking upwards as if I were looking from the bottom of a well, deep and tenebrous, towards the light and hope of the air above. It had to be reached, and I must not take a breath. Frantically, I began to swim, only prevented from breathing in the salt water by an agonizing effort of will. In my chest was a throb like the intermittent touch of a red-hot iron and every time it came, it seemed to shout out 'Don't breathe, don't breathe, don't breathe!' My eyes had closed tight, and I had very nearly lost consciousness. How I managed it without taking a breath I will never know. Some might say luck, some providence, and some God, but suddenly I was out, my head was above water, and into my empty lungs I gulped the precious air of Life. Never was nectar more divine than the clear air which lay over the murderous deep.

As I opened my eyes and looked around, the most wonderful sight I have ever seen greeted my eyes. There, not ten yards from where I was spluttering and kicking, was our dinghy, and Tom was in it. Of *'S' for Sugar*, nothing was left, no floating wreckage, no oil, nothing. Later on, Tom told me that the dinghy had been released automatically and after he had got into it, he had looked around for me, and when for a time he saw nothing, he thought that I must have gone. A feeling of complete exhaustion came over me, and I nearly fainted. Tom caught me and held me up, for I had no strength, and he told me to remove my parachute, which I had forgotten to do. He helped me into the dinghy, and I lay there panting and sick, weak as a child. All I could say was '*God, but we're lucky!*' and repeated it over again, '*God, but we're lucky! God, but we're lucky!*'

Poor Tom, he had not fared too well in the ditching, for a great ragged cut from his lip to his chin showed where his teeth had once been, the flesh gaping open horribly so that he could scarcely talk, and one of his fingers had been almost severed. That I too had been wounded I knew not, for I was past feeling pain. Only exhaustion and the desire to be sick remained. No, that is not quite true, there was also the overflowing thankfulness for our escape. It may sound strange to feel nausea and gratitude simultaneously, but that is how it was.

Tom was marvellous. Everything which could be done in the dinghy he had attended to, and he passed me a paddle. We were only about 200 yards from the shore, a barren desolate coast which rose like a battlement from the sea, a few outlying rocks between it and our dinghy. Just before ditching we had flown past a valley, which would have been far more suitable as a landing place than these sheer cliffs and cutting rocks which could so easily sink our fragile craft, and towards it we began to paddle, at least Tom did, for all I could do was to lean against the side of the dinghy flapping my paddle in the water. We made good progress, but could see no signs of life at all from the island. This was a good sign, because we would be able to contact people easily enough in our own good time, carefully approaching someone whom we thought we could trust, whereas an immediate chance meeting might prove disastrous.

A strong current must have dragged us inshore, because though we were fast approaching land, we were getting no nearer to the mouth of the valley. Soon the dinghy was very near a great jagged rock just off the coast, and the waves were throwing us up and down in a most alarming fashion. We were unable to control the dinghy, and it was dashed against the rock and damaged, the air hissing and bubbling out of it. This was rather terrifying, for we were so weak, but by helping each other we managed to cling to the rock, securing our position, and thence waded ashore, taking with us our box of rations. Tom had a knife, with which he ripped the dinghy even more, and we buried it beneath rocks to hide our passage. Its period of usefulness had been short, but its work well done, for it had saved two lives. Without it we would never have made land alive.

Now we stood wounded and soaked on a small strip of land, in front of us a very steep ascent, behind us the terrors of fire and water from which we had almost miraculously been delivered.

Chapter 11

GEORGE

It was in the afternoon of Halloween that we came to the isle which is called Naxos, the home of Dionysius. Nowadays, as I have already said, he is St Dionysius, and as is the case in our own country when a person of importance accepts a title and [ascends to] the House of Lords, he has in the past few centuries receded somewhat from public life on the island. Nevertheless, his presence is still very much felt. His temple still stands as the first building in the little town we had just passed, and in the veins of the descendants of those who worshipped him there, still lingers the fire of his forgotten mysteries.

Something of his presence came to us and stayed from the moment we set foot on his shores until the time we left. His was the creed of drink and be merry with never a trace of tomorrow we die. An excellent philosophy! Soon we were to meet a very fine disciple of his, but that comes later. I mention Dionysius now, partly in gratitude for his rare hospitality, and partly for the strange way that he influenced me as I wandered through his domains.

That I was drunk during my whole stay on the island I would not deny, but it was not with alcohol, at least not most of the time. I was drunk with an almost mystic exhilaration which was purely pagan, made up of adventure, beauty, and with the romance of Old Times. Who but the god of revelry should be thanked for that?

Tom looked at me, and I looked back. We were a strange pair!

He was still wearing his flying helmet, and, as uniform, a battle dress top with shorts, and flying boots. I had on a blue leather coat, which through many lucky ops had come to be known on the squadron as my 'flak proof jacket'. With a very slight feeling of consternation, I realized that I was in civilians, and if caught was liable to be shot. I did not even have my identity discs. In fact, a thorough search of my pockets disclosed nothing but a rabbit's foot and whistle on a chain, useful in an emergency, but no doubt somewhat spent after recent exertions, a packet of Craven 'A' cigarettes[1] which had seen better days, and a few coins. Luckily, Tom was better equipped, as he had managed to rescue his escape kit and purse.[2]

We stood at the foot of a cliff taking stock of everything before embarking on a new life with no assets but the clothes on our backs and the box in our hands, no guidance nor orders, no authority to which we could revert nor friends to help us excepting those that we might find through our own initiative. We were gloriously free, a thousand paths lay before us for our choosing. We were our own judges and our own masters, and our responsibility was to ourselves alone.

Above us the clouds had gathered to screen the summit of the great hill which lay on the northern side of the island, and evening was drawing on. Briefly, we conferred on our immediate actions, coming to the decision that our arrival ashore had escaped detection, and that even if we had been seen, we stood a reasonable chance of avoiding capture as long as we did nothing foolish.

The first thing to do was to find out the lie of the land. From our present position, we could see little except for a small stretch of coast which would have warmed the heart of an enthusiastic mountaineer. We had no alternative to trying to climb up and find out what lay beyond. Before starting, we hid our rations amongst the rocks. Then, choosing the way which looked the most promising, we headed upwards.

The climb was less difficult than we had anticipated, and my strength had returned fully to combine with an unconquerable urge to adventure. Tom, on the other hand, was feeling a bit tired by this time, and his wounds which were bad were causing him much suffering, but together we managed very well, and with the exception of the last few yards, which for a time proved a barrier, little difficulty was met. At last Tom found a way around this obstacle, and we lay panting on a grassy ridge some 200 yards wide by 300 long. Beyond it the hills still rose, blocking out the view. This tiny plateau was one of nature's hidden places lost among the cliffs, looking out to sea. Nestling in the middle of it was one of those goat houses so common in the Greek islands.

Maybe we were mistaken in assuming that the stone built hut was a goat house, for it might have been the chosen retreat of a hermit where he could contemplate forever the perfect beauty of Delos and Mykonos,[3] twin isles far out to sea, bathed in the purple loveliness of the evening sun. Theirs was a different appeal to the majesty of Crete, something far more gentle and dainty. Crete lay impressively like a lion on watch, but they were sparkling, ever-changing jewels, set in a sea of lapis lazuli.[4] In daylight they were emeralds, but in the evening they turned to amethysts[5] before fading away into night. I have never seen anything more lovely.

Perfect as was our hideout, for all directions it was cut off by ascending or descending cliffs. Our problem still remained unsolved, unless we just waited around to be rescued, which scarcely seemed practical, and so we resumed the hard climb upwards. At last we reached the top, to find ourselves looking down into a valley, the same one towards which we endeavoured to steer our dinghy. Down to our right, far below, we could see the twisting coastline from where we lay, the river bed appeared to be dry, although we could trace its course as it wandered away in the direction of the hills, shortly to disappear. For a long time we gazed in perfect silence, and as the incongruity of the situation struck me, I laughed. We were such a strange pair of intruders!

'*We won't leave this place unless we can get a boat to go home*,' I said, and half meant it. There seemed no chance of getting any kind of boat anyway, and the whole spirit of the place was so friendly after the desert, so welcoming after the sea that one could not help feeling gratitude for being there, peace, and happiness.

Over the far side of the valley was a square house, and a larger one stood higher up. They must have been about a mile and a half away. The scenery was of great rocks, interspersed with trees and in the valley were gardens, tiny crannies of cultivation amongst eternal mountains. Of people there was not a sign and no sound disturbed the hush of evening, except for the distant pealing of invisible bells. Far above us, wandering herds of goats were leaving their mountain pastures to find in the valley protection from the dangers of night, and it was from these that came the tinkling echoes.

The peace of nature had come to this happy island, and no discord of eye or ear was present to mar it. From our lookout down to the valley, and from the valley to the mountain, all was at rest. Serenity remained in this land.

Even we were not entirely out of place, for our story was no new one. Like shipwrecked sailors we had accepted death, and to us had been granted the reward of those to whom the romance of exploration is still alive. Ours was the tale of Ulysses, and even as he had been the first to hear this call to adventure, so we were the last. Out of the sea we had come, and its once menacing waves had swept us to the shores of a beautiful desert island. The romance of exploration is not yet dead.

This was the old Eden, where man was nature's child and nature all-providing. Here at last the uphill struggle for existence could not stifle the sweetness of life. Presently, we would find a limpid brook softly bubbling from a cleft in the friendly rock, and by it we would sit to eat the fruits which a generous Earth would of itself provide.

It was a fleeting impression, but an encouraging one for which we were the richer. There were other things, though, to which we must attend. Rising to our feet, we climbed down the hill again, and turned back towards the deserted hut.

It had been built at a place where there was a marked dip in the land, like a giant stair, in order, no doubt, to use the natural amenities to save work. The building materials must have been a very secondary concern, for they were purely local, and it boasted nothing as elaborate as cement. Approaching it from behind, it was miserable, for from its flat roof which was flush with the ground grew thistles and scrub, and one could walk over it without realising that it was there at all. In front, though, where the dip came, there was a very low door.

The place was so isolated from the rest of the island, and we had suddenly begun to feel the cold, for it was late Autumn and we were wet, that we decided to make a fire in the hut, smoky it would be without even a hole in the roof, to dry out our clothes. Tom had his waterproof escape purse which contained matches, and we had no difficulty in getting fuel, for quantities of dead thistles only needed uprooting, and they very quickly set fire to the more solid branches which lay about. Tom started the fire, and I collected the wood, and passed it to him through the narrow opening. It did it take long to blaze up, and the heat it gave was more than compensation for the smoke which was a bit thick. It was better that it should stay inside though, even if it did hurt our eyes than that it should rise in the clear air to attract unwanted attention.

We took off most of our clothes, hanging them on branches near the fire. Soon the water in them began to evaporate, the steam rising to mix with the smoke, and as the flames took a firmer hold of the wood, flying sparks caused a certain amount of damage, but it did not matter very much, though it kept us on the move extinguishing minor conflagrations in our shirts and trousers. As a final treat, we ate a Horlicks tablet[6] each, and settle down more or less in comfort to work out a plan.

The probability was, we decided, that up to then we had completely avoided detection, at least from close up, because if the inhabitants were not all asleep, someone must almost inevitably have seen us ditching from the hills. First priority would have to be given medical aid, because Tom's face was very bad, far beyond any improvisation that we might accomplish with our first aid kit.

Of course, he was quite as keen as I was to avoid capture, but we both realized that if we could find no help reasonably soon, he would have no alternative to giving himself up, because as he was at the moment, apart from the risk of infection, he could not even eat ordinary food.

Our most obvious course seemed to be to wait until it was dark, and then for one of us to approach either of the houses we had seen in the valley, putting our trust in the patriotism of the Greeks to hide and help us. That it would be easier for one than two was clear, and as my wounds were far less serious than Tom's, I was the obvious choice. Apart from this consideration, I had the advantage of speaking French, which we thought might well come in useful. Our plan, then, was that Tom should remain in the hut, whilst I looked for help, but that under all circumstances, even if I were captured, that I would come back the next day.

It had always been impressed on us that under any circumstances we must only approach solitary persons, so that they should not be deterred from their desire to help by the fear of betrayal or indiscreet talk.

In one respect our plan was altered. The countryside was so deserted, and also so wild and rough, that the chances of having a serious fall or of getting hopelessly lost outweighed, in my opinion, those of being seen in daylight and recognized as British by the Germans. Our new decision, then, was that I should set out just as soon as my clothes were reasonably dry, and that I would wear my brown shirt and trousers, which were not very conspicuous.

For a while we sat and talked. We had only met the day before and even then in a most cursory manner. We knew very little about each other, although the past half hour had brought us so close together.

Tom told me that he was married, and that his wife was in Bristol, and both of us were worried about the blow it would be to our families when in a few hours they would get those curt telegrams which begin '*The Air Ministry regrets* ...' – so short and seemingly so final.

We realized too, that although we would at first only be reported as '*missing*', that should we remain in hiding without being taken prisoner, time would add the words '*believed killed*' to the original. That was the most unpleasant part of our position.

Tom obviously liked to talk about his wife. He was one of those steady individuals whose thoughts rarely strayed from their home, and now in a crisis it was there that his mind had instinctively returned. I knew his courage, but thought him too conscientious to have an imagination. I was to be proved wrong.

He belonged to that type of Englishman that foreigners are always apt to underestimate, through their inability to understand a character essentially different from their own. Not unpleasantly, this has proved unfortunate for them. Reserved and betraying no strong emotion, neither nor hate, friendly but never demonstratively so, completely loyal and decent, but very shy of praise. Silent straightforward men in whose silence many have been tempted to assume nullity until too late.

It was of men like Tom that Napoleon spoke when he called us a nation of shopkeepers.[7] Hitler, who was a far cruder man, merely called them decadent because instead of boasting, they were quietly content to live and let live. Napoleon's estimation was perhaps the closer, but he should have known that a man will fight far longer for his shop than he will fight for the glory of war.

The sun was still up when I left Tom, setting out to find an unknown friend to whom I could trust our lives, but it lay pale and red, warming for a last time its sleepy flock of islands before leaving them to plunge into the sea. For a while it seemed to pause in meditation, half sorry to leave them, and half pleased to see their evening smile as mistily they faded into sleep.

As I began to climb down the slope towards the valley, I passed under a high rock, at the foot of which grew a pine tree. Its shape and appearance were both distinctive, and mentally I noted it as a clear landmark to guide me on my return. Occasionally, I had to jump down from inaccessible rocks, especially towards the end of my descent, but on the whole the way was surprisingly easy. Of course, there was no path, and I had to take very great care, both in taking cover and in avoiding dangerous ground, but I felt sure of success.

At last as my footsteps led me deeper into the valley, signs of cultivation began tentatively to push their way into the wilds and all around the browns and greys of the hills had turned to green. It reminded me of England as she used to be, lush and green, as she was when one thought of her from far away. A long association with parched fields and open deserts may have made this more noticeable.

The little house was at no great distance now, and cautiously I approached it from behind. In the garden nobody worked, and no smoke rose from the chimney. The house was deserted. It was not the derelict garden, returning to nature as it was, which told me that here at least no help could be hoped for.

As I drew nearer, I could see trees growing inside it. Already their tops protruded above the walls and the roof had collapsed. There was something very sad about this total abandonment.

Swinburne might have stood where I stood now when he wrote *A Forsaken Garden*:

> In a coign of the cliff between lowland and highland,
> At the sea-down's edge between windward and lee,
> Walled round with rocks as an inland island,
> The ghost of a garden fronts the sea.
> A girdle of brushwood and thorn encloses,
> The steep square slope of the blossomless bed,
> Where the weeds that grew green from the graves of its roses,
> Now lie dead.[8]

Man had trespassed too far into nature's preserves, and had been pushed out again. Farther up the valley he might live, but not here. Naxos might indeed have been a deserted island.

Turning to the left, along the river bed, I followed the curving slope of the hill towards the other house, which was no longer visible. The way was at first extremely rough, for the boulders which throughout the ages had been thrown down the mountain, had accumulated at the bottom.

Soon, however, I found myself on a path, still going in the same direction. It was no more than a goat track, but it was at least reasonably flat. I had not gone far along it when there was a sudden sharp rise in the ground before me, the path disappeared amongst the trees.

Climbing up, I found myself in a woodland glade, the last rays of the dying sun casting long shadows on the leafy ground, and there at last was the stream. Up till then, I had not seen it, and indeed from above it looked as if the riverbed were dry.

In the rainy season the waters would no doubt rush down from the hills to swell into a torrent, but now it was still, calm, and limpid. In great dips it came down through the trees, like a stairway, every step a clear inviting pool, and all around birds were singing.

Suddenly, I realized that all the sea water I had swallowed had made me very thirsty, and kneeling to the ground, I dipped my face into the stream and drank in deep refreshing draughts of soothing water. Never had any liquid seemed so delicious. When I raised my head and looked down at the water, it was red with blood, reminding me that I was wounded, but the pool held a magic which could transform misfortunes into adventure, and as I went on my way refreshed and happy, I felt like singing, which would have been a pity, for apart from the fact that mine is the sort of voice which makes clergymen descend from their pulpits to make me stop, in this setting at least: '*Heard melodies are sweet, but those unheard are sweeter.*'[9]

As the house that I was looking for lay on the other side, I had to find a place to cross the stream, and there, before my eyes were stepping stones. The unexpected sight recalled very vividly a little scene of the night before.

We had been sitting in the mess, drinking and discussing the difficulties there would be after the war, not very confidently I fear, and the adjutant of 603 Squadron had said: '*The man who counts is the one who can make stepping stones out of stumbling blocks.*'

That had only been 24 hours before, but the props of service life had already disappeared so completely that it seemed like a message of encouragement and hope from very far away. The words rang in my ears, even as when I did my first solo: I could still hear my instructor saying '*You're on your own now*,' long after he had gone.

I crossed over, suddenly to come up against a wall. Thinking that I had unwittingly come out directly behind the house, I drew back quickly to the protection of the trees, only to realize almost immediately that the wall was a support for a road which followed the inclined slope of a hill.

As I stood irresolute amongst the trees, a new sound broke into the hush of the sunset: the clear voice of a boy singing. The song was strange to me, wild and mysterious as the island itself. Even birds paused to listen as the hidden singer filled the glen with melody.

Forgotten now were Tom and my quest, all that I longed for was for a little while contained in the wood, the stream, and the music. There was a perfection about such an end to the day, rightness which stirred the soul and made it overflow with a joy which came very close to tears.

Presently the song stopped, and from behind the wall came the sound of two people in conversation. Although I could understand nothing of what they said, I knew that they were not talking German. Still mindful of approaching only a solitary individual, I kept myself well hidden, looking round for a way to circumvent them.

Not wishing to go back on my steps and with a wall in front, the only direction remaining was to the left, up the stream. That path was a hard one, for it was steep, entailed moving over rocks worn and smooth and slippery by running water. They were of a slate-like composition, and erosion had cut them into symmetrical shapes. Creepers hung down their sides, at times impeding progress and at times making useful ropes to which I could hang and climb the easier. As soon as it was feasible, I branched away from the stream, in the direction where I judged the house to stand. My calculations were exact, for it did not take me long to find myself on a path leading up to its door.

Approaching it from behind I tried to imagine what kind of inhabitants it would have, and judged that they would be the simplest country people, which was all to the good, for they were the backbone of any race, and Greece was no exception. Having little to lose they do not count the cost, and what little they have to give they give abundantly.

The house was small and dirty. At one time it had been whitewashed, many years before by its dilapidated appearance. The roof was flat, covering a single storey, and at the end towards which I was approaching a tired goat house leaned against the main pile as if for support. Whoever lived there was obviously very poor. A selection of gardening tools lay beside the door, a solitary black hole in the wall which had once been white. It was open and I looked inside. There was little to be seen, for it was very dark and I doubt if there was a window. I knocked, wondering whether the open door argued the presence of the owner or the confidence of complete poverty.

Almost immediately a boy of some 16 years old appeared, round faced and amazed. I raised my hands in a token of surrender and he began to talk fast and excitedly in Greek, of which I understood nothing, but it struck me as obvious that he had not fully appreciated the situation. There was no reason why he should have, and to him I must have been a terrifying sight, wet, dishevelled, and covered with blood. It was obvious that things would have to be explained in a very special manner, for even if no help were to come from him, I had now committed myself, and his silence, when I left, was essential.

Our only means of conversation lay in gestures, and so extending my arms like a small boy playing at aeroplanes and transforming myself into a Beaufighter, I gave with great feeling the sound of two Hercules engines, mixed flak, and an awful crash, followed by subdued groans.

The boy, thinking no doubt that he was confronted by a dangerous madman, rushed into the house, shortly to reappear with another boy who looked as if he might be his brother. With even greater feeling I repeated the performance, and when I had finished, pointed out to sea and repeated Xenophon's famous cry '*Thalassa! Thalassa!*'[10] – my only Greek word!

The lads were obviously impressed, and after a certain amount of whispering between them, I learned another: '*aeroplano*'. My cause seemed at last to have been understood. The next step, and this was a most important one, was to find out whether it was a cause sympathetic to my youthful audience.

Embarking on a new line, I traced a swastika in the mud before the door, indicating with no room for doubt that it did not represent my politics. Having finally spat on it, I saw with a glow of satisfaction the youths do likewise. We left it in a depreciated condition.

I began to extol the virtues of the '*Inglesi*' (English), contrasting them with the degradation and general moral turpitude of the '*Germani*' (German). No doubt they missed most of the particulars, but the general feeling was clear, and so putting a finger to my lips and glancing round several times furtively, I impressed on them the need for utmost secrecy.

Without more ado, we entered the house.

My first guess had been correct. There was no window, nor was there any furniture except of the very crudest kind: a packing case for a table, and as seats a few round logs. Above a cold, ash-strewn hearth, a hook supported an iron pot, and near it were some faggots. From the smoke blackened ceiling, onions drooped mournfully. A goat which had slipped in and was nibbling with little interest at a faggot was chased out, and I was asked to sit down.

For a while the boys talked together in undertones, then the elder made signs for me to get up, pointing to the wall opposite the door, thus indicating that he wished to take me somewhere else. The only thing now was to trust him implicitly, hoping for the best, and so with many signs as to the secrecy of our venture we left the other lad to ponder on the amazing sight he had witnessed. I was not sorry to go elsewhere, because I did not fancy staying in that house, waiting till Greece might once again be free.

My guide led the way along a deserted path which wound up the valley. The going was still rough, but the land had become less wild. We met no one on the way, and soon the path curved towards the right, and began to go downhill. We must have walked about a mile, when the rocky ground fell away into a garden, surrounding a white house, and sloping, rather surprisingly, down to the sea. As we had been going up the valley most of the time, I judged the sea to be far behind. Two or three people were working in the garden, and I stopped instantly, looking for cover. The boy seemed in no way concerned, but I insisted on repeating my previous method of approaching from behind. Slowly and cautiously we advanced, until at last we were in the garden, and could examine the men working in it without being seen. There were two, and one of them looked like a schoolmaster or doctor, in that he was wearing town clothes. The other was far more roughly dressed, and was doing most of the work. I thought that the relationship between them was probably that of master and man.

I was in a great hurry to get Tom, and in view of the confidence of my guide, decided to waste no further time on caution, but to go to the first man as if a friend. It is the approach which very often works the best, for all men like to be trusted. Leaving our hiding place, we walked towards him, and whilst the boy explained what he knew, I held out my hand, and smiled as well as my face would permit.

The man immediately seized me by the arm, propelling me into the house. He dismissed my guide and closed the door.

He pulled up a chair, and beckoned to me to sit down. Then, with a broad smile, he crossed the room and opened a drawer. I wondered what he was looking for, and was not left long in doubt, for he came back with a photograph of an immaculate and extremely dignified officer in the Greek Air Force. He pointed at the photograph, and he pointed at himself. Now George (or Giorgos), for such was the name of my new friend, had a considerable beard as well as a number of gold teeth continually flashing in a merry smile, and neither of these attributes appeared on the photograph, so it took me a short while to realize that George it was. We shook hands many times, and he seemed even more pleased to see me than I was to see him.

He left me, and went through to another room. I heard him say a few words, and shortly he came back, carrying a bottle, a glass and some cotton wool. His smile broader than ever, he said '*whisk*' and poured me out about half a tumbler full. No doubt he was thinking of the English word 'whisky'. Changing his mind, he went back and got another glass, to drink with me. The drink was very strong, though in no way harsh or unpleasant. When we had finished drinking each other's health, George took a piece of cotton wool, and dipping it in the '*whisk*' he swabbed my wounds with it. Next he produced a bandage, but before he could put it on I made him understand that I would first like to see my face in a mirror. He brought me one, and I was amazed at what I saw.

My nose looked irreparable. On one side, and in front, it was completely detached from my face, and hanging down. The alcohol stung, and the discomfort was still far more noticeable than any pain. George wrapped a bandage right around my face and when this was done and my eyes just showed over the top and my mouth at the bottom I began to explain my story as clearly as possible. As my experience was now greater, and my Greek vocabulary had been doubled, and moreover as George's appreciation was somewhat speedier than my previous audience, only one performance was necessary. Continuing, I told how Tom, my 'comrade', was not dead, but in hiding and that the aircraft had left no trace as it disappeared beneath the waves. At first, as I talked about my 'comrade', George looked very sad, and said '*morto*', assuming that, as I was alone, I must be the only survivor, but when I said '*no morto*', he lit up again immediately and seemed delighted.

By signs he showed me that we would go and look for Tom but only when it was quite dark. Opening a door in the corner of the room, he asked me to come through. We were now in a bedroom, obviously his. Opening a cupboard he took out his best clothes and handed me a towel. When I had dried myself he insisted on my putting them on. He made the bed up with clean sheets, and wanted me to lie down, but afraid of losing a minute in the search for Tom, and knowing that once on the bed I would sleep almost immediately, I declined.

These may seem normal acts of hospitality to those who are unaware of the terrible privation in Greece, where clothes, sheets, and soap were unobtainable but in truth they displayed a generosity which I have not seen excelled.

Everything which had happened since crossing his threshold had combined to make me take an instant liking and admiration for George, quite apart from the fact that all he was doing, and so cheerfully, as if it were a joke, would cost him his life if he was discovered and caught. He was a true descendant of the men who had made Greece great; the visionary adventurers who first gave beauty to the world, and left an inheritance of liberty. The men who guided themselves by a single star and strove for a single aim: perfection, seeking it in all things. In human relationships, where all were respected except '*the man who could neither read nor swim*'.[11] In the arts and government, in oratory and in architecture, all was inspired by beauty and left as a perpetual monument to the founders of a golden age.

George had many of the characteristics of his forefathers. Thoughtful, even sentimental at times, but always full of vitality and passionately alive, he understood hate and love both in full measure. He could nurse hatred secretly, keeping it hidden deep in his heart even to the end against anyone who had wronged him. His feeling for the enemy he did not conceal, for he was demonstrative, and whenever the Germans or the Italians were mentioned, he would make a gesture of drawing a knife across his throat with an expression which held such depth of passionate loathing that it was frightening. For his country or his friends he would have died, for they meant liberty to him, and liberty he loved above all else. As a companion he was light-hearted and exuberant, excellent company and always full of fun, enjoying to the full his wine and song and the company of women.

As I did not wish to lie down, we passed through into a third room, the kitchen. In it, sitting before the fire was an old lady. She was very beautiful, as those that grow old gracefully are. Her hair was white, and her face was lined, but the very lines traced a pattern of happiness, dignity, and calm wisdom. She sat on a three-legged stool cooking a meal. Her flowing skirt reached to the floor, and over her shoulders she wore a triangular shawl tied around the waist, and a kerchief was wrapped around her hair. As we came through the door, she looked up from her work and smiled, and it was that smile which made me realize how beautiful she was.

She rose from her seat and walked towards me as if I were her son. I held my hand out towards her, and she took it in both of hers, and reaching up she kissed me. She spoke a few words, of which I could understand nothing but the music, and by her gestures I gathered that she was calling down a blessing on me. Drawing another stool up to the wide fireplace for me to sit down, she continued with the meal. The old lady charmed and amazed me. That she should display such kindness yet be capable of so complete a lack of curiosity that when George had brought me into the house, instead of coming to see what I looked like, she had just thought I would be hungry and had begun to cook me some food.

The meal consisted of fried sweet potatoes and mint tea, both sweetened with wild honey, and they were very good. Of course, things like sugar, meat, and butter just did not exist. The Germans, and even more so the Italians, had seen to that.

The most common word in all conversation was '*tipota*' and so I asked what it meant and the answer was a cross between '*narpoo*'[12] and '*sanfareyan*',[13] in other words whatever was '*tipota*', be it 'meat' or 'matches', no longer existed. The potatoes or '*patates*' as they called them, formed the main basis of all meals. For the first time, I think, I understood what war does to the ordinary decent people and the courage and resolve which is brought out in them by adversity. The room was small, the open fireplace occupying the whole of one end, and it was sparsely furnished. There was one small window, and from the ceiling hung strings of onions, wartime substitutes for the hams and sausages of more prosperous days.

As my impatience to fetch Tom grew, so the twilight seemed to drag on interminably. Several times I signalled to George that the time had arrived, and on each occasion he showed that we could not go yet, insisting that it should be quite dark. Night came at last, the glow from the fire lighting up the room, and seated by the fire my head had begun to nod. George saw how tired I was, and said that he would go alone, but I was not to be left out, and he would have been unable to find the goat house on his own, so we both rose, and he lit one of the most primitive lights I have ever seen. It was a sphere with glass sides held together with wire and inside it a home-made candle flickered hesitantly. With a last word to the old lady we opened the door and left the house.

Outside the night was dark and cool, and the wind brought us the sad sound of the sea creeping around the edge of the little garden, and as we made our way faithfully guided by the flickering lantern, I remembered that it was Halloween. George led me by the arm up the path, which was very difficult, even with the help of the light. It was a wise move which had prompted me not to wait for dark to seek help. After a short while we branched away to the right. Now the path as I remembered it should have curved to the left, so I said that we had gone to the wrong way, but George explained as best he could that there was something which he must do before finding Tom. What it was I could not understand, but when we had walked a considerable distance, he motioned to me to stop and to wait, and he disappeared into the darkness.

For a long time I sat by the deserted path, and as the minutes slowly succeeded each other, impatience gave way to concern, and concern to alarm. The night was too dark and furtive to be natural. I held my breath for a while, the better to hear any sound which might come down the path which George had followed, but none came. Even the wind seemed to have dropped. I looked up the hill, and it mirrored the blackness of the valley below.

Only the faintest haze of light divided sky from the land, for the moon had not risen, and no stars shone through an oppressive ceiling of low cloud.

So close was the night that I felt held in its grip, a prisoner surrounded by evil things which I could not see. I was afraid now, afraid of the danger which cannot be seen.

Could it be that I had been wrong all the time about George, and that when he came back, a German patrol would come with him? My intuition said 'no', but fear is stronger than intuition on a night like that. If everything was alright, why, then, had he left me?

A footstep behind me made me start violently, jumping to my feet and turning towards the noise, ready to run. In my hand I held a rock and I suddenly realized that I was also ready to kill. It was George, and as he relit the lantern he smiled, as if to say that everything was alright. I felt ashamed of ever having doubted him, and also of having given way to what was no more or less than the fear of the dark.

We resumed our path, and a long slow one it seemed to be now. So much longer than when I had followed it by daylight a short while before. Often I stumbled, and each time George held me up. He wanted me to sit down a while and rest, but that would have been the end. If we were to find Tom that night we must hurry and not pause, for I well knew that a minute's relaxation would bring the sleep I both feared and longed for.

We were going down now, though where we were I knew not, for George was leading. With caution and in complete silence we passed the door at which I had first knocked. That seemed like an age ago. Now I must find the way. No longer could I lean on George and follow. We crossed the stream by those same stepping stones which had encouraged me not so very long ago. I could hardly believe the difference a few hours had made to that lovely wood. Eerie and tenebrous now, we were glad to be through it on the path leading down to the deserted house and the sea. It was very hard to tell our position, for the night betrayed little, but the time came when I judged that we had descended far enough, and I signalled to George that we must now turn off and begin the upward climb towards the goat house, or '*micro casa*' as we were calling it now.

Slowly we climbed, picking our way and mounting laboriously amongst the rocks, and I clung to the bushes and scrub to steady myself, for I felt very weak, but George was always there to help me when I stumbled. Our exertions were rewarded, for the path, or rather the trackless rock strewn way we followed, led us to the foot of that same rock with the pine tree beside it which I had kept in mind as a landmark just a few minutes after leaving Tom. We were very lucky to have got so far without losing our way, and I knew that Tom could not be far. We paused only for the time [it took] for me to look around again and attempt to regain my bearings before resuming the last lap of our journey.

I tried to retrace my footsteps, which should not have been difficult, for the distance was only a few hundred yards at the most, but our hideout remained hidden, engulfed by the night. Something was wrong, as if the landscape had changed, and yet the rock was there, just as I had left it.

We walked along the edge of the cliff, but it was too dark to recognise anything. George seemed perturbed about the little house, for he knew of none where we were. This was not surprising, for it was so hidden that only chance or great familiarity with the cliffs would disclose it.

At last an idea came to him and he led me a fair distance further on, until we came to the deserted ruins of a house, but it was not the right one. I was worried about Tom as we walked up and down. We returned to the hanging rock. There was no moon, but now the stars shone intermittently through the gaps in the running cloud.

Once more we resumed the search, and I called him by name: '*Tom! Tom!*' but no answer came, only the dull thud of the waves attacking the rocks, and the disquieting whisper of a dark night.

Crossing to the edge of the cliffs and lying flat we looked down, but little could be seen except for a dancing line of surf rushing forward to hurl itself against the shore, breaking, and creeping back again. Very faintly out to sea, a luminous swirl gave warning of the jagged rocks which had punctured our dinghy.

Sea, land, and sky were all as black as a subterranean cave, and somewhere hidden in the shadows lay a little house which we would never find.

With a great longing for sleep we continued to search.

'*Tom! Tom!*' George too had begun to call now, his voice sounding unnatural as he framed the unfamiliar sound. No answering call rewarded us as we groped through the desolation of dark rocks, seeing nothing, hearing nothing, and feeling only exhaustion. He wanted to stop until the next day, which was the obvious thing to do, but a feeling within me which had no reason sensed an impending calamity if we were unable to find Tom. For a long time we continued, searching and calling, from rock to cliff and back again, but neither sight nor sound rewarded our endeavour.

At last, no longer able to stand, I sat down, or rather stumbled and stayed where I was. Complete weariness prevented me from continuing the search. George told me to rest a while, secretly relieved, I think, that we were stopping at last, and he said that I was a very good '*comarado*' [comrade], which would have made me feel quite proud, if my brain had been working properly.

He explained that he would get the boys I had first met to look for Tom as soon as it was light. To go on any further would have been ridiculous, for I had obviously lost my bearings, and indeed I had no more strength to continue, so we started for home. George led me by the arm, and I leaned on him with my eyes closing involuntarily at every few steps. Occasionally, I went to sleep to be rudely awakened as I stumbled. I would have fallen, had it not been for him, but always he was there, steady and cheerful. I felt rather ashamed of my weakness, but the day's work must have used up a great deal of nervous energy.

Of the journey back, nothing sticks in my mind, for it slept, even though my body had to keep moving, but at last we were home.

George put me to bed, and too tired even to say 'goodnight' or 'thank you' I was asleep.

Chapter 12

THE HOUSE BY THE SEA

31 October 1943

Tom woke me up next morning. It was already late, and the sun was shining through the window. My mind, completely refreshed by a deep dreamless sleep, slowly took stock of the unusual surroundings as if I was making a discovery. The sheets, the ceiling above my head, the window, all the suggested leave in Cairo or Alex[1] for they were not of the desert, but the bandage round my face, Tom standing wounded and dishevelled at the foot of the bed …

Suddenly, everything came back to me – the crash, George, our fruitless search. How pleased I was to see Tom! Jumping out of bed, I shook hands with him, and he told his story.

He too had felt very tired, and so when he had been left alone, he had stoked up the fire, and had lain down beside it, and there he had slept undisturbed, completely deaf to our calls, until morning, when one of George's friends[2] had located him and brought him to the house. It could not have been a very comfortable night, and he did look very untidy, nor did I like the look of his wounds which, being unprotected, had become dirty. He seemed quite happy though, and took my place on the bed.

There was a knock on the door, and in came George, a bottle in his hand. He looked very spruce this morning, with his black hair bundled back tidily, his beard gone, and his gold teeth glistening a morning greeting. With many words which we judge to be enquiries about our well-being, he put the bottle down on the table beside the bed. Thinking that this was a very good way to start the day I looked around for the glasses, but my hopes were unfounded, for opening a drawer, George brought out a roll of cotton wool, which showed that at the moment the '*whisk*' was medicine, and Tom was given the same treatment that I had received the previous evening, except that he did not take my precautions against possible internal injuries.

Breakfast was brought in. With the exception of one Horlicks tablet, Tom had had no food or drink since lunch the previous day. In spite of his hunger, he was quite unable to eat until George had made him a hollow tube out of bamboo through which it was possible to suck liquid foods, which confined him to soup. When we had finished, the curtains were drawn, and Tom was left to sleep.

George and I went through into the kitchen, where the old lady asked us to sit down in front of the fire. Although the sun was shining brightly, the window faced the mountain, and the air was cool, for it was November. Taking from a jar a handful of dry tobacco leaves, and from his pocket some forms, which he showed me with great delight to be Italian propaganda leaflets, George proceeded to cut the paper into strips and rolled some cigarettes, the standard Naxos brand. Even paper was practically unobtainable now that the Italians had gone, for the Germans seemed more capable of protecting their decrees than their lamentable predecessors. Paper money was in good supply, for being completely worthless it neither circulated nor became worn.[3]

As a souvenir, George gave me a note which in ordinary times was worth more than £10, but which could buy nothing. On it was a reproduction of the lovely Winged Victory, and I still have it with the signatures of about everyone I met on the island. The cigarettes were not very good, or maybe I just could not appreciate them with my nose out, and for Tom, of course, they were impossible, so for a while we both gave up smoking.

On the previous night I had attempted to explain to George the pressing necessity of getting a doctor, and now that Tom seemed worse than ever, and the danger of infection was very great, I suggested it again.

There was no need to worry, all arrangements had apparently been made, although there would be some delay owing to the fact that the doctor George had sent for lived in the town of Naxos, whence a guide would fetch him as soon as it could be done without raising the Germans' suspicion. An additional complication lay in an after dark curfew which was very strictly enforced.

Common sense dictated that we should not leave the house, but indicating that he wished to show me something, George led me to the window of the living room, which overlooked the garden and the sea, and pointing out the various islands, he told me their names. His voice was far off now, amongst the islands themselves, and proud as if they were all his. He obviously loved them, for they were his home, and he was familiar with them all: he might have been talking to them, not me. I could understand his great hate, for it was born of a deep love which had been defiled, men who love lightly cannot live for revenge. Nothing at that moment would have induced me to mention the Germans.

Looking from one to the other, and hearing the names I knew so well from history repeated in the strange musical tones of the islands themselves was a true delight. For tens of centuries, men had stood where we were, and looking out to sea had seen those same islands, and had repeated the words that George was using now: '*Paro*', '*Milo*', '*Delo*' (for the 's' is not sounded in Greek) and many others, each one telling a story which goes back through the ages to where history fades away into mythological romance.

Paros lay close into us,[4] so close that I judged it to be a part of Naxos across a bay. The slope of the valley concealed one end of the island, deceptively hiding the water that lay between. Behind it was Melos,[5] one time home of the great goddess Aphrodite, out to the right lay Mykonos, reputedly the loveliest of all the Greek islands, with the two tiny isles of Megalo and Micro Delos in its shade. Delos is deserted now, but it was the birthplace of Apollo when jealousy had driven Leto,[6] his mother, down to Earth. For its hospitality, Apollo had honoured it above all the other islands, and to him it had remained sacred.

From Naxos worshippers had sent nine marble lions to guard his sacred lake, and of these five are still on watch.[7] Great treasures accumulated there, and Great Kings and many conquerors have come to Delos throughout the ages to destroy and to carry away, but now they and those they plundered have gone, and only the legend remains. The port lies derelict, the ruined town gives witness to the past, and of the great god's statue only enough is left to tell of mighty sacrilege, but the legend remains, and it was true. Even as on the day of Apollo's birth a miracle had covered the island with flowers and gold, so it lay now, and I could see it.

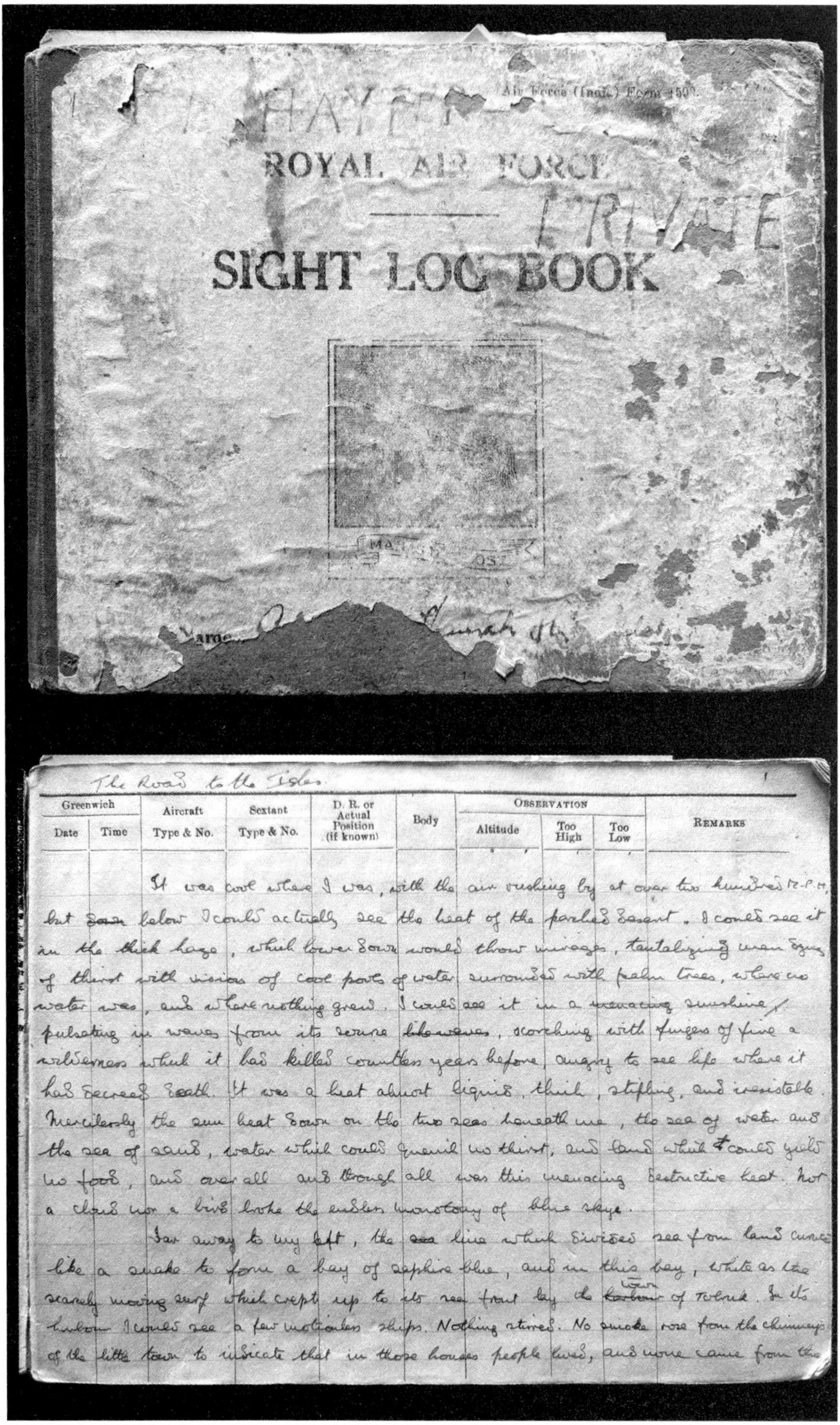

1. F/Lt Bill Hayter's handwritten journal, first kept in an old RAF Sight Log Book and later complemented by a second version, lay hidden for nearly eighty years. (Hayter family archive)

Above: **2.** BCATP pilot training class, Canada, 1941; Hayter centre, third row; Charles Allberry top left. (Patricia Staunton)

Left: **3.** Canadian Catherine 'Ann' Mills, Hayter's romantic partner from pilot training to the post-war years. (Patricia Staunton)

Above: **4.** Bill Hayter in an Avro Anson during SFTS training, Canada, 1941. Photo by fellow trainee and academic, Charles Allberry. (Patricia Staunton)

Right: **5.** Bill Hayter proudly receives his wings on 21 November 1941. (Hayter family archive)

6. Bill Hayter photographs his closest No. 47 Sqn friends in high spirits, North Africa, autumn 1943. (Hayter family archive)

7. Bill Hayter with his closest No. 47 Sqn friends at Carthage, Tunisia, September 1943. Names on the back: '*Arthur Unwin, Johnny Edwards, Doug Smart, Fletch, Titch Hayden, Smithy, Lew Rossner, Nobby Greentree*'. (Hayter family archive)

Right: **8.** Tom Harper in his flying suit, while with No. 604 Sqn, UK, 1942. (Harper family archive)

Below: **9.** Tom Harper, rear-seat Beaufighter navigator/observer; .303in Vickers K gun removed. (Harper family archive)

10. Tom Harper captures an attack on Ju 52 transports. Note on back: '*Ferrying troops from North Africa to escape the Allied advance. Photo taken prior to attack by our Beaufighter*'. (Harper family archive)

11. Period photograph of Chora, Naxos, its harbour targeted by *Beaufighter Strike* on 30 October 1943. The *kastro* (castle) crowns Chora's ancient acropolis, a circular thirteenth-century fortress protecting a medieval town. (Hayter family archive)

12. A 5,000-drachma banknote signed by Hayter and Harper's rescuers, including George Sideris, Dr Bardanis, the R1 LRDG patrol, and *ML-359* captain, Lt G.W. Whittman, RNVR. (Hayter family archive)

13. Lt D.J. 'Jack' Aitken (on chair) and his LRDG men training at the Cedars, Lebanon (background photo). On back: '*Missing links in Lebanese Mts. R1 Patrol after a 10-day scheme, August '43*'. (Brendan O'Carroll archive)

14. Crew of the RN motor launch *ML-359*, which ferried the R1 LRDG to and from Naxos, enabling Hayter and Harper's escape. (Brendan O'Carroll archive)

Above left: **15.** George Sideris and Bill Hayter, Cairo mid-1944, in a studio portrait celebrating their friendship. (Hayter family archive)

Above right: **16.** Bill Hayter steps into the cockpit of a legendary Spitfire while serving as a flight instructor in the UK. (Hayter family archive)

Less far afield, George's own island of Naxos looked very lovely in the sunlight which, on this October morning, might have been borrowed from July. To our left and to our right were the mountains, with the house and garden resting between them. The lower slopes rose in terraces, where by endless endeavour some meagre reward could be dragged from their stony slopes. Higher up were the arid pastures of mountain goats, clumps of shrubs and thistles, with an occasional tree growing precariously among huge broken boulders and bare rock. Behind us the valley undulated, green and fertile, until it too was swallowed up at last by the gaunt, greedy, hills. Far above us a brooding cloud still hung motionless at the top of the mountain. It was the only cloud in the sky.

Before us the ground sloped gently down to a beach, bordering a tiny bay, which must at one time have been the mouth of a valley, though now the stream had dried up. This piece of land was intensely cultivated and terraced, so that walls took the place of hedges, and the flowerbeds were at different angles, like a flowery staircase from the house to the sea. A bamboo plantation bordered to the right, concealing the house from the glances of curious strangers, and in front of the house was a well. It was George's garden, and he explained that he had not only designed it, but also laid it out himself, with flowers around the house and vegetables further down. Through the open window came the sweet smell of roses, which grew in profusion outside. They were the first I had seen since leaving England. A colourful abundance of flowers of many kinds were hanging thickly down from the walls or looking out happily from the crannies. I told George how beautiful I found it, and thinking what a perfect place it would make for a honeymoon, I longed to go outside.

If only I could make myself understood to George, I was thinking, when an inspiration came. It was true that I knew no Greek, but there was something he would understand. The names remembered from Greek mythology would be as familiar to him as English history was to me. It was here in Naxos that Theseus had deserted Ariadne, the tragic princess who, because she loved him, saved him from the Minotaur.[8] It was about that very desertion that the most perfect couplet in French literature had been written:

Ariane, ma sœur, de quel amour blessée,
Vous mourûtes aux bords où vous fûtes laissée.[9]

That seemed a good place to start, so saying 'Ariadne' I went through the motions of winding a thread as Theseus had done to guide himself through the labyrinth. George understood at once, and was delighted. After Ariadne then came Icarus[10] with George flipping imaginary wings, and pointing at me, much pleased with his joke. At last we could carry on the conversation as heroes and goddesses followed each other, and little by little I began to learn more words.

Leaving the window we sat down, and slowly with many signs and repetitions we began to discuss ways and means to escape. However pleasant and comfortable it was enjoying George's hospitality, it was far from safe. It was our duty to leave as soon as possible, for if we were caught George and his whole family would suffer for it, whatever might happen to us. Tom had some maps in his escape purse, and careful not to waken him, I tiptoed into his room and brought them back.

They soon dispelled any illusions I might have had as to our proximity to friendly territory. We were right in the middle of the Cyclades, the central group of islands in the Aegean, and all the islands surrounding us were held by the enemy. It might have been feasible for us to reach Cos,[11] but it had just fallen after a very gallant resistance. That only left us the possibility of Turkey, with the risk of being interned if we were not captured on the way, or reaching the island of Leros. It was lucky that we knew it to be in the hands of our troops. I say 'lucky' because up to then, it had only played a very minor part in what has since come to be known as the 'Leros Campaign' and the situation in the islands was so fluid that it was hard to know which islands were garrisoned at all, and if so, by whom.

George did not know at all which isles were occupied and which were not, nor for that matter very much about the war situation at all, for he had no wireless and little news came to Naxos except by way of the Germans, and that, of course, was disregarded. The last news we had heard had been that the fall of Rome was imminent – which was not the case – and so, exaggerating the propaganda of which we had been the victims, we said that Rome had fallen.[12]

George, who had an intense dislike for the Italians, immediately fetched the bottle to celebrate this, and it made him very happy, so maybe it did not matter. Having finished, we returned to the study of the maps. They were so beautifully printed on silk, and intended for just such an eventuality as this, but George expressed so great admiration for them that when we left we had not the heart to take them, and they stayed in his possession as treasured souvenirs.

After a while, Tom woke up and joined us. He crossed over the window and leaned against it, looking out towards the hills. Suddenly he drew back into the room, exclaiming '*Look out, someone's coming up the path to the house!*'

We were preparing to hide but George, who had gone to see for himself the cause of the alarm, remained unperturbed as he opened the door to let the stranger in. The man was a friend of George, rather lugubrious in appearance, and speaking little, he had come officially to settle a business matter I believe, though there is little doubt in my mind that his real desire was to have a look at us, and in this matter George saw to it that he was not disappointed.

All through the morning we were like exhibition pieces on view, and as George showed us off with pride, introducing us to the more favoured of his friends, and telling our story to all, Tom and I grew worried and frightened. Our presence, however secretly kept, was a terrible danger to this house. I felt it quite impossible to understand his complete confidence in all these people, and even if they were all to be trusted, they were bound to talk, and it would not be long before our presence would be common knowledge from one end of the island to the other. The sense of loyalty was magnificent, never have I seen it more highly or more worthily expressed, but here, where secrecy was of utmost importance, I could see trouble looming ahead for the friendly islanders, and I was right, though how it was to come I could not foresee. One can keep a secret or a museum, not a secret on show in a museum, and that is what George's house had become.

We had explained our hiding of the case of rations among the rocks at the foot of the cliffs, and it was not long before it turned up, carried by a stalwart youth whom we had not previously met. It was a large case, but proved rather a disappointment for we had described all its marvellous contents in most glowing terms without being too sure what was in it ourselves. Chocolate, sweets, concentrated foods, and far more besides we had promised in abundance, but on opening it we were most mortified, for in it was the barest minimum of food and a super abundance of water as well as the most inordinate quantity of red Verey cartridges and a pistol to fire them.[13] The punishment for our boastfulness served us right, and we had no cause for complaint against the manufacturers, for after all, it was designed for the people floating in dinghies not for landlubbers, but it was embarrassing.

There was little left inside now, and the emergence of a large first aid box with red crosses on top and sides passed almost without interest despite holding it up with a show of enthusiasm we were far from feeling. The whole thing was a failure, and I felt that we had let everyone down. We had offered food to the hungry, and given them water. Tom was going through the case for a last time, to make sure that nothing had been missed when he withdrew from a recess in the side something which would not only save our face, but also raise our prestige higher than ever.

It was a flag with a telescopic mast. Its success was immediate and complete. Patriotism carried the day, and hunger was for a time forgotten. As we drew out the mast, suppressing our smiles with difficulty, its appearance was greeted with applause, all present assuming, I am sure, that it was the Air Force flag which we carried around like good Empire builders to establish our hold on any pieces of territory that we might chance to conquer. It impressed them as being an exceptionally good show, but we never saw the flag again, for it was carried away, as far as we could understand, to form a rallying standard for a band of guerrillas up in the mountain. The purpose of the flag, which was red with a white circle in the middle, was, of course, to make the dinghy more clearly visible to rescue parties.

Amongst the small quantity of food that there was piled on the floor, were some sweets. I mention them because they were to play quite an important part in the future developments on the island. It would have been far better had they not been found.

Our next visitor, whom we could see clearly from a mile away, was staggering along the mountain path, laboriously carrying a huge yellow bundle on his head. Something about the bright yellow seemed very familiar, and an idea as to what his burden might be passed through my brain, to be dismissed immediately as ridiculous.

The man paused for a rest without depositing his load, as if it was too precious to be placed on the ground. As he came on again, slowly and with arched back, and he drew nearer, my suspicion returned, to give place to a certainty when, with pride at a job well done and panting a little, he deposited the remains of our dinghy on the floor before us.

I could have shouted at him to wake up, to realize that there was a war on, to stop being such a damned fool, for I was worried and scared, but he wasn't. He sat resting, a look of contentment on his wrinkled face, a vivid illustration of a passage I had once read: '*The perfect peace of the eye closing upon its accomplished work.*' That stupid old man was really happy in the thought that he had done us a service, and to have done anything but thank him would have been as bad as beating a well-meaning child for making a mistake.

We had taken such pains to conceal it, the rocks and Tom's knife had made sure that it would never float again, but it was ours, so the man had brought it back to us. It was rather touching.

Tom looked around, amused. '*Well Bill, do you remember yesterday when we were worrying about finding someone who wouldn't be too afraid of the Germans to help us?*'

'*Yes I do, and at this rate by tomorrow the only help we'll ever have to worry about will be the help we can get from our patron saints in Heaven, and they'll be precious little of that when it's found out that we have half the lives of an island on our hands.*'

'*The trouble,*' Tom went on, '*seems to be that they've missed all the security lectures – you know, "He talked so this happened". Let's have a chat with George, and get him to bury the thing when the old boy isn't looking.*'

George was leaning over the dinghy examining it; the compressed air bottle used for inflation seemed to interest him particularly.

'*Oxygen?*' he said as we approached.

Simultaneously we realized the hopelessness of our task. George would no more bury that dinghy than he would have thrown his bed into the sea.

'*No oxygen, dinghy vapour morto finish.*' We tried to explain the results should the Germans see it. Peering at the dinghy we said '*Germani*' and went on with a gesture which included everyone in the room '*morto*'. We even drew our fingers across our throats.

'*Kala*,' said George: meaning 'good' as he put it under a chair for future examination. We gave in. Trying to teach the Greeks the very elements of caution or suspicion of their neighbours seemed a hopeless task. If this sort of thing went on, though, someone was going to be shot before long.

The two shepherd boys I had first met came soon after, and with them they brought a young girl who was, I think, their sister. We gave them some chocolate and sweets from the rations, but apparently they had only come over to say 'good morning', and soon left, though the girl stayed to do the cooking.

The door had hardly closed behind them when an old man walked in. He was remarkably straight and had a white beard which curled wildly round the lower part of his face. Entering unbidden, and with a staff in his hand, he might easily have been one of the nice prophets. His coat was of faded velvet. Round his legs, leather thongs secured his trousers in the Saxon style, and his shoes were obviously home-made. He seemed to be a man of some importance, quite apart from his commanding personality, for unlike his predecessors, a chair was immediately brought forward for him and he sat down. We had several drinks with him together. He drank slowly and solemnly and at last rose to his feet holding his staff as it were a weapon far more than a prop for his old age. Unlike his predecessors too, he had something constructive to offer, for he was already on his way to fetch the doctor from the town, and had come to get final instructions from George.

When we were introduced to him he kissed us in greeting. We had noticed that this appeared to be the custom on the island, but had so far not joined in. As company came with regularity, and one young girl had already made her appearance, it seemed too good a thing to be left out of though, so we resolved to join in heartily at all future opportunities. As long as we were willing to do our bit and kiss father, we thought that he would not object to our showing the same courtesy to his daughters. The plan worked admirably, and by the time we left there were one or two very charming young ladies who had no cause to believe that English custom was wildly at variance with their own.

The old man left at last, a note from George to the doctor hidden on his person. We could not expect him back for a considerable time, owing both to the distance to be covered on foot and the difficulties which were to be expected in the town. Amongst other notices prominently displayed in Naxos by the Germans, was one saying that anyone aiding allied soldiers in any way would be shot. George took great pains to explain things to us, and it was surprising how easily we understood him without the use of conventional language.

There was very little which we could do after lunch, and it seemed wrong to be stuck inside when all was so lovely outdoors. We had no alternative but to sit about the house '*loungin' around and sufferin*'"[14] until the doctor should arrive, but everyone went so far out of their way to entertain us that we didn't feel at all bored.

We started to learn Greek, seated by the fire and pointing at objects, and when the old lady had told us their names we would repeat them after her, and she would either correct us or say '*kala*', which means 'good'. Sometimes, if our lessons seem to be going well, she would laugh and say '*poli kala*', and we would all pause for a while and drink some mint tea, the honey melting deliciously in the bottom of the cup. That would be our own cue to say '*poli kala*' making the old lady laugh again, and we would resume our work. Not infrequently George would stroll in with a bottle of '*whisk*' and insist on our having some in our tea.

When we grew tired of learning Greek, a gramophone was brought in, and with a file George sharpened up the needle, which was '*tipota*'. The noise which came from the old sound box was not highly musical, but it was amusing, and so was George, for closing his eyes he would sing the rather nostalgic tangos to his own very obvious delight.

The records were very old, and must have reminded him of previous occasions when he had heard them: of years ago when they had been the latest tunes in Athens, and he had been a young officer, or more recently when a lazy caique had brought them to the island, to be played at village dances, or be played on the accordion, and the young men of the island had sang them as serenades.

George leaned further back in his chair, his eyes still closed. The music had reached its end, but the record still revolved, grinding stridently. At last it stopped with a clatter, but George went on singing. Slowly and sadly now came the words we could not understand.

'*You're an old sentimental, George.*'

The song was finished, and he thought that we were praising him. '*Kala?*' he said, and then sang it again. Once more his chair was tilted back, and in mind he was very far away. *Sou Matia* was the name of the song, and it meant 'Your Eyes'. Like Shelly, George believed the sweetest of songs are those which tell of the saddest thought. His laughed again and tried to give us an explanation.

'*Mesdemoiselles, poli, much very much.*'

Was the word he wanted 'many' and not 'much'? But no, he could not be thinking of more than one mademoiselle when he sang *Sou Matia* so soulfully. Perhaps his wife for whom he longed was in his thoughts.

'*Madame, George?*' I asked.

He burst out laughing. '*No madame, tipota. Poli mesdemoiselles, ver' much madame ávrio.*'

'*Avrio*' means 'tomorrow', but like the Spanish '*manana*', a tomorrow which rarely comes.

Yes, I thought, the word should have been 'many'. Wicked old George!

His collection did not include Greek tunes alone, in fact it was highly representative. They were Strauss Waltzes, the soulful lament of the *Volga Boatman*,[15] and a surprise – *Mother Machree*[16] and *Loch Lomond*[17] on the reverse. How could we do anything but show the highest appreciation for the last two? And so it was, more fools we, for they were played over and over again in our honour, until the most noble purpose to which the much sung loch could be put, in our eyes, was that of a drowning place for the aged 'colleen'.[18] Worse was to come, though, for it was not long before George was singing them to his own words.

In spite of the music, life was good. We were enjoying ourselves, partly because it was so exciting to be fugitives, especially in this land where difficulties seem to solve themselves so easily, and where the people were so delightful. Through all the terrible privations of war, through hunger and suffering, doubt and fear, their ideals of freedom and democracy had not only stayed alive, they had spawn and spread, nurtured on hope, changing men who had been apathetic into patriots, and patriots into heroes.

Every man was a soldier, every woman who could cook a meal, every child who could carry a message, was one too. They were all ready to die, conscious of the complete demand set upon them by the times and of the greatness of their calling. The men were there, the call had been answered, and the course was clear to all, but with neither arms nor leadership they were doomed to failure. Their glory and their tragedy rested alike in the hopelessness of their situation.

Their courage and trust in one another were outstanding, far higher than in many countries which had not known enemy occupation – I can think of no other country where trust of one's fellow man was so complete or justified. But outstanding too, alas, was their foolhardiness. However justified their trust in the fellow men, it was too complete, for it was to result in discovery by the Germans, but when trouble came, it was the child of foolishness, not of treachery.

Yes, life was good. A merciless sun no longer beat down on tents amidst the bare and endless sands, for here roses bloomed beneath green trees, and beyond the trees, the sea was very blue. Tom and I both felt deep contentment, and knew the emotional joy of life won back from death. We knew that we loved life, and that the day before we had nearly died. Knowing how close we had gone to death, we were really grateful. It was a feeling that few came to know, and there are many who cared not to understand it, but they are those who have never understood the miracle of life.

We were fugitives in a foreign land, possessing nothing but life, but because we were alive, the whole world was ours, the earth and the sea and the sky above, all the things that we know and had nearly lost, everything which made up our lives, every sight and sound, every incident and every memory, all hopes and fears, friendships and sorrows – all are possessions, for all are lost in Death, whatever may come to replace them.

Like Ulysses, we could say: '*I am a part of all that I behold.*'[19]

Would that life might always be like that, and consciousness of it always as intense, for then it could never be replaced by the commonplace acceptance of mere existence or the joyless uniformity of the mediocre. Boredom is the chief enemy of man, not suffering, for boredom kills the mind, and in the mind is life. The bored of the world are the living dead. Suffering can be a spur to immortality.

That lovely day passed all too quickly, and the last rays of the dying sun had seen the hills of Paros change from glowing green to purple and had disappeared, leaving the island's still outline to fade into the background of stars, but still the doctor did not come.

We sat down to supper, but jumped up in the middle at the sound of shooting outside. It was coming from the town, and overheard we could hear the deep roar of engines. Our Wellingtons were attacking the harbour. Leaving the house we went out to look.

The night was starry, and we could follow the flight of the aircraft by watching the curved lines of tracer at their points of intersection, occasional flashes would light up the air brilliantly, showing the release of a stick of bombs. An aircraft passed over the target, to be caught neatly by the flak, and we could hear the drone of the engines change to a whine as the pilot pushed the nose down and gathered speed. He passed straight over where we were, only pulling out at a low altitude, and we could see the blue flames of the exhausts. Another Wellington, going in the opposite direction made a low-level run across the harbour, and now the high-pitched rattle of machine gun fire cut distinctly into the booming of the heavier guns, for once the tracer went from air to ground.

We were all so interested in watching the raid that none of us heard the sound of a horse approaching the house until our guide appeared, leading the doctor.[20]

We all went into the house, and were introduced. He was dark, rather fat, and very jovial, and to show that he was a doctor, he wore horn-rimmed spectacles and carried the usual little black bag which knows neither country nor race. He shook hands with everyone, looked with pleasure at the meal on the table, and after taking the briefest glance at our faces, sat down to eat and drink. He talked a great deal, brandishing his knife to emphasize his points, and appeared to be very amusing, because the others laughed a lot. It was very infectious, for Tom and I were soon laughing wholeheartedly, not at jokes which we could not understand, but at the amazing and picturesque vivacity of the doctor. He knew a very little French, and pointing his knife at himself he said '*Docteur de la montagne*.'[21] I hope that he was not going to use that knife in the coming operations, '*montagne*' or no '*montagne*'.

We wanted to know what the situation in Naxos was, and also if there had been any survivors from the Mitchell which had been shot down. No one had survived, the doctor told us, and taking out a pen and paper he began laboriously to trace what he knew of what happened in the port. It was, of course, an extremely difficult and unreliable process, and so I have corrected the account slightly in the light of future information.

The ship we had attacked had burned, but it had not sunk. Nevertheless, about 20 casualties had been taken from it [either] dead [or] seriously wounded. To evacuate the latter, the Germans had brought a three-engine flying boat into the harbour,[22] and had loaded the injured on board.

They had made the mistake of trying to include more men than the flying boat was designed to carry, with the result that in its overloaded state it had failed to take off. Apparently at the end of a long run, as it was leaving the harbour wall, the pilot had attempted to drag it off. It had staggered into the air, only to turn over, crashing into the harbour and killing its every occupant.[23]

This had all happened in full view of the town, and all the Greeks were amazingly elated about the whole thing. They regarded us as heroes, as if we had shot the plane down ourselves.

Personally, I felt rather sorry for the poor blighters who had been wounded one day, only to be killed the next, for it was a Red Cross plane after all, and they were out of the war, but it certainly did make us very popular. The piece of paper on which all this had been explained was an amazing sight, covered with figures, burning boats, little men with crosses at their heads and others without arms and legs, and at the bottom the flying boat upside down.

The doctor said that he did not intend to operate on us that night, because of the absence of light, so we began to form a plan of escape. We decided to leave the island by caique at night, and we were going to take with us all the details of military installations which might be of use to the Allies. The doctor promised to find those out, and to obtain photographs of them. Our eventual aim would be to get to Leros, although it might be necessary to stop off at Ikaria,[24] rather than travel through the Aegean in daylight, which would be inviting interception not only from the Germans, but also from our own Beaufighters. Of course, there would be difficulties in navigating at night, but we thought that we could make it, and the others were willing to get a caique somehow.

Late into the night we plotted, drinking quite a lot and laughing too, once again the ridiculous position struck me, for there we sat with candlelight making plans which rendered us all liable to be shot by the Germans, who were only a few miles away. At any moment a guttural order to open the door may interrupt us, and yet it seemed more as if we were schoolboys thinking up a rag to annoy an unpopular master. Everyone was in the best of spirits, and George kept jumping up from the table to replenish our glasses with wine, which he poured out of a goat skin.

At last the time came for us to go to bed, and it was not until then that we realized that there were only two beds in the house. The old lady had left us earlier in the evening to sleep with some neighbours, but still that left four of us, without counting George's servant who slept in an outbuilding. Tom and I decided that the least we could do was to share one of the beds which were quite big, but George and Dr Bardanis would not hear of it, and Tom was more or less forced into the bed I had occupied the night before, and I into the other, which was in the living room, and we were very soon asleep.

1 November 1943

If nothing new had created my awakening eyes in the island of a hundred surprises, I would no doubt have been disappointed and a trifle hurt, but of course it did. For a little while I had been lying half-awake listening to the subdued chatter of kitchen utensils and the muffled sound of a house emerging from sleep, all of which indicated that though work must go on, the guests should not be disturbed.

Very cautiously I opened an eye, determined, if need be, to close it again and go back to sleep. Having opened it and seen, I brought the other one in for corroborative evidence, and it was true. There in front of me was a slim blonde girl in a blue dress whom I have never seen before. Seeing my open eyes, she disappeared, to return almost immediately with a cup of mint tea.

I groaned, and I don't think I did it because I was dead; in fact, on looking back, I feel pretty sure that I was not responsible and that it was Dionysius who prompted me to do it. What she thought I don't know, but she put a cool hand on my forehead, and felt my pulse with her other one. So far I seemed to be doing remarkably well!

Had I taken the trouble to look into a mirror, I would have realized that it was not impossible that she thought I was dying. Quite apart from the fact that I had not washed, shaved, or brushed my hair for two days, I had no nose to speak of, two beautiful black eyes, one with a large cut across the eyebrow, a cut across my forehead, and my jaw bone sticking out at the bottom. Such is vanity.

There I lay in a horribly flirtatious mood, thinking that I had made quite a hit and feeling fit as a fiddle, and there she stood looking down on the most horrible remains of a face, thinking that I was suffering. She smiled, and I smirked. That must have finished it, for she disappeared feeling, I fear, rather ill. I drank my tea.

Such was my first meeting with Varvara, George's niece[25] (the girl who let her contempt for the enemy overcome her caution but who made up for her mistake by her own bravery).

At last George and the doctor came in, ready for breakfast, and so Tom and I got up. I do not know where they had slept, and felt ashamed of myself for having spent the night so comfortably.

After the meal we had prepared for the work in hand. The doctor seemed to be in no hurry at all, for after a brief conversation George left the room and came back with two ancient shotguns. I pointed at them and then at Tom, and raised my eyebrows, pleased to have a joke I could explain so easily. The doctor laughed, shaking his head and saying '*perdica*', which means 'partridges'. They were going on a shooting expedition, so with the last injunction to bring us back some *'Germani'* we watched them walk up the hillside to disappear amongst the rocks.

They were back again within an hour, replenished by the walk but with game bags empty, and on their return they found Tom and I sitting before the fire like condemned men in their cell. We were not looking forward to our operation. The doctor was now more jovial than ever, and repeated his favourite phrase of '*docteur de la montagne*' several times as he laid out on the table the bottle of '*whisk*', a curved needle and a piece of thread.

By this time my nerve had completely gone, so Tom went first, sitting in a chair facing the living room door, which was kept open for the sake of light. The mental suffering was awful, and instead of talking to Tom and trying to encourage him, I retired to the kitchen, for as far as seeing blood goes, I am the most awful coward.

For well over an hour Tom was in that chair, not only being sewn up, but also having teeth pulled out where they had been knocked so far out of place as to be repairable, and yet stayed in. Not once did he groan or even speak, and yet must have gone through pain far worse than what I suffered after him.

He appeared at last in the kitchen, but as his face was swathed in bandages it was impossible to assess the results of his operation. For myself, I had realized the object of making an excuse which would avert fate and protract my mental anguish. The only thing which presented itself to my mind to put off my operation was a meal, so saying I was hungry we sat down to lunch, although the idea of food was loathsome to me.

Tom could not eat for a time, and so he went to lie down. After lunch there was neither retreat nor escape, and I took my place in the chair facing the door, and awaited for the worst. News of the operation had apparently spread to the neighbours, because a considerable group had gathered around the chair and stood by to watch or encourage. In my frame of mind, their presence seemed fiendish, like tricoteuses at the guillotine.[26]

The doctor began by washing all my wounds very carefully with alcohol. Then taking up the needle, he threaded it and began. I tried gripping the arms of the chair to steady myself, because it would look so bad if all these people who looked on us as heroes realized just how cowardly I was. Tom had been brave about it, so I would follow his example. But not for long. The pain was very great, and at the first stitch in my nose, I let out a groan which, unlike the previous one, I really meant.

In fairness to myself, it may be mentioned that it was my turn, because sights and groans from a sympathetic audience had been feeling the air with distressing sound for quite a while. They might have been a band of professional mourners and weepers.

Faintly now, with my eyes closed, their voices penetrated into my brain, and trying to take my mind off the present I thought of home, and of times when I had been really happy. A voice which was of my own making repeated the word 'chloroform', and for the first time in my life I fainted.

I no longer felt any pain, and in my ears was a sound like running water, broken into by people talking.

For some reason the voices annoyed me, the anger swelling up inside me and changing into fury, vanishing immediately as I awoke, just in time for the very last stitch, and my operation was over. The onlookers could not have realized what had happened, for they patted me on the back and complimented me on my courage.

Someone brought me a mirror, and looking in it I saw a nose twice the normal size. It looked ghastly. I thought that no nose at all would be better than that. The doctor must've seen my look [of] disappointment, for his face which had been wreathed in smiles dropped suddenly, and he said that although he was only a '*docteur de la montagne*' that it would be alright.

I felt really ashamed of myself for showing anything but the highest gratitude to this man who was so cheerfully risking his life to help me, well knowing that his payment would at the best be our thanks and, if we were discovered, to be shot by the Germans, so I said that he was a '*très bon docteur*', and that the operation was excellent, which seemed to please him, and we all had a drink.

Chapter 13

THE PATROL

Strange news had come during my operation. The son of the man who had gone to Naxos to find the doctor had located some British troops on the island. Tom, assuming that the soldiers must belong to a Commando raiding party, had sent them a note requesting their help, an answer to which came two hours later. This is what it said:

> W.O. Harper. Your message received O.K. Are you injured? I will get in touch with my H.Q. and try to arrange your evacuation. Send more details of your lying up place. We can't move about in daytime ourselves, and I suggest you don't. Send this man back this evening.

It was signed J. Aitken, Lieutenant.

I wrote a reply saying amongst other things that conditions and company were so pleasant, and that drink was so plentiful that we felt no inclination to move about in the daytime at all, or at night either for that matter. We were, in fact, quite content and invited him down for a drink. I told him that our wounds were not serious enough to impede our movements unless it meant moving back to the hated desert, and as a parting shot asked him if he knew whether we were liable to pay income tax in our present condition.

This note I addressed to the Officer Commanding British Land forces, Naxos and signed W. Hayter, O.C. RAF Naxos.[1]

I did not want anyone to think that we could not manage by ourselves if we had to.

We were setting down as really good correspondents, and soon after dark our messenger reappeared with another letter, addressed, I was much pleased to see, to the O.C. RAF Naxos. The contents of this note were as follows:

> I have arranged for your evacuation. Stay where you are tonight, and tomorrow send this Greek up to get me here at 1700 hours and I will come and collect you. You will perhaps have guessed that I am not here for fun, so you can understand why I do not contact you in person tonight. You will, I know, be very discreet. So long.
>
> J. Aitken

I seemed to detect a slight hostility in the note which made me regret my facetiousness, but I found out later on that Jack Aitken had had as much amusement from reading it as I had had in making it up.

We were to leave this place, then, where I, at least, had felt so happy and so completely self-confident, and 'a headquarters' was to evacuate us. There was something I resented about the whole idea, though it does me no credit. I felt no gratitude for the planning of an escape in which I had had no part. That the initiative could have passed from us to an unknown body which was to direct us seemed like an attack on our liberty.

When we explained the news to George, however, he appeared well pleased, and repeated '*submarina*' and it was evident that he had, or thought he had, some knowledge of the submarine.

Time had already begun to drag, and evening, when it at last came, found me standing by the window, looking out half sadly as I tried to make a mental picture of a scene which I hoped never to forget. George came up behind me and for a long time he too gazed in silence at the lovely islands gleaming like jewels beyond the roses beneath us.

From the garden to Paros, and far out across a dancing sea to tiny Delos we watched a vision of perfection softly fading into night. The appeal of the islands' loveliness was not only to the eye, for like great music they held that mysterious call which is neither of sight nor of sound that belongs to the soul.

George spoke at last. He must have seen my longing to be outside, for he asked me if I would like to go down to the seashore. Until then neither Tom nor I had left the house.

Wearing an overcoat and a scarf around my head to hide the bandages, I followed George through the front door. We walked slowly past the rose garden down the sunken path. There was quiet as evening drew on, quiet and cool and sweet. No, I did not want to leave. I liked being a fugitive, and ways and means of becoming an escapee had already been planned, at night and by candlelight as they should be, but to be a refugee under the guidance of 'a headquarters' held no appeal for me.

We passed through the bamboo thicket, and through the vegetable garden, beyond it were some outbuildings we had not seen from the house. We paused there a while to say a few words to the doctor's horse, which was tethered outside a small stable.

Right at the bottom of the garden was an ivy-covered wall. We climbed over it, and continued down to the beach. It formed a very small semicircle of golden sand, in complete privacy for on both sides it was bordered by rocks. We stood no danger of being seen except from the sea.

In the middle of the beach was a small upturned boat, grey with age. In it were several holes, and it was obvious that through lack of paint and timber to mend it with, it would never sail again. We sat down on it, and neither of us said a word. A cool evening breeze blew softly from the sea, and tiny waves lapped musically against the sandy shore.

I tried to analyse my own thoughts and to know what it was that had made this spot above all others so delicious to me. It was indeed strange that in my most uncomfortable and dirty position I could sense a freedom and an inward fire which I had never known before.

There were so many questions and such unsatisfactory answers. All I could think of was that happiness was of this place, and that all who came here, if they paused to look, would find it as I had done. But that was wrong – I had not found happiness, I had not even looked for it, it had come to me freely of its own accord.

Was it to leave me now that I must depart, or would it stay a little while? On the morrow we would be gone, but someday I might return. Would it be only to find that a lost mood can never be recaptured? No, I would never return. It would be better to keep the memory of a spell than to risk allowing disappointment to take away the memory by breaking the spell. For a little while I had been allowed to wander in fairyland, now I must return to the world.

Slowly, as the first stars began to shine, we turned our backs to the sea and followed the flower-bordered path up to the house. The doctor's horse whinnied as we passed the stable, and we let it in for the night. The call of an owl from a tree above us proclaimed that for it day had begun. We could just see its outline against the sky as it waited and watched, and hooted as if impatient with us for being out so late.

2 November 1943

Our day of departure dawned, and we got up and had breakfast. Everyone seemed sorry that our stay had come to an end, and even the doctor forgot to laugh when he dressed our wounds.

It was on this day too that the old lady left. She had come for a ten-day visit, and this was the last one. So, putting her belongings in a bag, and with many smiles, kisses, and blessings, she left us to return to her village and to her deserted garden. She at least would say nothing of what she had seen when after her long day's work she would stop by to chat with her neighbours. She would smile sweetly as old ladies do when telling their friends of a pleasant holiday.

The doctor stayed with us right up to the time we left, and spent part of the afternoon sketching Tom and me, complete with our bandages. They were rather good sketches, though anything but handsome, and we asked him to give them [to] us, but laughingly he put them away in his little black bag, saying that they were souvenirs.

That was the starting signal for a real souvenir hunt. The first casualty was the banknote George had given me, which was so solemnly signed by everyone. But at supper time, when we were expecting to be fetched, anyone looking in through the window would have seen an extraordinary sight. It was a curious scene, half comic and half sad which only war could have produced.

George and the Doctor, and Tom and I, were seated around the table like a four at bridge. In the middle a dim lamp flicked, sometimes as if it threatened to go out, and sometimes lighting the room quite brightly, showing up four thoughtful faces and four pens poised above blank pages. Everyone else had withdrawn to the kitchen to let us concentrate before we were writing letters. That Naxos did not have a postal service with the possible exception of our young Greek friend was unimportant. We were writing to each other.

> And when it came to Christmas, the cards on his shelf …
> Were never from his near and dear, but only from himself.[2]

They were letters, moreover, the receptors would be quite unable to read because of the language. Tom wrote to the doctor and I wrote to George and we both signed each letter. We thanked them for all that they had done, adding a bit for them to show to our forces when the island would be liberated to help them in obtaining any assistance which they might need.

It was to be a long time before they could have been of use, and before then, another document had been signed, this time in the office of the German Commander in Naxos. It was a death warrant for one Capt. George Sideris, sometime of the Royal Hellenic Air Force, for having given refuge to two of the enemies of the third Reich.

> George Sideris – Naxos
> Nothing I could say could possibly express the gratitude which I feel for you for the generous and wholehearted manner in which you and your friends helped myself and F/O Hayter RAF when we were forced down near Naxos on October 30, 1943.
>
> To any Britisher who may meet Mr. Sideris, I request that they trust Mr. Sideris and do what they can to help him should he be in need of assistance.
>
> Good luck Mr. Sideris, Dr. Bardanis, and everyone. Maybe we shall meet again in the future.
>
> T. Harper W/O RAF
> W. Hayter F/O

As I have already said, George took great pride in having been in the Air Force, and he wrote us each a letter on the back of a photograph of himself in full dress uniform. Both letters were identical, for he copied the second one from the first, which did look rather naïve at the time. He said how pleased he was to have helped us, and wished us good luck. The doctor's letter was rather poetic, here is the translation of what he said:

> Dr. Emmanuel Bardanis: Naxos
> I consider myself very lucky to have had the opportunity to offer my medical services to 2 heroic children of England. Thomas Harper and William Hayter, who disregarded the safety of their lives and came to Naxos with their aeroplanes on 30.10.1943, specially to overcome the enemy who had enslaved Greece, and by a stroke of bad luck, and God's help in their future flying raids and safe return to their bases.
> Naxos 2.11.1943

Our messenger had been gone a long time, but still no sign of our would-be rescuer had appeared. We played the gramophone for a long time, and I changed back into my own clothes.

The evening meal came and went, and we were drinking a glass of wine when suddenly and completely without warning the door was flying open and we found ourselves gazing at the rifle held in perfectly steady hands and pointing towards us. Its owner must have been satisfied with what he saw, for the rifle was lowered and he advanced into the room. Obviously he was taking every precaution not to be caught in a trap. Behind him came our young Greek friend who had acted as postman. The man rested his rifle against the table. Already George was pouring him out some wine. He did not seem to notice it.

'*Are you ready to go?*' were his only words.

Tom pushed the glass towards him. '*You'd better have something to drink. There's some food too, if you're hungry.*'

The sound of something frying in the kitchen showed that Varvara had thought of that.

'*No thanks, I never drink when on duty. Tell them that and we must be getting along immediately.*'

Unbending a little, he passed some cigarettes around, the first real ones which could have been in the house for a very long time. He did not smoke himself, and seemed very impatient to go.

There was something about him which distinguished him from everyone else in the room. He was so completely the man of action. It was not that he was necessarily braver than the others, but he was far more disciplined. We were amateurs at war, and civilians in our ways, and to us the idea of having a few drinks before going was natural. To him it was a weakness, an unnecessary break in the plan and consequently an extra danger of which he could not but disapprove. There should have been tension between us, but somehow there was not, because the man was a leader. From the moment he entered the room he was in command, and we were ready to obey the orders he gave.

His appearance was in no way remarkable. He was bearded and dirty, and in the place of a hat he wore an army scarf tightly rolled over his ears. Whether he was the Lieutenant or one of his men could not be told, for his army coat was devoid of insignia. The buttons had either been dulled on purpose or had not been polished for months. It was the uniform of a man who could live in hiding behind the enemy lines. He was not old, probably in middle twenties, and laughing eyes showed that humour held a higher place than ascetic in his extremely forceful personality. He was used to taking instantaneous decisions, and to seeing them carried out without waste of time, implicitly sure of himself, a born soldier.

He picked up his rifle, slung it over his shoulder, and moved towards the door.

'*We must go now, you had better say goodbye.*'

My cigarette was only half finished, I took a last deep gulp, gazed intently around the room, blew out the smoke and placed the end in the ashtray.

'*Goodbye Dr Bardanis. Merci très bon docteur, poli kala, goodbye Varvara, poli kala, poli kala.*' We kiss them on both cheeks. Our rescuer had already left the house. George and the Greek youth came out with us.

We set off into the night, moving up the same path which I had followed twice before. George stayed with us a short distance, and I think that he would have liked to come the whole way, but with the last goodbye he too left us, carrying with him our deepest gratitude and sincere friendship. It was all we had to give. The four of us went on.

We moved fast, and the night was very black. The Greek was leading, sure of foot along paths where he had followed mountain goats since the days when he had first learnt to walk. Next came our new friend with Tom behind him, and I was last. When we came to the ford we did not circumvent it but waded straight through. In silence and with extreme caution we filed past the first house I had knocked at, and then turned right towards the mountain and away from the sea. The path was rough and very steep. With the bandage around my face I could not breathe, and my unstudded leather shoes slipped very easily on the rocks. Only my obstinate pride prevented me from asking them to go slower.

Suddenly, we stopped dead. Those in front had sensed something suspicious, and I heard the metallic click of a safety catch being put to fire. Apart from that, I heard no noise except the pounding of my heart. Investigation showed that it was a false alarm, but it gave us a brief moment of respite before we moved on again.

The path twisted and turned, following the rugged contours of the hills, as a guide with tireless energy led us ever upwards. My bandage, which had come loose anyway, I removed, after which I felt slightly more comfortable. Tom, who saw that I was having difficulty, moved behind me, and still we went on climbing, our heads bent low the better to pick out and avoid the many obstacles that littered our path. For the most part, there was nothing more dangerous than rocks to stumble against or thorn bushes. But once, as my unpractised foot displaced a stone, it was several seconds before an answering echo came up like thunder from the valley far below, causing us all to start and to hug more closely to the hill side of the path. The noise was shattering in this secretive silence, undisturbed even by the murmur of the sea, and the valley, like some giant loudspeaker, multiplied and amplified it until the world seemed full of betraying sound. Without pausing, we pressed on towards the mountain which loomed darkly before us, obscuring the sky.

Suddenly the path fell away to the right, and we scrambled down it to find ourselves in a little wood where the busy tinkering of fast-running water proclaimed a mountain stream. There was another ford just below a waterfall, and through this we hurried and continued to descend. The softest of night breezes caused the pines around us to rustle gently, and beyond the trees, far down to our left, a few faintly glimmering stars robbed the sea of utter darkness.

The downward slope was steep, and it was not long before we reached the bottom of the valley. Soon after this, our guide left us, which showed that we could not be very far from our destination. Unfortunately, though, we took the wrong path, and to get back to the right one we had to climb down an almost vertical slope, hanging as best we could to the thorn bushes, creepers, and projecting rocks which covered the hillside. When we reached the bottom, we were at last on flat ground, a table of cultivated land with a house nearby.

Slowly and with extreme caution, we bypassed the house, and went on for a few minutes, gradually descending towards the sea. The path was far easier now, bordered by trees, and beyond them were what we took to be terraced vineyards. A sudden challenge, low and from very close at hand, made us freeze in our footsteps. Looking around I could see no one. The sound seemed to have come from beneath our feet. The words had been indistinct, but the message was plain enough. If it were a trap, then we were well and truly caught, for we did not even know in which direction danger lay.

'*Is that you Mac?*' our rescuer whispered urgently.

The answer came: '*Okay, boss.*'

There was a rustle in a clump of bushes just to our left, far too small to conceal anyone in itself, and a man emerged and joined us. In the crook of his arm he carried a Tommy gun.

'*Everything is alright boss. Smithy's got through on the wireless, and he has a message for you.*'

He looked at us curiously, probably trying to assess our wounds. When he spoke his voice was friendly: '*I'll help these chaps down, boss.*' And then turning towards us, '*You're alright to climb down aren't you?*'

We said '*Yes*', meaning 'No', for we were standing on the edge of what looked like a precipice. Our position was very similar to the one from which we had just first looked round the island, with the sea scarcely discernible, but weltering angrily far below. The night was very dark and there was no moon, but somehow the booming of the waves was more comforting than the silence of the hills.

'*Follow me closely, and for Christ's sake, keep away from the edge.*'

Even as he spoke, Mac was pulling aside the bush from which he had emerged to disclose a shaft or chimney formed by a fissure in the rock and perfectly concealed by shrubs and creepers. He had already disappeared downwards as Tom and I followed with a prayer of thanks for being saved from a climb down the face of the cliff. Progress was extremely slow, it was not easy in the dark, but we did not have far to go, and there were many helping hands at the bottom. The sudden end of the shaft came as a complete surprise, for instead of taking us down to the sea edge, it led into a cave which opened out on one side to the stars.

Feeling thoroughly exhausted, we sat down. There were about eight men there, we could only see them as dim forms walking about, but they greeted us most friendlily, and one of them, called Smithy, who was the wireless operator, said that he had been in touch with H.Q. and that we were to be ready to embark early in the morning, and so we would have to get down to the seashore immediately. At this moment 'the boss' appeared feet first down the chimney, and after a brief conference, led us to the mouth of the cave.

Tom and I rose to our feet with a concealed groan, and looked outside. After the blackness of the cave, the night seemed full of a faint blue light. A glance upwards made us thankful for the chimney, but beneath us the way was not anything like so difficult. There was, of course, no path, but the way was quite practicable, and we followed the others down the steep slope to a river bed and down the river bed to the seashore. The men all carried haversacks on their backs, and weapons in their hands. One of them mentioned the fact that as the wireless was already down there, they need not worry about carrying it.

We were about 100 yards from the sea, still in the bed of the river, when 'the boss' gave the order to halt, and so discarding their packs and weapons the men sat down. As they settled down to rest, chatting in whispers, I wondered what they were and placed them mentally as Commandos. That they were admirably trained was obvious: the challenge, the wireless message, the soundless descent to the sea, and the most instructive obedience to a whispered order, everything had been flawless.

I had yet to see their almost uncanny power of anticipating trouble, their loyalty, and above all, their deep philosophy which found its outlet in cheerfulness. Their free and easy ways were amusing at first, small things like calling their officer – for our guide was he – 'the boss', but a little time was needed to combine amusement with admiration and respect for a most gallant and efficient fighting force. Men such as these are the salt of the earth.[3]

From the very start, Tom and I felt and admitted our own complete ignorance and puerility in this form of warfare, not that it was in any way impressed on us by the others, and we tried to adapt ourselves to the patrol not as entirely useless guests, but as very junior members under training. In consequence, we also called Jack Aitken, for such was his name, 'boss', everyone was soon calling us Tom and Bill, and we could not have been on more friendly terms. It would indeed have been ridiculous had we expected our ranks to mean anything under such conditions, and worse than ridiculous had we in any way tried to use them.

Guards were set, and those who were not watching lay down to sleep, for the ship was not expected until very late. I asked if I might do a watch, but the boss said that everything was arranged, and that he would not need me. Actually, I think that this was just a polite way of telling me that I would not know what to do. The two who were on guard lent us their beds, which consisted of a ground sheet and one blanket, saying that they would not disturb us, as they would use the ones of the men they relieved.

We were about to settle down when Mac came over to us and asked if we would like a smoke before going to sleep. Tom declined, for it was impossible for him. I was rather surprised, and asked how we could smoke without attracting attention. For the second time that night, Mac said '*follow me*' and we went and sat on the rock with two of the others, put a blanket over our heads and had one of the stupidest and most amusing smokes I've ever had.

One of the men kept us in fits with falsetto whispers of '*Lookout girls, I think the headmistress is coming,*' or '*Come on girls, let's be really daring and have a pillow fight!*' It was most amusing, and the atmosphere of smoking in secret certainly belonged more to the fourth form at St Hilda's than to full-grown men in an enemy land.

Unfortunately, at this stage, it was noticed that, whereas the others were seated on the bare rock, I was comfortably supported by my Mae West, an admirable and well-named piece of equipment which had become my chief source of joy. It was in vain that I offered honourable amends, and even the temporary loan of the desired garment. I was dismissed to bed as a typical pilot whose one motto was '*I care not what happeneth unto thee Jack. I'm alright.*' Like Mad Carew,[4] I went out into the night beneath the stars, soon to fall asleep, my head resting on the voluptuous pillow.

It was a fitful slumber, lulled by the whispering moan of the sea and the eternal silence of the stars, but disturbed by the cold of a heavy dew and by innumerable pebbles beneath me, which necessitated an almost continuous change of position. I was wide-awake as soon as I felt a touch, and guessing that the ship must have arrived, I sprung to my feet. Such was not the case, for the hour of its arrival had long passed, and the boss wanted us to be back in the hideout before the first betraying glimpse of dawn.

I folded my bed roll and gave it back to its owner with thanks, and asked what I could carry. I was given the wireless which was housed in a canvas bag so that it could be slung over one's shoulder, and we started the upward trek. All went smoothly enough as long as we stayed in the river bed, but when we left it and began to climb, it was extremely hard. Luckily for me, my position of wireless bearer gave me a favoured place, for no one wanted me to fall, and at the least sign of stumbling, anyone near rushed to support me. Had they not, I shudder to think what would have happened to the wireless, sturdy as it was to prove. At one stage, progress was so difficult that it was necessary to move sideways, and extremely slowly at that, but it minimized the chance of slipping. At last, we came to a narrow ledge skirted by a low wall, where a goat path crossed our way, and resting there awhile, we waited for everyone to reassemble before continuing.

The next step consisted of crawling on our stomachs through a thicket of thorn bushes, but when this was negotiated, it was only a short way to a large rock, which was in front of and slightly below our cave. The boss told us to lie down until dawn, and most of the men, who were experts at it, had soon made themselves comfortable positions, but Tom and I sat side-by-side with our backs to the wall of rock waiting for the dawn and cursing the ship for not turning up. The rocks struck into the tender parts of our anatomy, we were cold and uncomfortable, and felt fed up and far from home.

The stars faded, and slowly a world of grey emerged from the black night, a pale, damp monochromatic world of the rock and sea beneath a gloomy sky. It paused a while between night and day in sad indecision, and then moved on. It was as if the sun still hidden behind the great hill had decided to pour its favourite gifts into the sad, cold valley until it overflowed with beauty. At first the sky lit up, still pale, but suffused with a hidden warmth, and objects took shape, and their shape to colour. Then the vivid red of a cloud caught in the sun's first ray, the blue of the sky, and the bright glow in the East heralded the sunrise. The hills caught in the bright light, the trees, the terraced vineyards all awoke in turn as they chased darkness and shadow deeper and deeper into the valley until they had disappeared altogether, and we could look once more at the smiling island.

At first the new day seemed to have very little effect on the patrol, but soon everyone woke up, and we began to prepare breakfast. The patrol had ample rations, for as we were told later, they had had no specific orders as to how long they were to stay. In consequence, the ship which had brought them had also bought many cases of food which had been left in the cave the night before. A fire was lit and we cooked some sausages and bacon and brewed tea, and when that was finished and we sat lazily in the sunlight munching biscuits thickly covered with butter and jam, life became more pleasant.

Poor Tom, on the other hand, was feeling very much worse, for his stitches had come undone, making him able to eat only with the utmost difficulty; and although he was extremely cheerful and never complained, it was obvious to us all that he was in considerable pain, more especially when he laughed, which he did not infrequently, great as the effort must have been. We had nothing to do, but everyone seemed determined to do nothing in as pleasant a way as possible, so we basked in the early morning sunshine smoking and talking, looking out over mountain and sea and telling yarns about past adventures.

They were all, with the exception of Smithy, New Zealanders. All had beards and their skin was hard and browned from long exposure to wind and rain, for to them a tent was a luxury only provided when they went on rest. Even as the weather and the great outdoors had left their marks on the faces of these men, so also their minds had been formed and stamped by the conditions under which they lived.

The End

Segue

How did they escape the island? Where did they go, stranded as they were in a region embroiled in conflict due to the strategic objectives of Operation

Accolade? And what ultimately became of George Sideris and the Greek islanders who had risked so much?

There is clearly more to this story, but Bill Hayter's personal account ends abruptly as he awaited covert passage off Naxos and further medical care. Why he stopped writing remains unknown, just as no one knew of his manuscripts' very existence until they were discovered some eight decades later.

As authors, we found the situation deeply frustrating, but we soon set to work. Tracing those connected to the story across Canada, Greece, France, and the UK was challenging but essential. Through meticulous archival research and conversations with direct descendants and others linked to the events, the missing pieces of the puzzle gradually began to emerge.

The key to what unfolded next lies in Hayter's final written words, where he described the rugged, resourceful nature of his rescuers. A logical continuation point seemed to be the remarkable story of the Long Range Desert Group (LRDG), whose operatives were instrumental in covert operations across the region. But to truly understand the events described in Bill Hayter's work, we must step even further back – to the enigmatic figure of Tom Harper, whom Hayter had met mere hours before catastrophe struck and they found themselves stranded on an Aegean island behind enemy lines.

Chapter 14

ALL HARPED UP

Possunt quia posse videntur.
'They can because they think they can.'
Virgil, *Aeneid* (c. 29–19 BCE, interpreted maxim)

On 27 August 1940, just two days shy of his 25th birthday, Tom Joseph Harper walked into the No. 2 Recruitment Office at Cardington, Bedfordshire, UK, and enlisted in the RAF. Tall, confident, and undeniably striking, he carried himself with a charisma that immediately caught the attention of his superiors. He was swiftly recommended for pilot training, an opportunity he seized with enthusiasm.

However, Harper's early aviation career quickly veered off course near the end of his time as a pilot under training at the No. 19 EFTS. After logging just one and a half hours of solo flying, his fledgling efforts were marked by two crashes that raised a few stern eyebrows – not to mention serious doubts – about his suitability for the role.

The final straw came in spectacular fashion. Flying his commanding officer's Tiger Moth, Harper misjudged the controls, and the plane spiralled from 1,000ft (300m) straight into the trees surrounding a nearby convent. Though he emerged largely unscathed, the incident became the stuff of family legend, particularly when the nuns, perhaps scandalised by the sudden intrusion of this dashing young man into their cloistered grounds, refused to admit him for treatment. The fiasco all but grounded his ambitions to pilot aircraft, but Harper, ever pragmatic, took the setback in stride. He accepted advice to retrain as a navigator.

It was a decision that would define his wartime service and reveal his true talents. On 7 July 1941, he was posted to No. 4 Air Observer and

Navigator School, and later attended air armament and wireless training. Meticulous and methodical, Harper excelled in the role, a testament to his natural aptitude for detail and discipline. His RAF uniform became a symbol of pride for his family, particularly for his sisters, who admired the transformation of their charming, intelligent brother into an airman who truly put the 'air' into *debonair*.

The trajectory that brought Harper to the skies began far from the theatres of war, in a small industrial village at the mouth of the River Avon. Born on 29 August 1915, he was the eldest of four sons in a family of nine children. Just a month after his birth, Harper was baptised at St Mary's Church in Shirehampton, a local landmark known affectionately as 'the Shire'. This baptism was part of a lifelong connection between the family and the church, the site of countless family milestones over the years. The Harpers' devotion to St Mary's was so profound that they later funded a commemorative window in its honour.

The family lived in Avonmouth, a working-class community defined by its docks and shipyards. Tom's father, Thomas, a painter at the Avonmouth docks, was himself one of nine children, a reflection of the large family tradition. His mother, Catherine Matthews, of Irish descent, was a steadfast and loving figure in the Harper household until her untimely death in 1939, when Tom was just 24.

From a young age, Tom Harper displayed promise. Encouraged by his father and teachers at Avonmouth Church of England School, he was urged to sit the entrance examination for the prestigious Queen Elizabeth Hospital School (QEH) in Bristol. Founded in 1586 by John Carr, a wealthy local soap merchant, the school was originally established as a boarding institution for orphans and destitute children, modelled on Christ's Hospital in London. Carr's vision of providing education and opportunity to the underprivileged became a cornerstone of QEH, and by Harper's time it had evolved into one of the city's most respected schools. Harper secured a place as a boarder and immersed himself in its rigorous academic environment. Wearing the school's distinctive blue coat and yellow stockings, a uniform steeped in tradition, he embraced the challenges it offered. On Sundays, he often walked the 10-mile (16km) round trip to visit his family, demonstrating both perseverance and his strong ties to home.

The Harper family made sacrifices to support his education, pooling resources to contribute towards the cost of his schooling. Free from household chores, he sometimes drew the envy of his siblings, but his success became a shared point of pride. By the time he left school, Harper had developed into a well-educated and ambitious young man.

His first job was as a stockbroker's assistant, followed by a position as a cashier at the Co-operative Building Society in central Bristol. It was during these years that he met Irene Elsie Balderson, the daughter of James Balderson – a carpenter and diver who worked on ship repairs and lock gates at the docks. Balderson had been born in London, and his family moved between various dockyards following his father's work before eventually settling in the bustling port community of Avonmouth. The couple became engaged in June 1940, but with the war already raging, Irene's father insisted they postpone their wedding until peace was restored.

However, the war allowed little space for such hopes. After completing his training and certification, he was posted to No. 604 Squadron at RAF Middle Wallop, where he began integration and operational training.

No. 604 Squadron had played a pivotal role in Britain's air defence during the Blitz, pioneering radar-controlled night-fighter operations. Its adoption of the Bristol Beaufighter Mk I in September 1940, large enough to be fitted with early airborne interception (AI) radar,[1] replaced the slow, poorly armed Blenheim and signified a turning point in night combat.

The Beaufighter, equipped with such radar and guided by ground-based GCI systems[2] – often with searchlights cutting through the night – could locate and track enemy bombers in total darkness. Crews typically flew 'lone-wolf' missions, relying on precise coordination between pilot and navigator/radar operator. Once visual contact was made, the aircraft's cannon and machine guns could unleash devastating firepower.

The squadron's fame rested on the teamwork of John Cunningham and his navigator/operator, John Rawnsley. Cunningham developed radar-guided tactics in 1940, earning the nickname 'Cat's Eyes' from a press myth he tolerated in the interests of morale.

By early 1941, he was an ace with ten victories, awarded the Distinguished Flying Cross (DFC) and Distinguished Service Order (DSO), and promoted to squadron leader, while Rawnsley received the Distinguished Flying Medal (DFM). Their growing renown drew King George VI to RAF Middle Wallop on 6 May, where he personally congratulated the pair. That evening, during a visit to RAF Sopley,[3] radar operators invited the King outside to follow an interception in progress. Though the action was too distant to see, he reportedly listened as Cunningham scored his twelfth kill – a Heinkel He 111.

When you've impressed the King, you definitely know you are on the up and up.

By September 1941, Cunningham had 15 victories and a bar to his DFC, while Rawnsley was awarded the DFC himself, their joint efforts praised in official citations as they advanced through the ranks.

By this time, the sustained heavy bombing that had defined the Blitz was over, replaced by more sporadic raids. The *Luftwaffe* had turned to the Eastern Front, while RAF bombing operations struggled for want of better equipment and tactics.

In spring 1942, Air Chief Marshal (ACM) Arthur 'Bomber' Harris relaunched Bomber Command with area bombing, incendiaries, and the 'bomber stream' concept to overwhelm defences. Advanced aircraft such as the Avro Lancaster and soon-to-be-deployed navigation aids Gee and Oboe[4] enabled concentrated attacks on industrial centres and urban areas, targeting both production and civilian morale.

The campaign opened with Lübeck on 28–29 March 1942, followed by Rostock in April and the headline-grabbing 1,000-bomber raid on Cologne in May – events that changed the nature of warfare.

As described earlier, Hayter was involved, flying No. 114 Squadron Blenheims in parallel operations in support of the wider offensive. The repercussions also shaped Harper's path as the *Luftwaffe* launched the Baedeker raids, named after the German travel guides used to select culturally significant targets, in direct retaliation. These struck English cities including Exeter, Bath, Canterbury, Norwich, and York, beginning with Exeter on 23–24 April.

W/Cdr Cunningham's No. 604 Squadron RAF now found itself squarely in the firing line. It was at this critical juncture that on 7 April 1942 Tom Harper joined its ranks.

With legends like Cunningham and Rawnsley as role models, Sgt Harper was expected to help sustain the squadron's success – from the back seat. Beaufighters had only two crew positions, making him a true 'third-wheel' trainee on his first flight aboard 7747, with S/L S.H. Skinner at the controls and F/Sgt F.W. Larcey as navigator/operator. This orientation flight was a short night flying training (NFT), from 1500 to 1545 hrs on 10 April 1942.

Many others followed, mostly piloted by Sgt Ward. They included NFT, AI practice, and circuits and landings (see Appendix 2 for a full sortie list). April 1942 squadron records noted: '*Difficulties of training new pilots and crews owing to shortage of serviceable aircraft ... Of the 28 available pilots, 12 U/T [under training].*'[5] All efforts focused on getting them up to speed to secure the squadron's long-term success.

Life in war-ravaged Britain was far from comfortable. On 21 April, the squadron gave up a barrack block to the Women's Auxiliary Air Force (WAAF), leaving '*about 160 men in tents in an adjacent field*'.[6] Spring temperatures ranged from 10–15°C by day to 4–8°C at night, with dampness adding to the discomfort. Dysentery struck No. 4 Barrack Block on 27 April, leading to it being '*put out of bounds*' and a sanitation briefing – no doubt leaving some airmen wondering whether their next sortie would be against enemy aircraft or the camp's plumbing.

Operational hazards were ever present: on 1 May 1942, P/O Howard-Williams and his navigator, Sgt Nordberg, bailed out into open sea after both engines failed 12 miles (19km) south-west of St Catherine's Point, Isle of Wight. Their dinghy deployed automatically, and F/L Hoy – later joined by W/Cdr Cunningham – helped direct the naval rescue. True to form, the Royal Navy pronounced them '*hardly wet*' on recovery. The squadron mourned the loss of X7963 – an almost new aircraft – but the pair were back the next day, '*uniforms a bit creased but otherwise none the worse*'.[7]

Just days later, on 6 May, P/O Spencer, flying solo, found he could not lower his undercarriage and executed a wheels-up landing '*in a cloud of dust before a crowd of interested spectators*',[8] with minimal damage credited to his skill. No doubt Harper was among the onlookers.

Defending Bath, Exeter, and Cowes, W/Cdr Cunningham[9] and F/Lt Rawnsley[10] pulled off a truly daring feat. On 23 May, Cunningham's signature tactic – approaching below the bomber's slipstream, hidden from the dorsal gunner – was tested against a Heinkel. The bomber suddenly lurched left, fired a broadside, then vanished into cloud. Directed by GCI, Cunningham and Rawnsley re-engaged. The German pilot twisted through seemingly impossible evasive turns, culminating in a nearly inverted dive, with Cunningham hot on his tail. At 900ft (270m), radar contact was lost in the ground clutter; they stayed locked on at a harrowing 340 miles per hour (547km/h). Cunningham only broke off at the last moment: '*E/A dived down with C.O. after him and obviously could not recover before hitting the ground.*'[11]

The He 111,[12] piloted by *Staffelkapitän* (S/Ldr) Siegfried Langer, broke through clouds and plunged vertically to destruction at 1705 hrs, killing all aboard: '*C.O.'s 16th enemy aircraft destroyed (HE 111) fell at Alverston, S.E. [south-east] of Shaftesbury.*'[13] Cunningham returned at 1830 hrs, having completed a unique, hard-fought 150-minute chase – downing the enemy without firing a single shot.

Tom Harper flew 29 sorties during April–May 1942, almost all with Ward. His 28th, on 26 May, was his very first combat patrol – a testament to the squadron's tough training ethos. Like Bill Hayter, Harper's first posting was a baptism of fire: not from direct combat, but from unfavourable conditions, relentless pressures, and high expectations, with his initial vulnerability magnified by inexperience and a steep psychological learning curve.

Amid the strain and danger of an emerging operational life, another story quietly unfolded – more personal, yet no less complex. Tom's relationship with his fiancée, Irene, was blossoming, but obstacles still loomed. Her father, James Balderson, still insisted major decisions wait until the war ended, and as an RAF airman, Tom struggled to secure leave. Irene, then weeks shy of her 21st birthday, required special authorisation to take the next step.

With determined friends quietly assisting, plans moved forward. On 6 June 1942, Thomas Joseph Harper and Irene Elsie Balderson were married at St Mary's Church in Shirehampton. Irene's parents attended, a subtle nod of support despite earlier reservations. Joy was brief. Tom was soon called back to duty, and Irene travelled to see him off – an act sharply criticised by her parents for '*chasing after a man*'.

Evidently, it was a very different world back then – where love was often seen as a pursuit, rather than something worth pursuing.

Harper's tenure with No. 604 Squadron was brief. By June 1942, he was reassigned to No. 216 Squadron RAF at El Khanka, Egypt, which flew supply runs and casualty evacuations with Lockheed Hudsons and Bristol Bombays. Given the stark contrast to combat service, the transfer was almost certainly an administrative error. Harper flew no operational sorties, and the posting proved entirely inconsequential.

He was redeployed on 10 January 1943 to No. 272 Squadron RAF, primarily based at Ta' Kali, Malta, which operated Bristol Beaufighter VIs. He spent just over three weeks at the squadron's Edku detachment in Egypt. His name is absent from combat records, but a 3 February 1943 entry notes: '*All the aircrew who were attached to us for training were posted to No. 603 Squadron and No. 252 Squadron who will finish their training.*'[14] His service record confirms the transfer to No. 603 Squadron on 2 February 1943.

Bill Hayter and Tom Harper's paths were beginning to converge.

Chapter 15

HIGH-FLYING HARPER

Καὶ μάλιστα γε τοῖς ἀρίστοις στρατεύεσθαι φιλοῦσιν οἱ ἀγαθοὶ.
'And indeed, good men especially love to campaign with the best.'
Xenophon, *Anabasis* 3.1.16 (c. 370 BCE)

By 1943, No. 603 Squadron RAF – motto '*Gin Ye Daur*' ('If You Dare') – had already earned its reputation. Formed in 1925 as a light-bomber unit, it became a fighter squadron in 1939, flying Supermarine Spitfire Mk Is. On 16 October 1939, Flight Lieutenant (F/Lt) P. Gifford, piloting Spitfire L1070, shot down a Heinkel He 111 east of Dalkeith while it was on an anti-shipping raid. Three airmen were captured; the fourth was killed. It was the RAF's first aerial victory over British soil.

In summer 1940, No. 603 Squadron moved to RAF Hornchurch, taking a central role in the Battle of Britain, with several pilots among the highest scorers. They returned to Scotland for the winter, and by May 1941 were conducting offensive sweeps over France. The squadron spent the winter of 1941–42 at home, before deploying to the Middle East in 1942 in two contingents.

The Spitfires reached Malta aboard USS *Wasp*[1] on 20 April 1942, remaining four months before merging with No. 229 Squadron on 3 August. Ground crews arrived in Egypt in June but, with Rommel advancing on El Alamein, were rushed to Cyprus on 26 June, supporting other squadrons for six months. They returned to Egypt before Christmas, relocating to Edku to receive Beaufighter Mk I and IV aircraft with fresh crews in early 1943, many of which were from No. 272 Squadron.

When Tom Harper joined on 2 February 1943, No. 603 Squadron was gearing up for convoy patrols and long-range escort missions along the North

African coast. The next day: '*A big day for the squadron since arriving in M.E. [Middle East]. The first flight of an aircraft allotted to the Squadron took place. The ground crews, after an enforced rest, were as "busy as bees" with the new arrivals.*'[2] Re-equipment with Beaufighters – a sharp departure from the nimble Spitfire VBs – expanded the squadron's capabilities.

With engines roaring, the squadron moved quickly into action. Early operations included convoy escorts and an anti-shipping patrol to Misurata, while other efforts focused on honing skills and cohesion. Despite poor weather, pilots conducted orientation flights, formation practice, air-to-sea firing tests, and naval exercises. Ground crews worked tirelessly as the squadron forged itself into a formidable force.

On 7 March 1943, some notables arrived with their acronyms: '*Distinguished Visitors to the Squadron today were Prince Bernhardt of the Netherlands (Hon. A/Cdre) accompanied by Sir W. Sholto Douglas, K.C.B., D.F.C., M.C., C.A.C.-in-C, Middle East. Officers and Aircrew were introduced to Prince Bernhardt by W/Cdr H.A. Chater, Commanding 603 Squadron.*'[3] The visit lifted morale and reinforced purpose – or at least that was the idea.

In the early hours of 15 March 1943, Sgt Tom Harper, navigator/observer aboard Beaufighter KL504, joined his new pilot, Sgt T.R. Beattie. Taking off from El Magrum airfield, Cyrenaica, at 0700 hrs, they formed part of a three-Beaufighter close cover patrol for convoy 'Survey'.

About an hour later, the convoy appeared roughly 125 miles (200km) north-north-east, off the North African coast. Six destroyers, eleven merchant vessels, two tankers, and a corvette moved under deceptively calm skies, with intermittent clouds and low visibility complicating patrols. Harper and the crews maintained vigilance until relieved by other No. 603 Beaufighters at 1100 hrs. At 1115 hrs, Harper's aircraft left the convoy and returned to Misurata West, touching down at 1200 hrs. This sortie marked his first operational mission with No. 603 Squadron.

Later, F/Lt H.M.P. Ashby, with P/O F.H. Pritchett navigating, faced a tense end-of-day challenge. At 1800 hrs, Ashby was vectored toward suspected enemy aircraft. In fading light and rain, they briefly sighted an aircraft that '*disappeared into a rainstorm*'. A second vector at 1810 hrs yielded nothing, but on a third at 1815 hrs, they spotted '*6 or 7 unidentified aircraft, possibly Ju 88s, going astern of the convoy about 5 miles [8km] away, heading south at sea level*', before darkness concealed them. Returning, Ashby and Pritchett narrowly avoided friendly fire as '*the convoy started firing on approach*', leaving the convoy '*still putting up an intense light flak barrage*' and returned safely to base.[4]

Throughout spring and early summer 1943, No. 603 Squadron settled into a routine of close escort missions from its new aerodrome, guarding convoys carrying troops, materiel, and vital supplies. Days blurred in long, often uneventful patrols, yet the constant tension of being 'on watch' – where danger could strike without warning – never faded.

A few moments broke the monotony. On 19 April 1943, F/Sgt J. Goodfellow, with Sgt L.G. Maynard in the rear seat, took off in the early hours alongside another Beaufighter to escort the 'Merit' convoy. Routine turned perilous when Goodfellow's aircraft developed mechanical trouble, forcing them to ditch 15 miles (24km) north of base. '*It was seen that 2 dinghies with one occupant in each were afloat,*'[5] the records noted – a calm account of a nerve-wracking ordeal.

The second Beaufighter piloted by F/Sgt R.H. Giles with Sgt L. Coulstock, returned to base to report the situation and then quickly took off again. For nearly two hours, Giles circled the dinghies, guiding a search-and-rescue Walrus to the scene. Once the survivors were aboard, Giles returned to base. Goodfellow and Maynard had been saved, thanks to their comrades' swift action.

Sometimes, you need a little help from your friends.

Less than two weeks later came a harsher turn. On 2 May 1943, nine aircraft were dispatched to protect convoy 'Liquid', a mix of tankers, merchantmen, and escorts. '*All aircraft were vectored onto bandits by the convoy, but nothing was seen,*'[6] the records indicate. The day passed quietly – until dusk, when three Beaufighters were sent up for cover. Among them was F/O Scantlebury in 'E', with F/Sgt James as navigator/observer. They never returned.

'*No news has since been received, and both Pilot and Navigator have been posted missing, believed killed,*'[7] the report stated, adding only that more than ten enemy aircraft were in the area. For the squadron, the loss of Scantlebury, from Bristol, and James, from Kalgoorlie in Western Australia, was another sharp reminder of the risks they lived with daily.

The pairing itself spoke volumes. Bristol, also home to Tom Harper, was a long way from Kalgoorlie, a remote, sunbaked gold-rush town Australians call '*in the middle of absolutely bloody nowhere*'. And yet here they were – two men from opposite ends of the Earth – sharing the same cockpit over the Mediterranean, caught in a global conflict.

The war drew men from every corner of the world: Māori from New Zealand, Gurkhas from Nepal, and countless others fought in North Africa and across Europe. Scantlebury and James were part of that wider story – ordinary men from distant places, thrown together by remarkable circumstances.

On 23 May 1943, Beattie and Harper, now both Flight Sergeants, flying Beaufighter X7741, were assigned close escort for convoy 'Naval' – a mixed group of merchantmen, destroyers, and a cruiser. Taking off from Misurata West at 1620 hrs, they were forced back within 20 minutes by engine trouble. The failure might have ended their mission – and their lives – but Beattie coaxed the aircraft down safely. Undeterred, they took off again at 1705 hrs in another aircraft and completed the mission without incident.

The months that followed ticked by with little to write home about – not that the censors would have allowed much detail anyway. Engine trouble occasionally forced early returns, but serious mishaps were rare. On 18 June 1943 an aircraft crashed on landing after engine failure, damaging another, though mercifully no one was hurt. Later, on 27 June, during low-flying VHF tests, a burst tyre brought down a Beaufighter's undercarriage on landing – again, without serious injury.

Throughout June, July, and August 1943, their days fell into a repetitive cycle of briefing, take-off, seemingly endless vigilance, and the welcome return, occasionally punctuated by sudden jolts of danger. This monotony must have worn at their spirits. Yet in a war short on certainty, the uneventful was a blessing. It was the ordinary sorties, not the dramatic ones, that kept them alive.

The double irony was that these 'quiet' operations often brushed against history. Although Harper did not fly on 2 July 1943, two Beaufighters from No. 603 Squadron that day provided cover for a formidable force – '*2 Queen Elizabeth-class battleships, 1 aircraft carrier, and nine destroyers*'[8] – ships that only days later supported the landings in Sicily.[9]

Harper's role was peripheral, but no less important for it. As noted on 8 July 1943: '*No. 603 Squadron, in cooperation with aircraft of the 252 Squadron, 272 Squadron and 227 Squadron and Lightnings of 96th Group U.S.A.A.F. from N.W.A. Command, covered convoys which later made rendezvous S.E. [south-east] of Malta at dusk on 9th July to form the main assault group for the invasion of Sicily.*'[10]

Following the fall of Sicily, it was time for No. 603 Squadron to advance towards the front lines in preparation for the Italian campaign. In early September 1943, the squadron relocated to the recently captured Borizzo airfield in Sicily, '*to operate under 325 Wing, 242 Group, N.A.C.A.F. [Northwest African Coastal Air Force], coming under 62nd Fighter Wing, U.S.A.A.F. for operational instructions and intelligence reporting*'.[11]

Tom Harper's first sortie from Borizzo took place on 9 September 1943, with F/O C.B. Megone at the controls of Beaufighter 'J', KL517, tasked with escorting convoy 'Elicit', which they failed to locate. Over the following days, three similar missions followed, escorting convoys of landing ship tanks (LSTs), landing craft tanks (LCTs), escort vessels, merchantmen, and occasionally destroyers. Two were piloted by P/O P.H. Miller, with the final sortie on 17 September led by W/Cdr H.A. Chater.

Having last flown with him on 12 July, the fate of Harper's regular pilot, F/Sgt T.R. Beattie, remains unclear. Aircrews were encouraged to stay together, fostering familiarity that bolstered morale and increased the odds of success. Separated from Beattie, Harper faced a definite disadvantage – coordination was not just a convenience but a matter of survival.

There is no record of Harper flying with No. 603 Squadron in October 1943. His service record notes he was 'discharged' and reposted to No. 47 Squadron on 26 October, a temporary assignment, described elsewhere as having been 'borrowed' from No. 603 Squadron. Whatever the reason, he returned to the Middle East, attached to Bill Hayter's squadron at El Adem, Cyrenaica.

The stage was set. Harper and Hayter first met during the preflight briefing at Gambut III on 30 October 1943. That day, they were introduced to the aircraft *'S' for Sugar* for the first time. Just hours later, their lives would become inseparably linked in a perilous venture over the Aegean.

Chapter 16

GEORGE'S WORLD

Εἶς οἰωνὸς ἄριστος, ἀμύνεσθαι περὶ πάτρης.
'The best omen is to fight for one's country.'
Homer, *Iliad* 12.243 (c. eighth century BCE)

In the remote village of Komiaki[1] on Naxos, the analogue radio crackled to life on the morning of 28 October 1940. Anxious residents huddled around the sole receiver, powered by batteries and a hand-cranked generator. A familiar chime sounded, then broadcaster Kostas Stavropoulos[2] calmly announced what everyone expected but nonetheless feared:

> This is Athens Radio Station. We are broadcasting the first War Bulletin issued by the Greek General HQ. Since 5:30 a.m. today, Italian military forces have been attacking our frontier troops along the Greek-Albanian border. Own forces are defending the homeland.

Throughout the island, news spread swiftly, signalled by the pealing of church bells. Few wanted another war, but as Russian revolutionary Trotsky once warned, '*You may not be interested in war, but war is interested in you.*'[3] And so it was. War had come – regardless.

A closer look at the life of George Sideris – one among millions of Greeks whose world was torn apart – opens a window into a turbulent era.

Born Georgios Ioannis Sideris in 1898 in Komiaki, a village perched high above the island's northern coast, Sideris was the eldest of eleven. He grew up amid hardship, where survival demanded quiet strength and perseverance, qualities that would later define him. His very surname, drawn from the Greek '*sidero*', meaning 'iron', seemed to foreshadow the unyielding spirit he would come to embody.

In 1917, amid WWI turmoil, Sideris volunteered for the Hellenic Army, serving as an infantryman against Bulgarian forces in Macedonia. By 1921 he had risen to warrant officer – remarkable for a man without higher education or military pedigree. There is no evidence he fought in the Asia Minor campaign (1919–22), though he was discharged in July 1923, shortly after its conclusion.[4]

Re-enlisting in 1924, he moved from infantry to army aviation as a quartermaster, later serving in the Finance Corps. With the creation of the Hellenic Air Force in 1930, he became one of its first officers, promoted to lieutenant comptroller in 1931 and discharged as captain comptroller in 1933. Historian Nikolas Levogiannis[5] told us that politics likely lay behind this departure – a claim the Air Ministry denied when Sideris sought reinstatement in 1945.[6]

Sideris' second departure from the military was shaped by two forces. In 1932, amid the Great Depression, Greece abandoned the gold-exchange standard, triggering its fourth default. Political upheaval and deep military cuts followed, compounding the trauma of the Asia Minor disaster – the 1922 defeat and mass expulsion of Greeks from Asia Minor (modern Turkey) – and the huge influx of refugees.

The second force was indeed political. Venizelos' 1928 government collapsed amid the crisis, replaced by fragile regimes. By March 1933 an anti-Venizelist coalition was poised to seize power, prompting Venizelist officers – led by the defiant Gen. Nikolaos Plastiras (ret'd) – to launch a desperate, ultimately doomed *coup d'état*. The revolt deepened military schisms, and Sideris, like many others, was caught up in events, even if only inadvertently.

Certainly, Sideris' predicament reflected less on his abilities than on the difficulty of pursuing a military career in a country tearing itself apart. Amid the chaos, retired general turned political leader Ioannis Metaxas rose to power in 1936, swiftly imposing a dictatorship – part of a broader European wave of authoritarianism. That Mussolini's fascist Italy served as a model for Metaxas would soon prove one of history's many paradoxes. Across the Continent, the Spanish Civil War raged, while revisionist Germany and expansionist Italy consolidated their regimes through ruthless authoritarian rule, signalling an ever-darkening horizon for Europe.

Sensing Europe's foundations cracking, Metaxas built walls of his own, literally. While reorganising and modernising the armed forces – hampered by time and resources – he pushed forward the construction of the Metaxas Line: a chain of bunkers, tunnels, and gun posts along the northern frontier. Modelled on France's Maginot Line, it aimed to stop – or at least delay – a Bulgarian invasion. Much of it still stands as concrete proof of Metaxas' fixation on sovereignty and defence. However, like its French counterpart, it failed for the simplest reason: it was bypassed.

Despite Germany's long-standing influence over Greece's elite – Metaxas himself had studied at the Berlin War Academy – geography ultimately dictated allegiance. Greece's vast merchant fleet and strategic location made one thing clear: in any coming conflict, it would have to side with those who 'ruled the waves', as Britannia still did, and as the United States soon would.

Of course, all three nations had yet to reckon with the deadly German U-boat menace that would soon be prowling the Atlantic.

In the name of diplomatic expediency, Metaxas pursued strict neutrality, hoping to delay Greece's entry into any conflict. His chief concern remained Bulgaria, the country's traditional revisionist rival. That changed abruptly on 7 April 1939, when Italy invaded Albania, transforming it into a de facto vassal state.

It was all part of Mussolini's delusion of turning the Mediterranean into '*Mare Nostrum*' ('Our Sea'), reviving the glory that once was the Roman Empire. No louder signal of his ambitions could be given: he had planted a 'Made in Italy' flag on Greece's very doorstep.

It was no secret that Greece stood little chance of matching Italy's military might. The *Regia Marina* (Royal Italian Navy) was among the world's largest fleets, with over 100 submarines. Greece, despite its proud maritime tradition, had only six – and no warship larger than the ageing cruiser *Georgios Averof*, itself built in Italian shipyards in 1910.[7] On land, Italy could field over 1.5 million men; Greece, barely 250,000. In the air, the *Regia Aeronautica* (Royal Italian Air Force) had more than 3,000 aircraft, while the Royal Hellenic Air Force (RHAF), so named since 1935, had an eclectic fleet of just 158 – many of them trainers.

The disparity was both stark and hopeless – a David and Goliath scenario, if ever there was one.

Defence plans were swiftly revised for the northern frontier, even as the government outwardly upheld peace and appeasement. Italian forces repeatedly violated Greek airspace and waters. On 15 August 1940, during the Feast of the Dormition on Tinos – the Italian submarine *Delfino*[8] torpedoed the light cruiser RHN *Elli*[9] while at anchor on Tinos, killing nine. The government stayed silent to avoid provocation, but the public knew exactly what had happened.

If Mussolini hoped to intimidate Greece, he miscalculated: the sinking neither cowed the nation nor milked it – it galvanised it, and when the Italian ambassador delivered Mussolini's ultimatum in the early hours of 28 October – '*Let us in or be swept aside!*' – Metaxas replied with terse resolve: '*Alors, c'est la guerre.*' ('So, it is war.')

The words were French, but the sentiment was unmistakably Greek. In the streets, it became a single roar: '*Ochi!*' – 'No!'

Defiance cannot get any simpler than that – just ask any teenager.

As the nation rallied, old divisions fell away. Greeks mobilised not for victory, but out of fierce determination to resist. Among those recalled was George Sideris.

Acting on ULTRA[10] intelligence, a limited number of RAF squadrons arrived in November 1940, and the Royal Navy secured Souda Bay, enabling Cretan forces to redeploy north. Metaxas only cautiously accepted aid, fearing German retaliation, particularly as RAF aircraft from Greek soil could threaten Ploeşti, Nazi Germany's vital Romanian oil fields. His sudden death on 29 January 1941 lifted restrictions, though major reinforcements would not arrive until March.

Meanwhile, Greek forces, lacking tanks or anti-tank weapons, used terrain and ingenuity to resist, eventually driving the Italian army deep back into Albania. It was the first Allied land victory of the war – Greece's finest hour.

Mussolini's imperial theatre had collapsed into farce, forcing Hitler to come to the rescue of his humiliated ally. For the first time, Hitler had to clean up the egg on Mussolini's face – but not the last.

Meanwhile, George Sideris, recalled as a captain, was posted to Larissa Air Force Base. Records are sparse, but his work focused on recruitment and mobilisation rather than administration. Yet he was not spared the violence of war. Larissa, a key supply and communications hub, soon became a target for the *Regia Aeronautica.*

Early raids on ammunition dumps, rail yards, and the railway station had little effect, lulling locals into a false sense of security. That ended on 21 December 1940, as people prepared for their first wartime Christmas. Three Italian bombers struck Larissa with no warning or resistance. Heavy cloud cover masked their approach, but blame fell on human error, with rumours that air wardens were playing backgammon in a café instead of watching the skies. The raid killed 61 civilians and injured many more.

Then, on 1 March 1941, a powerful earthquake struck Larissa, killing 40 and injuring over 100. Nearly 10 per cent of buildings were reduced to rubble, 60 per cent damaged, leaving most of the population homeless. Italian bombers returned the next day, heartlessly finishing what nature had begun. Many fled; others stayed out of necessity or stubborn resolve. And yet, worse was still to come.

On 6 April 1941, Germany launched *Unternehmen Marita* (Operation Marita), invading Greece and Yugoslavia – Mussolini's bailout courtesy of Adolf.

Larissa, home to the vital airbase, came under fierce *Luftwaffe* bombardment. Sideris witnessed the onslaught at first-hand: death and devastation raining from above followed by the acrid stench of TNT- and ammonium-nitrate-laden bombs. The city lay shrouded in smoke and despair – a grim mockery of its former self.

Though a WWI veteran, such devastation was unfamiliar. Unlike confined front-line battles, which characterised that war, Larissa – on the Thessalian plain, Greece's 'breadbasket' – endured the ruthless impact of modern warfare, echoing the fates of Warsaw, Rotterdam, and London.

By 12 April, German troops entered an empty city, seizing the airbase to strike at British and Commonwealth forces retreating south. In scenes reminiscent of Dunkirk, Allied soldiers scrambled for evacuation to Crete or Egypt. Rear units of Australians and New Zealanders fought valiantly, but the general exodus was chaotic – dubbed Operation Demon, a name all too fitting.

On 20 April 1941, Lt Gen. Georgios Tsolakoglou, with Greek forces exhausted and outflanked by Germans advancing on Athens, began unauthorised talks with *SS-Gruppenführer* (Maj. Gen.) Sepp Dietrich, bypassing the Italians. Without approval from C-in-C Alexandros Papagos, he sought to avoid surrendering to the Italians. The armistice was signed in Votonosi, Ioannina, on Easter Sunday, 20 April 1941. The next day, 21 April, in Larissa he signed 'under duress', as he later claimed, the surrender of the Greek Army, although he was not the C-in-C.

Furious at being sidelined, Mussolini threw a tantrum, forcing a third, unnecessary tri-party signing on 23 April, in Thessaloniki.

Whoever decided that 'bad boys shouldn't cry'?

Tsolakoglou became quisling prime minister until the Nazis removed him for incompetence in December 1942. After the war, he was convicted of collaboration – few tears were shed when he died in prison in 1948.

Athens fell on 27 April, marking Axis control over Greece, though fighting continued in the Peloponnese. In just three weeks, the *Wehrmacht* had overrun the mainland – achieving what Italy had failed to do in six months – and captured around 7,000 British and Commonwealth troops, sealing a humiliating defeat.

The following month, Crete fell in *Unternehmen Merkur* (Operation Mercury), the largest airborne invasion yet. Expecting a seaborne assault, Allied forces were unable to hold key positions. As Hayter notes, many who could not flee the island – soldiers and civilians alike – went on to join the resistance. George II, King of the Hellenes, and his entourage fled into the mountains on the very day of the invasion, at first protected only by a single platoon from the 18th New Zealand Battalion. He was evacuated two days later by HMS *Decoy*[11] to Egypt.

In other words, checkmate.

On the mainland, the Greek soldiers were disarmed and allowed to return home, officers even keeping side arms – an unprecedented leniency reflecting Hitler's focus on *Unternehmen Barbarossa* (Operation Barbarossa), the imminent invasion of the Soviet Union. The occupation was divided: Germany controlled key cities; Italy ruled much of the mainland and many islands; Bulgaria took northern regions.

By the time Sideris returned to his farm, some 700 men from Italy's *6ª Divisione di fanteria 'Cuneo'* (6th Infantry Division 'Cuneo') had already imposed a harsh regime on Naxos, commandeering resources and enforcing strict movement controls. The occupation triggered a humanitarian crisis: rationing, fuel shortages, and the devaluation of the drachma crippled trade and fishing – the lifeblood of the Aegean since antiquity – culminating in the 1941–42 famine. As 1942 unfolded, Italy's declining fortunes worsened logistics, fuelling more looting by its soldiers and harsher treatment of the local population.

From the outset, Sideris joined the resistance. In a 1954 report, he wrote: '*... the idea of Freedom was not indifferent to me, so from the first days [of occupation] I had begun efforts to create a National Resistance group ... to act and fight the common enemy with what little means were at my disposal.*'[12]

He linked with networks formed by returning Naxian officers, including the *Stratiotikon Tmíma Náxou* (STN, Military Detachment of Naxos), founded by Maj. Detsis and tied to British Middle East Command. Listed as No. 222, Detsis noted of Sideris: '*He supplied valuable intelligence on enemy vessel movements, enabling Allied air attacks and rescuing two English airmen ... Excellent performance ... Recommended for the O.A. [Outstanding Acts] Medal.*'[13]

Sideris' farm, overlooking the Icarian Sea, was ideal for intelligence work. Operating under the *nom de guerre* (war name) Byron, he undoubtedly aided the British. Though respected locally, his claim of working for British Intelligence throughout the occupation contrasts sharply with his SOE file, which records his only official service '*for GROTESQUE*' as 12 December 1943 to 5 February 1944 – just eight weeks.[14] His direct British involvement may have been brief, but STN, the group he served throughout, almost certainly collaborated with, or operated closely alongside, SOE and Apollo.

Founded by lawyer and future MP Ioannis Peltekis, after SOE recruitment, Apollo was among Europe's most effective sabotage and intelligence networks. Between 1943 and 1944, it supplied intelligence on

Axis shipping and air activity, smuggled downed Allied pilots and Italian officers to safety, and carried out over 100 major sabotage acts, including disabling or destroying 72 enemy vessels. At its peak, some 400 operatives and six W/T operators maintained daily contact with SOE Cairo. Its success made it a prime *Geheime Staatspolizei* (Gestapo) target; by mid-1944, over 70 members were arrested, several executed, and operations suspended. Remnants, however, continued to thwart the Germans until their eventual withdrawal.

Sideris' peripheral but significant role illustrated Apollo's decentralised, layered cell structure, designed to preserve the network if parts were compromised. How vital he was would become clear when he himself needed rescuing.

Chapter 17

THE LRDG ON NAXOS

Οἱ δὲ ἐν σκιᾷ μαχόμενοι.
'They fought in the shadows.'

Inspired by Herodotus, on the Battle of Thermopylae (c. 480 BCE)

Forged in the harsh North African desert, the Long Range Desert Group (LRDG) was founded in 1940 by Maj. Ralph A. Bagnold.[1] His obsession with sand culminated in *The Physics of Blown Sand and Desert Dunes* – hardly a 1941 bestseller to grace coffee tables – yet it was the scientific blueprint for desert mobility and the audacious tactics the LRDG had mastered.

Formed from rugged New Zealanders and later joined by British and Rhodesian volunteers, the LRDG never exceeded 350 men, yet served within an army of millions. Their mission – long-range reconnaissance – included mapping terrain, tracking enemy movements, and rescuing downed airmen.

They first used modified Chevrolet and Ford two-wheel drives – stripped-down models that, counter-intuitively, outperformed 4×4s in desert operations. Faster, easier to maintain, and more fuel efficient, these trucks carried the ubiquitous jerry can,[2] giving them the range for long missions. Armed with Vickers K machine guns, Boys anti-tank rifles, 37mm Bofors guns, 2in mortars, and wireless sets, LRDG patrols were agile, self-sufficient, and deadly. Later, specially modified Willys-Overland 4×4 Jeeps extended that reach, enabling even deeper strikes across vast distances.

In November 1941, the LRDG rescued 21 survivors of Operation Squatter, a disastrous night parachute raid braved during a violent desert storm. Over half the original party had become casualties; some were too injured to be saved as the rest limped to safety. Realising that if the LRDG could extract men, they could also strike into danger, the visionary leader of the ill-fated jump enlisted their help – a marriage made in deadly heaven. Eventually equipped with their own vehicles, they parted ways with their beloved 'Libyan Taxi Service'. The LRDG endured – watching, rescuing, striking – after having helped forge Lt David Stirling's[3] legendary Special Air Service – the SAS.

The end of the North African campaign in May 1943 posed a dilemma for those in the upper echelons: disband the LRDG or harness its hard-won expertise?

Battle hardened and adaptable, the men were sent to Lebanon to retrain in mountain warfare – a far cry from the desert. Their mission remained long-range reconnaissance and special operations across the rugged mountains of southern Italy, Yugoslavia, Albania, and Greece.

Training was punishing. The LRDG mastered skiing, pack animal handling, and operating in small, self-sufficient patrols carrying all supplies and heavy wireless sets. Fitness and resilience were vital.

The Aegean offered a new challenge: fragmented islands, sheer cliffs, and dense undergrowth. Covert patrols infiltrated enemy-held islands by caïque, motor launch, or submarine, gathering intelligence on German garrisons, airfields, and naval activity – all relayed in code to Cairo to map Axis operations across the region.

On 26 September 1943, the eight-man R1 patrol landed on Naxos. At the time, Leros was under British control but bombed constantly by the *Luftwaffe*. Tasked with monitoring a likely German seabourne invasion route, the team was commanded by Lt D.J. 'Jack' Aitken and included Lance Corporal (L/Cpl) M.F. Fogden, Trooper (Tpr) C.B. Mason, Signalman (Sgn) B. Smith, and Privates (Pte) J.S. McIntyre, L.G. Dean, A.V. Emery, and B.W. Lambert. They carried personal weapons, a wireless set with batteries, 21 days' rations, and seven days' water.

Aitken also had two letters in Greek: one from the General Officer Commanding (GOC) Aegean, outlining his policy for the island, the other instructing locals to assist with mules and water, but otherwise leave the patrol alone. Stealth and secrecy were, of course, of prime importance.

They departed Leros on 25 October aboard RN Fairmile motor launch *ML-359*, commanded by Lt G.W. Whittman, RNVR, spending most of the next day hidden in a cove on Patmos to avoid *Luftwaffe* attention. At dawn, they reached Naxos, offloaded and camouflaged supplies and then pressed inland.

From a high-ground observation post a few miles from the coast, reconnaissance began. Sgn Bill Smith later recalled in a 1979 LRDG Association Newsletter: '*Now and again the Germans tested their machine guns, but the only other sound was the distant tinkling of sheep bells, and all around was the smell of wild thyme. The war seemed far away, and those off watch made up for the sleep lost on Leros.*'[4]

Their peaceful afternoon on 30 October 1943 was shattered by the roar of an Allied air raid – the very strike in which Bill Hayter and Tom Harper flew aboard *'S' for Sugar*. From their observation post, Smith recalled: '*Two B-25 Mitchells and two Beaufighters from Libya strafed the area. We saw only three planes fly away, but reckoned the missing Beaufighter might have slipped west, close inshore and out of sight.*'

Revealing themselves was out of the question, so the R1 patrol stayed on mission, observing and preparing reports. Nevertheless, their position was soon discovered.

'*A day or two later, the sheep moved our way, and the shepherd boy stumbled upon us. He recognised us instantly and, with one shout, was off. Greeks soon arrived, bearing food and wine, seemingly ready to celebrate liberation – or so it seemed,*' Smith wrote.

Local food and wine were a welcome break from army rations but a serious risk. '*We tried to convince them we had plenty; that we were teetotalers; that although we should be happy to take on the Germans (odds over 100 to one!), for grand strategic reasons we were under orders to restrain ourselves and they must do likewise; and finally, would they please get off the skyline and make less noise?*'

Language barriers made the task nearly impossible. '*Since none of us could get much beyond "Good morning" in Greek, this was a tall order and, in fact, a losing battle,*' Smith recalled. Still, the celebration continued. '*Soon bottles were waved in time to patriotic choruses. R1's capacity was by no means negligible, but we confined ourselves to the "sippers" Allied solidarity demanded,*' he added with humour.

Amid the hullabaloo, a diminutive Greek appeared, every inch an important messenger, handing Jack a slip of paper. Smith watched as Aitken maintained control. '*Not surprisingly, of Jack's many qualities, grim determination prevailed and his sense of humour was temporarily eclipsed. He did not take kindly to the interruption and took the note with a scowl, growling: "Must have been on the bloody ouzo!"*'

For all the wine and spirits being waved in celebration, it was Aitken's remark that probably proved the driest. Despite the unhelpful and untimely arrival of the note, any suggestion that its writer must have been drunk was quickly dispelled once it was read:

> To Officer Commanding British land forces Naxos from Officer Commanding RAF Naxos:
>
> I understand that you have recently arrived here and have the means of returning to the fleshpots of civilisation. If that is so, I should be grateful if you could make two seats available for my navigator and myself.
>
> My navigator damaged his jaw when our Beaufighter ditched and I am anxious that he should receive medical attention as soon as possible.
>
> You can trust absolutely the bearer of this message, who is one of the Greeks now sheltering us, and you can safely confide to him the details of any rendezvous you may wish to arrange.
>
> W. Hayter
> Pilot Officer RAF.
>
> P.S. Do you happen to know where one has to pay income tax for the period spent on Naxos?

Hayter's words might read as bravado, even flippancy, but they were chosen carefully. For Aitken, it was the first news of the airmen's plight. Importantly, the humour reassured him the note was genuine, not a German ruse to compromise the patrol.

Decades later, Smith still appreciated Hayter's wit, concluding his article with: '*I've often wondered whether Bill tried it on with the Inland Revenue, and if so, what happened!*'

There is an old adage: only two places on Earth don't need spies – Japan, where no one speaks to strangers, and Greece, where everyone does.

On wartime Naxos, news of the airmen and the patrol would have spread like wildfire, making every moment a race against German discovery. Yet, despite near-famine conditions, the Naxians brought what little they had. The patrol's hideout soon saw a steady stream of visitors. Their generosity, offered at mortal risk, revealed the courage and warmth of the local people – choosing compassion over fear.

C'est la guerre! (Such is war!) – or at least the bizarre circumstances it can create.

Before long, three well-dressed Greeks appeared, speaking a mix of broken Italian and French. They sought proof the patrol were Allies and questioned their intentions. After some effort, Aitken convinced them, and the men introduced themselves as resistance veterans of the Greco-Italian War. Unarmed but experienced, they shared crucial intelligence on German positions.

Though likely using first names or pseudonyms, these men were in fact Manolis Korres, Konstantinos Matzakos, and Manolis Alibertis – the trusted '*bearer of this message*' Hayter mentions, responsible for liaising between the downed airmen and the patrol.

On 2 November, troubling news arrived: one of the three Greeks had been arrested the previous day. Fearing for his safety, the others insisted the patrol leave immediately. That night, Aitken moved his men under cover of darkness. Guided by a local, they collected the airmen from Sideris' farmhouse in Kampos at 1900 hrs. '*They had been well treated and were fit to travel*,' Aitken reported.[5]

This was the pivotal moment – Bill Harper and Tom Hayter had finally been rescued.

However, evacuation was delayed by rough seas. On 3 November, Aitken noted: '*Hiding all day so as to give the Greeks the impression that we had left the island. The sea was too rough for us to be evacuated that night.*' Frustratingly, the storm persisted, but by 5 November the seas had abated, and Smith put out the call. Aitken recorded: '*Sea much calmer. 2200 hrs. Picked up by ML. The dinghy was swamped and lost, but the assault boat proved very effective*.'

Aboard *ML-359*, they did not head straight for Leros but remained hidden in neutral waters off the Turkish coast for most of the following day, avoiding prowling *Luftwaffe* aircraft. They arrived at Leros two hours after sunset. Aitken's final entry confirmed their arrival: '*1930 hrs arrived back in Leros. Disembarked ALINDA BAY.*'

Bill Hayter and Tom Harper were finally safe – or were they?

Throughout the ordeal, their injuries must have troubled both airmen far more than Hayter admitted – especially Tom Harper, whose wound was severe and whose stitches had '*come undone*', as Hayter notes. On reaching Leros, they were taken straight to a medical facility. The island hosted a key *Regia Marina* base at Porto di Portolago (now Lakki),[6] complete with a well-equipped naval hospital, though it is unclear if they were treated there.

Hayter's surviving field medical card confirms they were cared for by No. 161 Field Ambulance under Capt. Jack Barder, receiving 3,000 units of anti-tetanus serum intramuscularly at 2030 hrs on 6 November 1943. His clinical notes, with explanatory comments, read:

> 6/11/43. Crashed into sea & sustained laceration nose, severe, 30/10/43. Seen by Greek doctor 1/11/45 who stitched nose under local anaesthesia. Good apposition, depth indication [wound edges aligned; depth appropriate]. General condition excellent. Sod. Bicarb [sodium bicarbonate] coating to nose [for healing and infection prevention]. Sutures [stitches] remained. Sulphanilamide formula applied [antibacterial treatment]. Evacuate setting [planned further care].
>
> J. Bigmond

We now know that the '*local anaesthesia*' was actually George Sideris' potent '*whisk*'!

Their injuries, while serious, may have been a hidden safeguard, sparing them from further danger – and perhaps even saving their lives.

By early November 1943, Leros was a beleaguered Allied outpost in the Aegean, held together more by determination than strength. The British garrison numbered just over 3,000 – a patchwork force including the Royal Irish Fusiliers, the Buffs (Royal East Kent Regiment), the King's Own Royal Regiment (Lancaster), a company from the Queen's Own Royal West Kent Regiment, elements of the LRDG, and Maj. Jellicoe's Special Boat Service (SBS). They had arrived mid-September to capitalise on Italy's surrender.

The Italian garrison under *Capitano* (Capt.) Luigi Mascherpa numbered about 7,600, mostly naval personnel with little land-warfare experience. Only around 1,000 were combat troops; the rest were technical, service, or anti-aircraft units. The British assumed command, hoping to make Leros defensible, but despite the Italian fondness for cement, fortifications were scattered, supplies scarce, and the garrison vulnerable to *Luftwaffe* raids.

From 26 September, relentless bombing began, sinking the destroyers HMS *Intrepid*[7] and RHN *Vasilissa Olga*[8] in harbour on the first day. Throughout October, the island endured up to eleven raids per day. Coastal batteries, naval facilities, and infrastructure were systematically destroyed, and morale plummeted. With Kos having fallen in just 24 hours in October, defenders braced for a similar fate.

Brigadier (Brig.) Robert Tilney arrived on 5 November and chose to defend the coastline rather than the interior high ground, leaving Mt Kleidi (Clidi) exposed. On 12 November, the Germans launched *Unternehmen Taifun* (Operation Typhoon, formerly Leopard), led by Müller, infamous for executing Italian officers after his conquest of Kos and already notorious as the 'Butcher of Crete' for self-explanatory reasons.[9]

Three German battalions from the 22nd Infantry Division – *III./Infanterie-Regiment 440* (3rd Battalion), *II./Regiment 16*, and *II./Regiment 65* (both 2nd Battalions) – landed at Vaghia (Palma) Bay, Cape Akra Pano Zimi (Pasta di Sopra), and Pandeli Bay, supported by a specialised amphibious company from *Division Brandenburg*. Despite early gains, British and Italian forces fought back fiercely, particularly at the Lagos and Ciano batteries.

The rocky terrain had left the British entirely unprepared when *I./Fallschirmjäger-Regiment 2* (1st Battalion, Paratrooper Regiment 2) dropped from just 300ft (90m) from slow Ju 52s. Many were shot under their canopies, while others broke bones or were killed falling onto rocks or into gullies. Survivors, however, proved impossible to dislodge, giving the Germans an inland foothold from which they divided the island's defences.

By 16 November, Tilney deemed further resistance futile and agreed to surrender at 1730 hrs. Mascherpa held out until 2200 hrs, with some Italian units fighting into the next morning. Despite heavy losses, many LRDG and SBS men escaped – fleeing by caïque, motorboat or even rowboat to Turkey, while others used their specialist skills to hide inland until rescued.

Weeks earlier, on 23 October, the LRDG had suffered heavy losses in a poorly planned assault on Levitha – five killed, 37 captured – their worst single-action toll. On Leros, patrols were stationed close to Italian artillery and slowly whittled down by *Luftwaffe* attacks. The German landing forced them into direct combat, hunting parachutists, engaging enemy forces, and mounting counterattacks as regular infantry.

The misuse of the LRDG at Levitha, their deployment on Leros, and CO Lt Col. John 'Jake' Easonsmith's death on 16 November led New Zealand to protest and withdraw personnel. Yet the British and Rhodesian members carried on, conducting special operations across Italy, Albania, and Greece until the unit disbanded in August 1945.

About 1,400 combatants from both sides died or went missing at Leros; nearly 3,000 British/Commonwealth and some 5,300 Italians were captured. The fall of Leros ended Operation Accolade and the Dodecanese campaign – only Samos remained, isolated despite reinforcement by *Ieros Lochos* (Sacred Band – Greek commandos).[10] Allied forces evacuated Samos on the night of 18–19 November, many fleeing through neutral Turkey disguised as civilians.

Having just escaped from Naxos, it would have been bitterly ironic for Hayter and Harper to be captured on Leros. However, fate had whisked them away to the Middle East for urgent medical treatment mere days before the German onslaught.

Miraculously, they had escaped twice.

Chapter 18

BETRAYAL

Timeo Danaos et dona ferentes.
'I fear the Greeks, even when they bring gifts.'
From Virgil's *Aeneid*, Book II (c. 29–19 BCE),
spoken by the Trojan priest Laocoön
as a warning about the Trojan horse

Following Bill Hayter's and Tom Harper's rescue from Naxos by the LRDG and their evacuation from Leros before it fell to the Germans, they were hospitalised in Egypt. Meanwhile, George Sideris' situation remained perilous. Those who had aided the British airmen – from shepherd boys to Dr Bardanis – now faced the grave threat of exposure and retribution.

Hayter's '*docteur de la montagne*' displayed extraordinary skill, stitching both airmen in the primitive conditions of Sideris' living room. He recalled: '*Later on in hospital, the job was finished by Major Oldfield, the most brilliant plastic surgeon in the Middle East, and his opinion of Dr Bardanis' work was that it was absolutely exceptional, so much so that he could not understand how he had managed it with the instruments at his disposal.*'

Sideris faced a dual peril. The first was internal – betrayal by fellow Greeks. While official accounts often downplay local collaboration, historian Menelaos Charalambidis notes that '*the official version that only a small minority of Greeks cooperated with the occupier does not comply with reality*'.[1]

Collaboration began at the top. Tsolakoglou's quisling government facilitated tacit cooperation across the state – from police to bureaucrats and academics. On Naxos, this threat manifested locally in a collaborator appointed by the Italians as civilian governor, widely despised by the islanders. Collaborators turned on neighbours and even family, denouncing those who resisted, spoke out, or hid food from marauding occupiers. Fear, desperation, personal vendetta, and greed all drove these acts.

The second danger was personal. Hayter describes Sideris as sincere, generous, and trusting – but not discreet, a trait ill-suited to the covert demands of espionage.

Sideris' SOE file notes his '*unfortunate habit of boasting to all and sundry about his exploits, thereby endangering not only himself but the Mission as well*'. As Hayter outlines, the farmhouse quickly became a magnet for curious locals eager to glimpse the British airmen he was sheltering – a fact that deeply worried both him and Harper. Yet the same SOE file acknowledges the real essence of the man: '*On the other hand, he was enthusiastic and well intentioned. His prestige on the island is high.*'[2]

For all his qualities, the inescapable truth was that too many had learned of the airmen's rescue and evacuation – it was only a matter of time before word reached the Germans. In a strange twist of fate, however, it seems George Sideris' life may have been spared by one of them.

Her name was Valli – the German-born wife of Michalis Milonas, a landowner with homes in Komiaki and Apollonas. In a 2020 video interview, Sideris' niece, Varvara Chorianopoulou-Levogianni, and her friend Elissavet Christou-Alimperti – both young women during the war – spoke of her courage. When Valli learned the Germans had discovered George's role in the escape, she acted fast. Through his cousin, Ioannis Korres, she sent word: Sideris was being hunted down.

Korres rode straight to Kampos, giving the warning just in time. Sideris was gone before the soldiers arrived.

He moved through the mountains by night, taking shelter wherever he could – barns, caves, shepherds' huts. The monks of *Panagia Phanerómeni* (Our Lady of the Revelation) turned him away at first, fearing German reprisal, but eventually offered a few days' refuge. Later, he found a more lasting hideout in a farmhouse in Afres, where Nikolas Levogiannis' father lived. His uncle Antonis, a fellow STN member, helped wherever he could. Others kept watch over the hills.

When the Germans failed to find him, they issued a death warrant on him in absentia.

Then, on 1 February 1944, they came again. An armed patrol left Apollonas before dawn with a hand-drawn sketch of Sideris' farm supplied by a local collaborator. By daybreak, they were in position – machine guns covering the two soldiers advancing on the house.

Unknown to the Germans, Sideris had temporarily returned from hiding. He had seen a fully laden German caïque offshore and wanted it reported to the British. While Varvara kept watch through her uncle's binoculars – the same ones he used to spy on maritime traffic – she saw movement: silhouettes in helmets, guns glinting.

Panic stricken, she warned her uncle. He ran – but not far.

From the hillside, George watched the soldiers descend on his home. His mother, Kiriaki Sideri – the elegant old lady Hayter had described – and his niece were inside. He waited – still, silent, watching. The torment must have been unimaginable. He was ready to give himself up if either were threatened.

The Germans ransacked the humble farmhouse, rifling through cupboards, overturning bedding, probing every corner – but they did not harm the women. George's mother sobbed uncontrollably, while Varvara stood by her side, silent but resolute. After two tense hours, the patrol withdrew. Before leaving, they delivered a message: George Sideris was to present himself immediately at their billet in Apollonas.

Curiously, they carried a photograph – a formal portrait of Sideris in his air force dress uniform. It was a copy of the same picture he had shown Hayter and Harper in his living room at their first meeting.

The hunt was well and truly up.

Around this time, the SOE launched two covert missions in the Cyclades. Operation Primer aimed to land a wireless operator and observer on the remote islet of Irakleia to establish a communications post. Operation Grotesque II sought to reconnect with agents on Naxos and resupply them.

Such missions were extremely perilous. Under Hitler's *Kommandobefehl* (Commando Order) of 18 October 1942, capture meant execution by firing squad, uniformed or not – anyone involved in resistance, sabotage, or covert operations was to be shot without trial.

Both missions sailed aboard the caïque *Armadillo*, captained by Lt K.J. Mackenzie, RNVR, with Maj. Barker in overall charge. They left Haifa on 4 January 1944, but storms forced a delay in Beirut before they reached Paphos, Cyprus, and crossed into the Aegean. On 19 January, in heavy seas, they sought shelter at the uninhabited islet of Anhydros. Mackenzie wrote: '*When we tried to enter a small cove, the surge was so violent we had to hack away the anchor and head for open water. It was pitch dark and snowing – squalls of intense ferocity tore down the cliffs – so I cruised in small circles until dawn.*'[3]

'Cruised' suggests calm seas and cocktails. In reality, he was clawing through a blizzard, desperate to keep the fragile wooden craft from being smashed to splinters.

On 22 January, they narrowly avoided a floating mine in the half-light before reaching Irakleia, where their local contact, Manolis Psaras,[4] met them. Under cover of darkness, Sgts Demoulas and Valavanis were moved inland by mule to their post.

The *Armadillo* then slipped towards the Makares – three barren islets just off Naxos' eastern coast. They cut silently through the dark Aegean, hiding in daylight as German aircraft passed overhead. That night, they crossed to Naxos, hoping for a signal from SOE agents at Cape Moutsouna. None came. Suspecting equipment failure, they returned to Irakleia, trapped again by storms.

On 1 February, they finally completed the mission – supplies delivered, agents repositioned, the original team extracted. Among those landed at Moutsouna was Lt Michalis Kairis. He handed Sideris a note: he was to be ferried to Irakleia, where a man known only as Kosta would lead him to a caïque for evacuation. Timing was uncertain. He might wait days – or weeks – surviving on scraps.

The wait stretched painfully. On 22 February, he was taken to Irakleia to hide, fully aware he could be discovered at any moment. By 14 April, food was low, extraction still uncertain. On 30 April, under darkness, he boarded a caïque and began a hazardous escape through the islands: Irakleia, Giaros, Gioura, Serifos, Anhydros, and Syrna – finally reaching Megisti.

Two gruelling weeks at sea brought him to British-held Cyprus – first Paphos, then Ammochostos (Famagusta). On 19 May 1944, he reported to the Greek Military Mission in Lefkosia (Nicosia). His long ordeal was finally over.

The Greek government-in-exile ran a refugee centre for those fleeing occupied Greece. On 23 May 1944, Greek Intelligence notified the Cyprus Refugee Centre of Sideris' arrival. For his vital assistance to Bill Hayter and Tom Harper, the British authorities spared him quarantine. A subsequent report painted a stark picture of his plight – he literally had nothing but the clothes he stood in. The centre provided food and some aid, yet support from the overstretched Greek authorities was not forthcoming.

Sideris kept a tiny pocket diary, recording key moments in neat, fragile handwriting. Alongside other artefacts, it is now preserved by Maria and Konstantinos Levogiannis, who kindly allowed examination.

The first entry recounts 1 February 1944, when he narrowly escaped arrest on Naxos. Only seven further entries follow – not for lack of events, but what he deemed most vital or safest to record.

The 17 May entry notes his arrival in Famagusta, where an RAF captain, Ashe, and a colleague met him and arranged accommodation in Lefkosia. He remained there for 52 days at the British military's expense. The bill came to £31 – a considerable sum at the time, and a quiet measure of the esteem in which he was held.

Yet Sideris remained penniless and adrift. He petitioned to rejoin the Hellenic Armed Forces: '*I arrived from Greece on the 17th of April 1944. Strangely, the resident Greek authorities informed me that the drafting of new arrivals had been cancelled, and I now find myself in an uncomfortable position, with neither money nor clothes.*'[5]

His hopes were dashed. Political tensions within the government-in-exile shredded cohesion in the Middle East. King George II, awkward and divisive, never connected with his people. Rifts between royalists and republicans, and the rising communist threat, spread discord even in Egypt, where most exiled forces were based.

Mutinies erupted in April 1944. Frustration over poor conditions, political infighting, and ideology tore discipline apart. With British help, the uprising was suppressed, but the damage was done. Of nearly 18,500 men, only 2,500 were deemed loyal and reliable. The rest were interned in desert camps or dishonourably discharged.

A diary entry of 8 July 1944 records Sideris' departure by air for Cairo. Though formally independent, Egypt was firmly under British influence, especially militarily. His route included stops in Beirut, Haifa, and Tel Aviv – all under British control or heavy oversight. Beirut, nominally Vichy French, still hosted significant British forces. On arrival, the British lodged him at the National Hotel in the city centre.

Cairo in 1944 was a city of extremes – a vital Allied hub where war met luxury. The Suez Canal made it strategic, and the streets swelled with soldiers, diplomats, and exiles, with hotels and cafés humming with rumours, politics, and espionage. Officers lived well, and black markets flourished, while ordinary Egyptians faced overcrowding, inflation, and exclusion.

For Sideris, newly arrived from an occupied Greek island, the contrast was stark – ease and comfort replacing hardship and constant threat.

Soon afterwards, he received news that lifted his spirits. On 13 July, the Greek government-in-exile decreed: '*George Sideris, a long-retired former Comptroller Officer, is eligible for service during the current war period.*'[6] Reinstatement seemed possible, though uncertainty still stretched ahead.

The final entry in Sideris' wartime pocket diary notes a visit to Port Said on 28 July 1944. At the northern mouth of the Suez Canal, the city pulsed with Allied ships and soldiers. Just two years earlier, Rommel's *Panzerarmee Afrika* – including the feared *Deutsches Afrikakorps* and substantial Italian forces – had reached as far as El Alamein. The threat had sparked panic in Cairo, with British officials torching sensitive files in a frenzy known as 'the Flap'; one day, so many glowing embers drifted over the city that it became known as 'Ash Wednesday'.

Standing amid the bustle of Port Said, Sideris must have reflected on the improbable path that brought him here – from Naxos' verdant hills, through narrow escapes and a covert voyage, to this desert city of war. The sea, the ships, the uniforms – all reminders of a global struggle that had swept up his quiet island. Thoughts surely turned to Kampos, to his mother and Varvara, and to the garden he once tended – now under ruthless Nazi control.

Yet he did not linger. Determined, he sought the two men whose lives he had saved. Against language barriers and wartime turmoil, he discovered F/O Bill Hayter stationed at an aerodrome outside Cairo. No detailed record survives of their reunion, but when Sideris appeared – alive and free – Hayter must have been stunned, and deeply moved.

It was no fleeting meeting. Over the following months, they spent meaningful time together, renewing the bond first formed on Naxos. Post-war correspondence shows a connection far deeper than their brief six days on the island could have suggested. Tom Harper may also have joined them, though evidence is lacking.

At some point, they marked their reconnection with a portrait. In a local photographic studio, two men in uniform – not just comrades-in-arms, but linked by fate and forged through shared trials – posed side by side. Their expressions convey more than formality: a profound sense of unity and loyalty, 'us against them'.

Time pressed on, and circumstances eventually drove them apart. They would never meet again.

On 8 August 1944, Sideris' long limbo ended. The Greek government-in-exile, led by Prime Minister Georgios Papandreou in coordination with British military authorities, decreed: '*We induct into the roster of the Middle East Royal Hellenic Air Force the escapee from Greece, who has since reported for duty to our military authorities, Reserve Air Force Capt. Comptroller George Sideris (SN: 5045), starting from 13 May 1944, the date he entered friendly soil.*'[7]

By autumn 1944, the Third Reich was crumbling. The Red Army's relentless advance through Romania and Bulgaria threatened to cut German forces off from the Fatherland, even as these former Axis powers switched sides. In Greece, a 27 August 1944 Führer directive outlined a phased withdrawal: '*loosening up of the occupation of the Ionian islands and of the Aegean islands, as well as of the coastal section*', though '*larger harbours*' were to be spared immediate evacuation.[8] *Deutsche Truppen* (German troops) fell back north through Yugoslavia, mainly on foot, harried by resistance fighters and battered by Allied air and naval strikes. They retreated with grim discipline, leaving a swathe of destruction in their wake – devastation that only swift action could hope to contain.

Amid this chaos, SOE operatives acted to limit the damage. Maj. Brian E. Dillon sought to halt a 150-strong German demolition team in Athens, saving the city's power station even as Piraeus was lost. Fellow operatives – Lt Col. L.F. 'Rufus' Sheppard, Capt. H.N. 'Harry' McIntyre, and Emil Sandstrom of the Swedish Red Cross – persuaded the Germans not to destroy the Marathon Dam, sparing Athens' water supply and averting further catastrophe for the civilian population.

When the Greek government-in-exile returned on 18 October under British protection, Athens was a tinderbox. *Ellinikós Laïkós Apeleftherotikós Stratós* (ELAS – Greek People's Liberation Army) communists refused to disarm, royalists pressed for King George II, and republican factions resisted. Violence erupted on 3 December when a mass protest in *Syntagma* (Constitution Square) was fired upon, leaving 28 dead and scores wounded. British Commander Lt Gen. Ronald Scobie, charged by Churchill to maintain order '*with bloodshed if necessary*',[9] had Sherman tanks rumbling through the streets and RAF aircraft strafing rooftops, yet ELAS, outnumbering them five to one, still held much of Athens and Piraeus.

On Christmas Day, Churchill himself arrived to mediate, narrowly escaping an assassination attempt linked to an ELAS bomb plot in the sewers beneath the Grande Bretagne Hotel in central Athens. Talks were moved to HMS *Ajax*[10] at Phaleron, tempers flared, and compromise remained fragile. Archbishop Damaskinos was appointed neutral regent on 31 December, imposing a truce, yet the country teetered on the brink of full civil war.

It soon plummeted headlong into that abyss. Peace finally returned in 1949, but at a heavy cost: Greece had deepened its wounds, dividing families, delaying economic recovery, and sowing mistrust that would last for decades.

It was, in every sense, a modern Greek tragedy.

The exact date of George Sideris' return to Naxos after liberation is uncertain, but it occurred sometime after April 1945. He received two formal commendations. Gen. Sir Henry Maitland Wilson, C-in-C of Middle East Forces, wrote:

> This is to certify that Georgios Sideris has, during the period December 1943 to February 1944, faithfully and loyally served the Allied Cause and thereby has contributed to the liberation of Europe.

Field Marshal Sir Harold Alexander, Supreme Allied Commander Mediterranean Theatre, added:

> This certificate is awarded to Georgios Ioannou Sideris as a token of gratitude for and appreciation of the help given to the Sailors, Soldiers, and Airmen of the British Commonwealth of Nations, which enabled them to escape from, or evade capture by, the enemy.

However, bureaucracy proved indifferent. His request for promotion to major was denied, and a 1945 appeal went unanswered. In 1954, his application for formal recognition as an SOE agent was dismissed, the ostensible reasons given being that he had never been on the payroll and that his certificates were mere propaganda. Consequently, his claim was lumped together with those of others merely 'trying on' for compensation. The final line, delivered with chilling detachment, left no room for doubt: '*Whether his assistance to RAF personnel should be referred to the Escaping Society*[11] *is, of course, no concern of ours.*'[12]

Regrettably, George Sideris died prematurely in Athens on 13 December 1963, aged 65 and is buried there. Officialdom may have overlooked him, but Hayter's journal attests to his courage and selflessness.

A quiet, yet very real hero.

Chapter 19

DECIMATION

Decimatio more veteri supplicium militibus irrogatum est.
'Decimation, according to the ancient custom, was inflicted as punishment upon the soldiers.'

Suetonius, *De Vita Caesarum* (c. 121 CE)

After plastic surgery and recuperation, Bill Hayter and Tom Harper returned to Gambut III, Cyrenaica. They had missed much of the action: the Beaufighters of Nos. 47 and 603 Squadrons had flown other raids – sometimes with B-25Gs, sometimes not – and had been highly active in the Battle of Leros.

Given that American help had been denied to Churchill's foray into the Aegean, the direct involvement of B-25Gs was unusual but not unprecedented.

In October 1943, the 321st BG of the USAAF's 12th Air Force, part of the 57th Bombardment Wing, relocated from Soliman airfield in Tunisia to Grottaglie aerodrome – near Taranto, Italy – becoming the first American medium-bomber group to operate from Italian soil. The 446th Bombardment Squadron historian, 1st Lt Sergius P. Neprash, happily noted in the 321st BG War Diary: '*Now that we were located in the forward zone in the theatre of combat, free rations of cigarettes and candy were issued each week.*'[1]

The perk, however, was short-lived. On 15 October, the group deployed a special 'G' detachment of North American B-25G Mitchell gunships to Gambut III, supporting Operation Accolade and the wider Dodecanese campaign. With Kos fallen in early October, it was plain to all that British forces were in 'a spot of bother', urgently requiring deliverance.

Other 12th Air Force units, operating from southern Italy, were diverted from the Italian campaign and Balkan operations to strike key Axis airfields in mainland Greece. In October 1943 alone, the USAAF carried out at least 30 attacks, deploying heavy bombers (B-17s, B-24s), medium bombers (B-25s), and long-range fighters (P-38s) against airfields and shipping, as well as providing convoy support.

Famously, in early October 1943, P-38 Lightnings of the USAAF's 1st Fighter Group were briefly detached from Tunisia to cover British naval forces in the Aegean. Their commitment lasted just three operational days, 7–9 October, but in that short span the strengths and weaknesses of the deployment were shown starkly. On 9 October, during a handover between squadrons of the 1st and 14th Groups, a brief lapse in cover over Karpathos (Scarpanto) Strait proved disastrous: Ju 87s of *I./Sturzkampfgeschwader 3* (I./StG 3, 1st Group, 3rd Dive Bomber Wing), flying from Megara on the Greek mainland, struck without warning, sinking HMS *Panther*[2] in less than a minute and crippling HMS *Carlisle.*[3]

Minutes later, however, a second wave of Stukas was intercepted by the newly arrived 37th Squadron. In the furious clash that followed, the Lightnings claimed heavy German losses, with Maj. William L. Leverette credited with seven victories – the most recorded in a single sortie in the theatre. It was a demonstration of what American support could achieve, yet almost immediately the fighters were withdrawn at the insistence of senior US command.

Their sudden absence left the Royal Navy once more exposed to daylight attack, and, as Churchill observed with bitterness, '*the enemy had air mastery, and it was only by night that our ships could operate without crippling loss*'.[4]

Could the modified B-25G gunships help? Their design was an exercise in rhinoplasty – the Perspex nose was shortened and replaced with metal, fitted with mounts for two .50in (12.7mm) machine guns (later variants had more). Into this unlikely space they crammed a modified 2.95in (75mm) M4 tank cannon – by far the largest ordnance ever grafted onto an aircraft snout.

As with many combat aircraft of the period, USAAF crews adorned their aircraft with names and artwork. In the 448th Bombardment Squadron,

B-25G 42-32487 was christened *Black Magic*, crewed by F/O Charles F. Keith (pilot), 2nd Lt William E.A. Winegar (co-pilot), 2nd Lt Joseph W. Shook (navigator), Sgt Richard L. Maddox (engineer/gunner), S/Sgt Bert A. Cobb (radio/gunner), and Sgt Charles O. Krueger (gunner).

The 445th Bombardment Squadron's B-25G 42-64579 bore the name *Flying Caisson*, a nod to historic field artillery carts and the aircraft's massive cannon. There was pride in these names and the all-American 'big is beautiful' ethos, but in reality, the weapon's slow manual reload limited its effectiveness: *Black Magic* only managed two shots over Naxos harbour.

It was the downing of *Flying Caisson* that Bill Hayter described during the attack on Naxos. Tragic as the loss was, Hayter and Harper – having met the crew only that morning and then facing their own crisis – were likely little affected. For the 445th, however, it was profound. Neprash wrote: '*Lt. Black, although the newest man, was well liked by all. Our hats are off to Lts. Black, Golden, and S/Sgts Horton, Ramsburg, Lang, and Wenrich.*[5] *We'll miss them.*'[6] Fate spared S/Sgt Jacob Leist, who was left behind on latrine duty for failing to muster that morning – his place on *Flying Caisson* taken by Ramsburg from 446th Squadron.

Sometimes it pays to be late.

Hayter returned to operational flying at 1310 hrs on 25 November 1943, piloting Beaufighter 'E' with F/O F.C. Miles as navigator/observer. On an offensive sweep over the southern Aegean, they spotted a few small vessels off Amorgos before returning safely at 1730 hrs.

For Hayter, it was more than a routine mission. Climbing into the cockpit after the trauma of ditching with Tom Harper, he must have felt a tangle of fear, relief, and determination. Every switch and instrument reminded him of the deadly weight of duty – the fragility of life in the air, the courage of those he had flown with, and the sheer will it took to survive. When the mighty Hercules engines spluttered into life, shaking the cockpit with raw power, he returned to the skies that had tested him so cruelly just weeks earlier.

In his journal, Hayter describes other pilots – men losing confidence or, worse, resigned to their fate. The war had worn them down; some seemed to accept death as inevitable. Was it the same for him – or an act of defiance against that fate and the attrition of war? Perhaps it was simply the need to follow orders and the quiet resignation it implied. These questions remain unanswered. As his eldest daughter, Anne, explained with frustration, he barely acknowledged his RAF role, much less shared his war experiences with family.

By the time Hayter returned, No. 47 Squadron had changed beyond recognition. Major losses over the preceding weeks had decimated his inner circle, leaving the unit a shadow of what it had been.

On 5 November, during a torpedo strike against three merchant vessels in Lavrion Bay, 37 miles (60km) south-east of Athens, six Beaufighters from Nos. 47 and 603 Squadrons encountered intense, precise flak. W/Cdr J. Lee-Evans, with F/Lt D. Heden as navigator/observer in Beaufighter 'D', was forced to ditch just '*north of the harbour*', starboard engine ablaze: '*The A/C [aircraft] was still partly afloat after 15 seconds and pilot should have escaped, but navigator may have been caught in flames which were spreading.*' Another No. 47 Beaufighter, piloted by F/Lt T. Graham with F/O H. Langdon, was seen '*to be well on fire and crashed in the sea near the position of "D's" ditching*'.[7] The crews' exact fates were unreported, although Lee-Evans was replaced as CO by W/Cdr J.R.H. Lewis DFC on 13 November.

The loss of W/Cdr Lee-Evans – 'Jimmy', as Hayter notes – was more than an aircraft downing. Leadership shaped morale – the force driving crews to face danger against the odds. Historian Max Hastings, in *Bomber Command*, noted: '*The morale of a squadron was almost always in direct proportion to the quality of leadership shown by the squadron commanders.*'[8] A respected CO inspired crews to press attacks with resolve and reduced losses. His absence reverberated far beyond the cockpit – felt in confidence, cohesion, and courage.

On 6 November, F/O Lewis 'Ross' Rossner – one of only two '*completely fearless men I have ever fought with*', according to Hayter – flew over the entrance of Naoussa Bay, Paros, with F/Sgt K. Levy as his navigator/observer. Moments later, their aircraft was hit. Flame erupted from the starboard engine before the Beaufighter slammed into a hillside north of Langeri Bay. No parachutes were seen; smoke spiralled as the rest of the formation broke away. 'Ross' – the born mimic who '*every time he spoke, one had to laugh*' – was gone.[9]

The mission quickly unravelled. S/L C. Ogilvie, flying with F/O M. O'Connor, came under attack from at least one of five Bf 109s, supported by Arado floatplanes. Tracer rounds lit the sky. Their Beaufighter vanished in the melee – another crew lost. In the same engagement, No. 603 Squadron's Beaufighter LX998 was forced to ditch – a story recounted more fully in the Epilogue.

Four days later, on 10 November, three Beaufighters from No. 47 and nine from No. 603 Squadron were dispatched on a low-level barge sweep between Amorgos and Leros. One aircraft peeled off early with a fuel leak and radio issues. Suddenly, two Bf 109s dove from above. In the ensuing dogfight, F/O J.S. Hayden and rear gunner Sgt J. McMaster were hit – '*shot into the sea*'[10] 15 minutes after first contact. McMaster's fate remains unrecorded, presumed dead, but Hayter's friend – 'Titch' Hayden – was confirmed lost. Only three months earlier, shortly after joining the squadron, Hayden had featured on the front page of *Stars and Stripes*. Now he too was gone.[11]

Two minutes later, another loss. No. 603 Squadron's Beaufighter LZ275, piloted by F/Sgt W.A. Eacott with P/O W.B.P. Pritchard, was seen smoking before crashing into the sea. No survivors.

By 12 November, operations had intensified. Two No. 47 Squadron Beaufighters joined three B-25Gs from the 310th (former 321st) BG and six more Beaufighters from No. 603 Squadron on a combined shipping strike. At grid 35°51'N, 23°54'E, they located a convoy. The American gunships went in first, their massive nose cannon blazing. No. 47 Squadron's torpedo-armed Beaufighters followed, releasing their loads from 1,000 and 800 yards (915 and 730m) off the starboard beam of a 3,000-ton merchantman. Both torpedoes missed.

As the aircraft turned away, flak erupted. F/O A.G. 'Nobby' Greentree, a New Zealander, flying with Sgt G. Freeman, was among the last to break. Their Beaufighter was hit and '*presumed to have ditched*'.[12] Both were later listed missing in action, presumed dead.[13]

On 13 November, F/Sgts R.G. Provost and H.P. Meadows of No. 603 Squadron suffered engine failure during another sweep. As Provost tried to ditch in heavy swell, the tail snapped off and the aircraft '*sank immediately*'. Though the dinghy inflated, '*neither crew was seen*'.[14] For hours it seemed they had been lost – until the stunning news arrived: both were rescued and flying again the next day.

Later that afternoon, seven No. 47 Squadron Beaufighters encountered twelve Ju 88s north-west of Leros. One formation was already bombing between Alinda and Gunia Bays. The Beaufighters intercepted a second formation at 2,000ft (610m) off Porta di Sotto. Under pressure, the Ju 88s jettisoned their bombs harmlessly into the sea.

S/L Muller-Rowland, with F/Sgt S. Anderson, led an attack from below and behind. His Beaufighter's starboard engine was shot up, trailing smoke and flame. He ditched in San Nicola Bay. Both men clambered into a dinghy – alive, barely. On the return leg, the formation ran into more Ju 88s east of Patmos, engaging again before continuing home to El Adem.

By 16 November, the strain was telling. Seven Beaufighters from No. 47 and one from No. 603 Squadron launched a sweep against a Siebel ferry carrying troops and equipment to Leros. Enemy cover included seven Arado 196s hugging the sea, four Bf 109s at 1,000ft (300m), and four Ju 88s below. Yet the Beaufighters pressed on.

The strike was devastating. '*All cannon fire*'[15] tore through the ferry. Last in the run, P/O R.H. Giles of No. 603 Squadron saw a glow where his rounds struck – then the ferry '*caught fire and blew up*'.[16] The barges were likely hit too. The formation was immediately set upon by Ju 88s and Bf 109s in a furious 25-minute dogfight. The Arados circled but did not engage.

At 1340 hrs, one Beaufighter crashed into the sea in flames; two more shared the same fate. Eventually, the Bf 109s broke off – '*possibly ammo exhausted*'.[17]

It had been a slaughter. F/O A.D. Bond[18] and (presumed) Sgt A.R. Cottle; F/O W.W. Thwaites[19] and F/O J.E. Lovell[20] and John 'Fletch' Fletcher[21] – Hayter's closest friend – with Sgt J. Dale[22] were all lost.

By 25 November, the faces around Hayter were unfamiliar. Friends had vanished into fire, smoke, and spray. Comrades with whom he had joked, shared fears, and braved pre-flight briefings were now names on MIA reports and future memorials. In three weeks, his squadron had changed beyond recognition.

However, the expectation was that he get straight back into it.

Hayter completed a handful of sorties with his new navigator/rear gunner, F/O F.C. Miles. On 27 November, flying Beaufighter 'J', they took part in a shipping strike off Nilaria, with no sightings.

On 4 December, six Beaufighters left Gambut III for an offensive sweep over the eastern Aegean. Hayter piloted 'G' with Miles navigating. Two Beaufighters returned early – one with an oil leak, and 'G' '*with unserviceable VHF radio*'[23] denying Hayter the chance to re-engage – the formation later attacked a high-speed vessel flying a swastika and four Arados, one of which broke up, its crew escaping by dinghy. Another was crippled and sank after its port float was shot off.

On 5 December, flying 'Z', Hayter and Miles conducted another sweep with only a sighting of a single Baltimore aircraft at deck level. After this point, Hayter's name disappears from No. 47's operational records. By March 1944 – just prior to the squadron's transfer to India and Burma – he is conspicuously absent. His combat flying career had ended quietly, likely following a transfer request.

While such requests from volunteers could be granted under certain conditions, the RAF in 1943 often viewed appeals based on psychological or morale grounds with suspicion. Command feared that if an honourable escape from front-line operations were too readily available, many airmen would take it – even at the risk of being labelled lacking moral fibre (LMF) – which could seriously jeopardise squadron morale and combat effectiveness. The very existence of an official route away from operations threatened to undermine the sense of duty and shared sacrifice that held combat units together, even under extreme duress.

The relentless tempo of missions and the constant threat of sudden death placed an immense psychological burden on aircrew. Hastings notes that many men experienced temporary collapse of morale during operational tours. In the UK, those treated with sensitivity were sometimes sent to the RAF convalescent home at Matlock for rest and recovery. A post-war medical report concluded that many genuinely wished to be rehabilitated and return to operations, driven by self-respect and duty. Conversely, genuine cases of LMF involved individuals who, with hindsight, should never have passed aircrew selection.

Hayter had, in fact, served in Bomber Command earlier in the war, before transfer to the Middle East and a more tactical role. Hastings estimates approximately one in seven operational aircrew were lost to flying duties at some point between training and tour completion due to psychological or morale reasons. In this context, Hayter's quiet withdrawal reflects a tacit acknowledgement of the mental and emotional toll of his combat experiences – particularly his near-fatal ditching off Naxos, compounded by the slaughter of his comrades during the Battle of Leros and the catastrophic failure of the Dodecanese campaign.

With no formal explanation recorded, his absence from combat flying may be the clearest surviving indication of just how deeply those events affected the young 21-year-old pilot.

Chapter 20

LOVE AND WAR

Ἔρως ἀνίκατε μάχαν.
'Eros, you are invincible in battle.'
Sophocles, *Antigone* (441 BCE)

On the morning of 12 December 1943, under the hard glare of the Egyptian sun, Bill Hayter arrived at Heliopolis. The posting marked a clear turning point. Combat sorties were behind him; his new work was quieter, though scarcely risk free given the mechanical frailty of piston-driven aircraft. Its importance lay elsewhere – in training the steady stream of RAF pilots bound for the front.

Now attached to No. 203 Group under Middle East Command, Hayter served as a supernumerary – not on permanent staff, but vital nonetheless. On Christmas Eve he was at RAF Shandur, a dusty outpost by the Suez Canal; later he moved to RAF Gianaclis near Alexandria, preparing airmen for the realities of operational flying. The work could be monotonous, but it was essential. Hayter's combat experience gave young pilots not only the skills to fight, but a chance to survive.

The posting also brought him within reach of George Sideris, who managed to track him down in the summer of 1944.

For much of that year Hayter remained on instructional duties, his only distinction coming on 29 September 1944 with promotion to flight lieutenant – a quiet acknowledgement of his steady contribution to the RAF war effort.

In early 1945, as Allied forces advanced across Europe, Hayter was finally posted back to the UK. On 23 February he arrived at RAF Harwell in Oxfordshire, later transferring to No. 13 Operational Training Unit at RAF Bicester to prepare bomber crews.

While Hayter drilled young airmen for the final phases of the air war, events on the ground hurtled toward their endgame. By spring 1945, Hitler's Reich was collapsing: his armies shattered, his empire in ruins, the Red Army closing on Berlin. In a last, warped act of control, he married Eva Braun in the *Führerbunker* on 29 April – hours before their suicides. The ceremony was brief, joyless, a hollow show of legitimacy as the Third Reich crumbled.

The relationship had always been hidden. For years, Braun was kept in the shadows, largely confined to Munich or the Berghof, his exclusive mountain retreat in the Bavarian Alps, while Hitler paraded as the celibate Nazi hero – Germany's 'eligible bachelor', a persona cultivated for political effect. Twice she had tried to end her life: once with a pistol in 1932, again with sleeping pills in 1935.

Indeed, Adolf had a disturbingly ballistic effect on the women around him. His half-niece, Angela Maria 'Geli' Raubal, 19 years his junior, fatally shot herself in 1931 with Hitler's own pistol in his luxury Munich flat – today, somewhat perversely, a police station.[1] Yet Braun – 23 years his junior – remained bound to him, ornamental, obedient, and almost invisible outside the inner circle.

In April 1945, she could have fled to the Berghof, where comfortable rooms in a bunker complex awaited. Instead, she chose Berlin, resolved to stay with Hitler to the end – a choice born of loyalty, fatalism, or lack of real alternatives, but terminal all the same.

In the last hours, the bunker scene echoed *Tristan and Isolde*, one of Hitler's cherished operas, where love and death are inseparable, and transcendence is found only in the grave. Steeped in Wagnerian fatalism, he staged his end as poisoned love, theatrical sacrifice, and destruction as art – the final act of a twisted *Gesamtkunstwerk* (total work of art) of purity, violence, and propaganda – all epitomised by Goebbels' 1943 cry: '*Wollt ihr den totalen Krieg?*'

After testing a capsule on his beloved German shepherd, Blondi, Braun took cyanide while Hitler combined poison with a shot from his Walther PPK. Whether it was capsule, bullet, or paranoia that killed him matters little after the millions he destroyed.

More to the point, they left no little Führers behind in their destructive wake.

Doused in petrol, their bodies were burned in the garden of the Reich Chancellery – not as a Wagnerian pyre, but as a crude attempt to deny the Soviets a trophy. Unlike Mussolini, who was literally strung up by the hordes, Hitler left no corpse for spectacle, only ashes and rumours. His reign ending not in grandeur, but in fire, poison, and a marriage as grotesque as it was brief.

In the immediate wake of Hitler's final curtain call on 30 April 1945, the Third Reich was effectively extinguished. In his will, he appointed *Großadmiral* (Grand Adm.) Karl Dönitz – architect of the U-boat campaign – as *Reichspräsident* (President of the Reich), not Führer, a hollow gesture signalling the regime's collapse. Dönitz's short-lived Flensburg government lasted only a few weeks.

On 7 May, Germany signed an unconditional surrender at Reims; hostilities officially ceased the following day, VE Day. Much like in April 1941, when Greece surrendered to Germany rather than Italy, Stalin insisted on a second, formal signing in Berlin, which is why VE Day is celebrated on 9 May in the Soviet Union.

News of the surrender swept across the globe: crowds poured into the streets, church bells rang out, and celebrations erupted, seemingly untempered by six years of unrelenting war. Even as the Pacific conflict continued, in Europe the guns fell silent, and for a brief moment the world seemed to hold its breath in relief and astonishment.

As the war wound down, countless soldiers, sailors and airmen returned home to rebuild their lives, while others remained in service. Among them was Bill Hayter, who, on 7 August 1945, was transferred to No. 6 Aircrew Holding Unit at RAF Kirton-in-Lindsey, which processed and billeted trained aircrew awaiting postings, courses, or demobilisation. His exact role is unclear, but he likely continued with flying duties.

By February 1946 he assumed administrative responsibilities with No. 7 Fighter Interception Squadron at RAF Pocklington, later joining the Aircrew Cadet Advisory Committee. Further postings took him to RAF Blakehill Farm in Wiltshire and RAF Fairford in Gloucestershire. On 24 June 1946, his status shifted from supernumerary to regular, confirming the value of his role in the RAF's transition to peacetime.

For his steady service, Hayter was awarded a Good Conduct Badge (B4-1205) and authorised to wear the ribbon of the 1939–43 Star with Rosette, ME (Middle East) Command. He resigned his commission on 8 March 1947, retaining the rank of flight lieutenant, and was officially discharged that September – though he had been permitted to travel earlier.

As previously outlined, Ann Mills had captured Bill Hayter's heart before he even completed pilot training at No. 20 EFTS in Canada. Through the war he kept in touch, sending (censored) letters and photographs whenever he could – and in late 1946, it was into her arms that he returned.

But had time, distance, and the weight of wartime experience altered what they once had?

By all accounts, their reunion was joyful. Surviving photographs show them together in the garden of Ann's home at 402 Mary Street, Oshawa – quiet, sunlit moments that hint at the pull of a shared past. Hayter had clearly hoped to build a future with her in Canada. A letter from McGill University, dated 6 January 1947 and addressed to the Mary Street residence, confirms that he had been accepted into the Faculty of Arts and Science. However, it was not to be.

As Ann's daughter, Patricia Staunton, later reflected, Bill and Ann's story is best understood through Thomas Wolfe's[2] *You Can't Go Home Again*:

> You can't go back home to your family, back home to your childhood, back home to romantic love, back home to a young man's dreams of glory and of fame … back home to places in the country, back home to the old forms and systems of things which once seemed everlasting but which are changing all the time – back home to the escapes of Time and Memory.

Wolfe's words speak directly to their experience. The war had been both the bright beginning and the quiet unravelling that followed. Brought together at 17 and 19 years of age in a world of urgency and upheaval, their bond was real – yet shaped as much by circumstance as by choice. When the war ended, their reunion was sincere but could not restore what had once been.

By spring 1947 they parted, not with bitterness, but with an acceptance that some loves belong to a particular moment in time.

One of Hayter's letters captures the tone of that parting:

> C/o Massey Harris
> Brantford Airport
> 11 Nov.
>
> Ann dear,
>
> I hear that you are now engaged, & would like to congratulate you & to wish, from the bottom of my heart, all the happiness I hope & trust will be yours.
>
> It is so much easier to see things clearly and dispassionately now than it was six months ago. I'm afraid that I must have hurt you quite a bit, I know that it hurt me, but as you see, things have worked out for the best … I can see no reason now why we should not be good friends, that is, if you are willing to forgive what has been largely forgotten.
>
> For myself, I am in Brantford for a while. It seems funny, with the 'drome closed down & deserted where it once teemed with noise, life, enthusiasm, & the great Unknown. Sometimes it seems terribly sad & final too. One should not look back.
>
> I still have the old car, but my ship having failed to drop anchor in a port of untold wealth, I think its days are numbered, & I am thinking of buying a jeep!
>
> Would you please thank your parents very much for bringing me my things back, & give them my love, & I hope to see you all before very long.
>
> With all kind thoughts,
> Bill

The letter's address points to Hayter's next step: employment with Massey Harris (later Massey Ferguson), the agricultural machinery firm that also produced military vehicles such as the M24 Chaffee tank. His exact role is unknown, but the intent is clear – he still hoped to settle in Canada, a country thriving after the war and full of promise. His fluency in French would have been an asset in that endeavour.

Why he did not pursue his studies remains unknown – perhaps immediate financial pressures intervened. A civilian job offered instant social and economic security, a first step into peacetime life far from war-torn Europe.

Yet life – *c'est la vie* – had other plans.

Bill Hayter was summoned home. Château de Sermet,[3] the family estate near Villefranche-du-Périgord in the Dordogne, required the presence of their only son. The choice was far from easy. Canada promised a fresh start, but obligations in France loomed. Having recently broken up with Ann, he knew the past could not be reclaimed. Post-war fortunes had shifted, and being an heir to a bona fide medieval castle no longer guaranteed security. Family ties, however, prevailed.

Yet Bill's temporary room in Paris hints at the struggle beneath the surface. A December 1947 note to Ann Mills, accompanied by a photo of the city's iconic cathedral, captures the uncertainty of that time:

> Dear Ann,
> I live just up from Notre Dame, right in the heart of the Paris student quarter, in a small one-room apartment on the fourth floor. It was a real find, even if there's no hot water, bathroom, central heating, or telephone.
> Time simply flies by before one has the chance to do half the things one intends. Paris is full of interest, if not quite as lively as of yore.
> Do drop me a line sometime and tell me all your news. I think of you often and wonder how life is treating you.
>
> Best,
> Bill

Following a brief engagement, Ann married Herman 'Herm' Heintzman in June 1948. As Patricia recalls, '*My mom was pragmatic and optimistic. She was not one to look back.*'[4] Together, Ann and Herm raised three children: sons Charles Robert and James Philip, and their youngest, Patricia Ann, nicknamed 'Spitfire' for her lively spirit and ability to hold her own against her teasing older brothers. Regrettably, Ann passed away in May 2022 at the age of 98, having faced dementia in her final years.

Bill also moved forward with his life. At 32, he married 29-year-old Lucienne Marie Aimée Bernard on 2 April 1955, marking a new chapter that offered stability and purpose.

The union faced delicate challenges. The church did not typically permit marriages between individuals of different faiths. Anne's grandmother, Joshuanna ('Anna'), had faced a similar issue in 1919. Anne Timsit-Hayter recalls: '*Because our mother was Catholic and our father was Anglican, they weren't supposed to be able to marry in the Church. However, our mother's brother happened to be a priest, and he helped make it happen.*'

Family approval posed another hurdle. Joshuanna insisted that Lucienne spend a year in England learning proper, fluent English before the marriage. Conventions and family expectations often shaped choices, and approval came only after these conditions were met.

The wedding was attended by around 50 friends and family, including the parents: Mark Cholmondeley and Joshuanna Hayter, and Jean-Pierre Louis and Charlotte Marie Élisabeth Bernard. Due to the denominational difference, the register was signed privately in the sacristy rather than before the altar. The ceremony was followed by a joyous reception at the home of the bride's parents.

A young family soon followed. When the first pregnancy was announced, Joshuanna famously exclaimed, '*You don't have babies unless you can afford a nurse!*' The family grew with the help of several au pairs, particularly Christine von Albedyhll, and experienced both profound joy and heartbreaking sorrow along the way.

Charles Edward, the firstborn, arrived in 1956 but drowned four years later. In 1957 came Anne Cécile Sophie, named in honour of both Bill's mother and his former girlfriend – a deliberate dual tribute.

In 1960 followed Marie Alice, known as 'Mali' – a free spirit who has lived in France and Canada while running her own business, which she still manages today.

Elisabeth Georgina was born in 1961 but lived only briefly. In 1964 she swallowed her grandfather's heart pills, mistaking them for sweets –

another tragedy that darkened the family's early years. Finally, in 1965 came George Denis, named after George Sideris.

Anne, Mali, and George were raised in privileged circumstances. In time, they moved to Paris, started families, and built lives of their own.

La vie continue (life goes on), even in the shadow of loss.

Bill's correspondence with George Sideris remained valued, if less frequent. Knowing someone in George's circle on Naxos would understand French – his mother had once written in that language, thanking him for the rescue and even suggesting the purchase of a small house in Greece – Bill often wrote in French as well. The following is a translation:

F/Lt. Hayter
SPAYNES HALL
GT YELDHAM
ESSEX
22 March

My Dear Friend,
What a pleasure it was to receive your charming letter, though it took such a long time to arrive. A month and a half, and by road – it's really ridiculous! I had been eagerly waiting for your news, and now I am so pleased to know that life is going well.

How your letter made me laugh, George! How I remember the sea, your famous fishing stories. Some details about the fishing … what size is it? Can you catch it at sea? What will be the price? Is it easy to catch?

I am really looking forward to seeing you again, George, and to revisit your beautiful area, where I was once so happy. It's something I could never forget.

Best wishes to your family and to Varvara. Tell them that I think of them very fondly.

With much affection,
Bill

But not all threads endure – some are severed too soon. With George Sideris' death on 13 December 1963, his correspondence with both Bill and

Tom came to an end, closing a meaningful chapter in their post-war lives – a friendship anchored in memory and shared history.

Though not inclined to farming, Bill managed the family estate with modern equipment. Life at Sermet was good. '*My parents loved entertaining and frequently hosted guests from all over the world,*' recalls Mali.

A former pilot with a taste for speed, Bill bought a Bugatti 35 and often raced around. '*He was always asking me if the light was green, if he hadn't seen it change – terrifying at the speeds he drove*!' Anne laughs. '*His colour-blindness meant he couldn't tell the difference.*'

Mechanics fascinated him. He drew meticulous technical plans and won medals in Paris, Brussels, and London for inventions including a rotary engine and a handless clock that tracked the movements of the moon and sun. '*He was a tinkerer and inventor at heart, with a solid grasp of how machines worked,*' says his son George.

The skill ran in the family. Bill's grandfather, Harrison Goodenough Hayter, was a noted Victorian civil engineer who built railways and docks worldwide. As mentioned, his father, Mark C. Hayter, tested aircraft during and after WWI. Of Bill, his son George reflects: '*My dad clearly grasped the mechanics of the aircraft he flew in the RAF – no doubt making him a better pilot.*'

Lamentably, the life of this remarkable man – pilot, author, estate owner, car enthusiast, inventor, husband, and father – was cut short. In July 1972 he returned from Rhodesia, gravely ill with liver cancer. On 14 October – Lucienne's birthday – he passed away at Sermet, aged just 49.

'*I was only 15 when papa died,*' Anne recalls. '*He had never spoken about the war. We knew almost nothing – only that he had been a pilot in the RAF.*' After his death, Lucienne left Château de Sermet for a smaller home in the village of Pomarède (Lot département, Occitanie), near close friends David and Margaret Barwick. The journals went with her but were forgotten – left in the attic to gather dust.

In 2006, tragedy struck again when Anne was hit by a lorry and left paralysed. She adapted with resilience, drawing joy from her daughters – Johanna, Olivia and Victoria 'Vicky' – and from simple pleasures: feeding the birds in her garden, reading, music, and the company of cherished friends.

After Lucienne's passing on 29 January 2019, the attic was eventually cleared many years later and the first of Bill's journals came to light. His children, long in the dark about his wartime experiences, were astonished by the vivid, reflective accounts. '*It was a true revelation into our father's past*,' is the mutual consensus.[5]

The rest, they say, is history.

Chapter 21

TEA, DUTY, AND GOLDFISH

Τὰ πάντα ῥεῖ.
'Everything flows.'
Heraclitus, fragment (c. 500 BCE)

While recovering from his injuries in Cairo, Tom Harper passed a group of Montgomery's battle-worn Eighth Army soldiers when a familiar voice called, '*Hello Tom, is that you?*' It was his brother, John Edward. Brief though the encounter, it must have lifted the spirits of both, offering a rare moment of warmth amid the harshness of pain, healing, and uncertainty.

With his strength gradually restored, Harper faced another challenge: rejoining No. 603 Squadron and taking to the skies once more. On 25 February 1944, he flew aboard Beaufighter 'H', NK400, piloted by F/Sgt C.J. Gould, departing from Gambut III on an offensive sweep over the central Aegean. They pushed through the Kasos Strait, past Santorini, Ios, Amorgos, and Astypalaia, before returning uneventfully. Mission accomplished.

However, it cannot have been easy. Pulling away from the earth, Harper must have felt both fear and relief. Like Bill Hayter, he carried the memory of ditching: the crash, the pain, the uncertainty of capture or rescue. And yet he was airborne once more, back in the same type of aircraft that had nearly killed them both. Returning demanded more than physical recovery; it required fortitude.

Keep Calm and Carry On.[1]

In March and April 1944, Harper flew eleven sorties with Gould – from offensive sweeps across the Cyclades, striking shipping off Mykonos,

Paros, and Naxos, to convoy escorts and U-boat hunts – still perilous even as *Luftwaffe* power waned irrevocably. The Beaufighter Mk X now carried rocket projectiles (RPs), far more accurate than torpedoes, though effective only at close range.[2]

Then, on 13 April 1944, everything changed.

At 0640 hrs, Gould and Harper lifted off as part of a six-aircraft sweep bound for the Gulf of Laconia, along the southern Peloponnese. Their target was a German Danube lighter.[3] But as they neared Cape Matapan, just 6 miles offshore, three Messerschmitt Bf 109s swept in – fast, lethal, and far more agile than the Beaufighters.

The clash was sudden and violent. Sgt R.T. Gosling's aircraft, with Sgt S.A. West as navigator/observer, was hit almost immediately and smashed into the sea in a spray of wreckage. The two remaining fighters then locked onto Beaufighter 'F', flown by Gould with Harper in the rear seat. Under intense fire, the pair dodged, dived, and fought back, their aircraft riddled but still airborne. Relief came only when F/Lt Pringle DFC, with F/O A.E. Ross as his navigator/observer, swung his Beaufighter into a head-on attack, forcing the Germans to break off.

Against the odds, Gould and Harper coaxed their crippled aircraft back to North Africa, landing at 1120 hrs. Their escape was narrow, their Beaufighter badly damaged, yet their survival stood as a testament to skill, nerve, and sheer will.

No. 603 Squadron's W/Cdr J.R.H. Lewis DFC later noted;'*On the 13th April in a fight with 3 ME 109s off Cape Matapan,*[4] *the squadron scored one ME 109 damaged – a very credible performance by the navigator responsible.*'[5]

Which navigator, though? The evidence points to Harper. His Beaufighter bore the brunt of the assault, both Messerschmitts raking his aircraft with fire. With one squadron-mate already down and Pringle engaged elsewhere, Harper alone had to defend pilot and self alike. The burden in that moment fell squarely on him. Hayter's journal shows he was not averse to using the rear-mounted .303in Vickers K gun, and in this desperate fight his bursts almost certainly broke the attack – the '*very credible performance*' later recorded by the squadron.

Eight days later, on 21 April 1944, Harper flew his final combat sortie. Alone with Gould in Beaufighter 'H', NE400, they scoured the Mediterranean on a five-hour U-boat hunt. Nothing stirred, and they returned safely at 1900 hrs. Harper's combat flying against the Axis had ended quietly but with resolute calm.

No. 603 Squadron continued operations over Greece and the Aegean until 28 November 1944, when they were recalled to the UK to re-equip with Spitfires from No. 229 Squadron – the very unit that had taken No. 603's Spitfires during Malta's defence in 1942.

What goes around comes around.

Harper was posted to South Africa, staying at a Personal Transit Camp some 14 miles (22km) from Cape Town – likely near Wingfield aerodrome. On 16 August 1944, he wrote home from '*In Transit, Cape Town*' about a fellow RAF colleague who urgently needed him to organise a same-day wedding. Harper dashed into the city, saw the event through, spent the night recovering at the Officers' Club, and returned to duty bright and early. The episode showcased his loyalty and resourcefulness – traits that made him so well liked.

Shortly afterwards, he was ordered to join No. 64 Air School, some 620 miles (1,000km) away. South Africa's Joint Air Training Scheme (JATS), the local equivalent of the BCATP, operated 38 Air Schools across the country, including key facilities in Pretoria, Germiston, Baragwanath, and Bloemfontein. They trained South African Air Force (SAAF), RAF and Allied personnel, producing over 33,000 aircrew, including 7,764 pilots, during the war.

No. 64 Air School, in Bloemfontein's Tempe suburb, opened on 5 February 1941 and operated until 20 December 1945. Its main role was training electrical and wireless operators, using aircraft such as the Avro Anson and de Havilland Dominie for practical instruction in wireless operations and navigation. With his training and experience, Harper was well placed to be an effective instructor.

Life in Bloemfontein was a world away from North Africa's harsh landscapes. Tom Harper, now a flying officer, quickly settled into a routine of instruction and relaxation, with cricket naturally the game of choice.

On 25 January 1945, he received a curious letter:

> Dear F/O Harper,
> Very many thanks for your letter dated December 18th, which has just reached me.
>
> I am pleased to advise you that your name has been entered as a life member on the membership lists of the Club, and your badge enclosed.
>
> The official membership card is currently being prepared, and I hope it will be ready for dispatch during the next two to three weeks. At the moment, it is being enclosed in its waterproof case.
>
> May I offer my congratulations, although rather belated, on your escape, and I hope you were none the worse for the experience.
>
> I have enclosed herewith a pamphlet in which you may be interested. The question of affiliation between the Goldfish Club and the Middlesex Flying Club is under discussion, and in the event of this taking place, it will mean special concessions and privileges for our members.
>
> Very best wishes for the future.
>
> Yours sincerely,
> C.A. Robertson

Among the wry distractions available to wartime airmen was the Goldfish Club, an unofficial association for those who had been dunked 'in the drink' and survived thanks to life-saving equipment such as rubber dinghies and Mae West lifejackets. Founded in 1942 by C.A. Robertson of the P.B. Cow company, a major supplier of air-sea rescue gear, it bore a dry English wit in its name and motto – 'Gold for the value of life' and 'Fish for the sea'. With time on his hands at No. 64 Air School, Tom Harper seized the chance to join.

Much of the club's original archive of over 9,000 members was lost after the war, when a former secretary's family, assuming no one would care, disposed of the records. Today, the club continues to welcome those rescued at sea, and thanks to the efforts of Art Stacey, its current chairman and membership secretary, the WWII database is gradually being rebuilt – '*an opportunity to reinstate them into the shoal*', as he put it.[6]

Whether Bill Hayter ever applied remains unknown, but the humour, resilience, and understated camaraderie of the Goldfish Club reflected the spirit of surviving a watery mishap at sea – and was entirely in keeping with the character of both him and Tom.

When the war in Europe ended in May 1945, the promise of demobilisation and returning to his wife, Irene, must have been tantalising. Yet the JATS programme took time to wind down, slowed by military bureaucracy, and many afternoons were spent on the cricket field under South Africa's sun-drenched skies.

These moments later became a source of light-hearted jibes for Irene – while Harper fielded at silly mid-on, she struggled on her own sticky wicket in the UK, still coping with wartime shortages. However, in true sporting spirit, Tom played a long innings, taking the teasing in his stride while waiting for someone to call stumps.

His wartime service earned him five medals – the 1939–45 Star and War Medal, together with the Africa Star, the Italy Star and the Defence Medal – each a tangible reminder of his courage and service across North Africa, the Mediterranean, the UK, and the wider conflict. The most personal, however, was a coveted LRDG Scorpion Badge pressed into his hand by one of his Naxos rescuers – a small token of respect that remains a treasured family heirloom.

On Tom's return to Bristol, he and Irene settled into a modest Clifton flat. His former employer, the Co-operative Building Society, had no vacancies, so Harper joined the bustling *Bristol Evening Post*, grounding himself in steady routine. Their first child, Richard, was born in February 1947. When the tenancy forbade children, relief came from Irene's father, who offered them a three-bedroom house in Avonmouth. There the family settled, and in June 1950 their daughter, Elizabeth Jane, was born.

Tom stayed at the *Evening Post* until 1962, then joined Fisons at their Avonmouth plant as an accounts and cost clerk. The meticulous, unglamorous work suited him, and he remained there until retiring in 1980. Apprentices honoured him with a handcrafted Beaufighter model – a tribute to both his wartime past and the respect he had earned – now promised to his grandsons.

Though reserved about the war, Harper kept a link through the Observer Corps, attending Sunday meetings in full uniform. '*He never really opened up about the war*,' Richard recalls. '*Only once, for a school project, did he mention being shot down over Naxos – barely a sentence*.' Like many combat veterans, he carried it home quietly, plagued by nightmares. Family noted the change: '*He came back quieter ... as if part of him had been left behind.*'[7]

In peacetime, Tom found fulfilment in steady routines. Gardening became a solace – first in the backyard, later on a rented allotment – teaching his children patience and care. Summers brought cricket with Shirehampton Cricket Club, where the children cheered from the sidelines. Faith and community were central: he sang in St Andrew's Church choir alongside family, with Irene's father as church warden. It was a portrait of post-war English family life.

In 1989, the Harpers moved to Wickham Bishops in Essex to be nearer their children. Surrounded by gardens and trees, Tom spent his final years there, passing away on 26 January 2004, remembered as a gentleman – thoughtful, kind, and rarely given to complaint.

Hayter described him as '*reserved and betraying no strong emotion*' – courageous and decent, preferring action to words. That steady resolve and practical nature shone in moments of crisis, and also in the quieter rhythms of family life. Irene Elsie Harper survived him by eleven years, passing peacefully on 17 October 2015. Together, they had built a life defined by quiet strength, enduring love, and the grace of ordinary moments – an enviable legacy carried forward by their children and grandchildren.

Chapter 22

STRIKE ON NAXOS

Alea iacta est.
'The die is cast.'
Julius Caesar, *Commentarii de Bello Civili* (49 BCE)

The skies were clear, the air sharp and bright – a pleasant autumn day. At 1400 hrs, the stillness of Saturday, 30 October 1943 over Naxos shattered with a cacophonous attack that would last only minutes, yet echo long afterwards.

From the west, skimming scrublands and hugging shadows came the strike force: two USAAF B-25G Mitchells and two RAF Bristol Beaufighters. They tore across the island's narrow neck, pouncing on the harbour below. Their mission: *Kriegsmarine* vessels and mayhem.

Several witnessed what was about to happen – including Sgn Smith from his LRDG observation post: '*Two B-25 Mitchells and two Beaufighters from Libya strafed the port.*'[1]

From above, it seemed deceptively simple. F/O Charles F. Keith, piloting B-25G *Black Magic*, spotted three ships and assumed they were harmless merchantmen. In reality, *GA-01* and *GA-54* were flak-bristling patrol boats, recently returned from a submarine hunt following the attack by HMS *Unsparing* and No. 47 Squadron the previous day. The *Kriegsmarine* War Diary notes that *GA-94*, once tied alongside *GA-01*, had been prudently '*ordered to leave due to the air danger*'[2] after taking on wounded from that same attack. That left patrol boat *GA-51*, used for 'coal replenishment', as a possible third target. However, amid caïques, schooners, and fishing smacks also lurked *Kriegsfischkutter KFK-4*, a militarised trawler – and this is specifically identified as the third target by *Kriegsmarine* records. As Hayter notes, two or three Arado 196 floatplanes also lay moored nearby, but the strike would be long over before they could pose a threat.

On the ground, *GA-01*'s watch spotted '*the four aircraft in a low-flying attack from starboard aft*'.[3] Sirens wailed, orders to open fire snapped out. *GA-54* reports: '*four enemy aircraft attacking in low flight ... coming from the rear, protected by a low mountain*'.[4] Gun crews scrambled, fingers on triggers, ammunition flying into breeches.

Keith recalls, '*The M/Vs [motor vessels] were sighted straight ahead and about 3,000 yards away.*'[5] The Mitchells struck first – 75mm nose cannon and .50 cals raking the harbour. Beaufighter *'L' for London*, flown by F/O John Fletcher with F/O T.E. Jones as navigator/observer, followed with a five-second cannon burst. Sparks and flames licked *GA-01*.

The *Kriegsmarine* archives capture the shock: '*The attacking aircraft opened fire with heavy on board weapons. GA-01 was approached directly by three aircraft.*'[6] The assault pressed to within 1,000 yards (910m). *Black Magic* managed only two cannon rounds before both Mitchells broke away – climbing, banking hard, trying to evade. Keith reports, '*There was no flak encountered until the ships [aircraft] turned off the target run and started to break for safety.*'[7]

Then hell broke loose.

GA-01 unleashed a storm – 20mm, 37mm and 88mm rounds slashing skyward. *GA-54* added its own fury: '*The first 3 aircraft were kept under fire ... clear hits were achieved from our boat, which were observed from the ship and from land.*'[8] Tracers cut red arcs; incendiaries shrieked past. Shore defences joined in, filling the harbour sky with flurries of deadly steel.

Keith confirms, '*We encountered a great deal of medium and heavy flak.*'[9] Most tore into the sea, near misses that sparked hope. Sgt C.O. Krueger, a gunner on *Black Magic*, notes with unsettling calm: '*I saw the first flak. It burst well away from us and to our right. From its range and size and color of explosion, I judged it to be 88 mm.*'[10]

From Smith's LRDG post, the scene was unclear. '*We saw only three planes fly away*'[11] – the two B-25Gs and Fletcher's Beaufighter.

Meanwhile, Hayter and Harper bore in with Beaufighter *'S' for Sugar*, dodging erratically to avoid fire. Hayter writes, '*Violently we started to weave ... down almost to the ground and up to about a hundred feet. We did not want to be caught like Paddy Finucane by some chance bullet.'*

During his own evasive manoeuvres, Keith radioed *Flying Caisson* to break left – no response.

GA-01 reports: '*Through the firing of all flak weapons, the aircraft received hits.*'[12] Fletcher witnessed the B-25G beside him, on a heading of 280° at just 100ft (30m), mortally struck by flak: '*I saw a big flash on the Mitchell ... it turned violently to port and commenced a gradual glide to the water. He flew straight in and the a/c [aircraft] broke up.*'[13] Hayter adds, '*The pilot must have been killed ... it seemed almost impossible that anyone could have survived the awful impact.*'

Just after their second left turn to a heading of 150°, gunners on *Black Magic* caught their last glimpse of Hayter and Harper's Beaufighter strafing *GA-54*.

Moments later, Krueger was the last to see 2nd Lt Gordon Black alive, '*I saw the pilot look up and both engines were turning and everything seemed normal ...*' *Flying Caisson* slipped beneath them, briefly vanishing from view, and Krueger refocused on the Beaufighters and the harbour. Moments later, he reports, '*about a mile to our rear, I observed a large splash in the water. In fact, it seemed to continue to rise as I looked*'[14] – but the significance did not register immediately.

GA-01 confirms the kill: '*One turned, with smoke developing, to starboard and crashed in the direction of north Paros into the water.*'[15]

Flying Caisson had disintegrated in a plume of sea spray, her entire crew instantly lost.

Meanwhile, Harper and Hayter were now close enough to strike. '*All this I saw in a flash as I set my sights on the ship ... Tom and I had the harbour to ourselves. I pressed the cannon button & noted the rhythmic thumping of the four guns beneath me.*'

Below, the enemy ship loomed black, tracer fire streaking from its defences. '*The ship looked like a destroyer ... thin lines of deadly trace rushing from it towards us,*' Hayter writes.

But they didn't flinch.

'*I stopped weaving ... held my thumb hard down on the trigger ... Straight towards her we went, all our cannon blazing continuously.*'

Shell after shell struck.

'*The cabin filled with acrid fumes ... flash after flash from the deck and superstructure ... no splashes in the water, which told that every shell was hitting the mark.*

'*Tom had manned the machine gun in the back, but it was not very much use as an antidote to all the flak coming up from the sides. Then, at last, we saw some results from our fire, as explosions shook the ship, and flames leapt up from her decks.*'

The damage wrought was devastating.

GA-54 reports: '*The fourth aircraft unexpectedly attacked from the rear and disabled the rear machine guns through on board weapons fire.*'[16] The aft 37mm flak gun erupted in a fireball. The *Kriegsmarine* War Diary confirms: '*On GA-54, one gun crew was incapacitated, and ready ammunition caught fire. A greater disaster was averted thanks to Maschinenobergefreiter [Able Seaman, Engine Room] Stiska, who threw a burning ammunition box overboard.*' The vessel itself was shredded: '*the bridge was completely riddled with bullets, as well as the superstructure and funnel. Four hits were located above the waterline at the stern.*'[17]

The casualties were severe. *Bootsmannsmaat* (Boatswain's Mate) Dehlenburg, *Matrosengefreiter* (Able Seaman) Hemgens, and Steudel were all killed outright. *Signalmatrose* (Signal Seaman) Engel, *Matrose Obergefreiter* (Leading Seaman) Tannreuther, *Steuermannsmaat Obergefreiter* (Quartermaster 2nd Class) Vogel, and *Maschinenmaat Obergefreiter* (Machinist's Mate 2nd Class) Waidenbahn were seriously wounded. Vogel later died after being evacuated to the hospital on Syros.

GA-01 had fared no better: its chartroom and radio room obliterated, hull punctured at the waterline. '*Fires broke out in the forward compartment, chart house, and crew quarters ... but both fires were quickly put out by immediate, decisive action. Equipment and goods were damaged by fire and water.*'[18]

Flotilla Commander *Korvettenkapitän* Adolf Brune was gravely wounded as he stood on *GA-01*'s bridge. He later died on Syros after a failed amputation. Radio operator Martin was also badly wounded and succumbed soon afterwards. Two crewmen were struck by 20mm cannon fire, others injured by burns and shrapnel. Despite the carnage, the crew's conduct was described as '*impeccable*'.[19]

Neither vessel sank. Both *GA-01* and *GA-54*, scorched and riddled with shellfire, limped to Piraeus the next day for repairs.[20] *GA-51* and *KFK-4* escaped entirely unscathed. On 3 November, *Kapitän zur See* (Capt.) Albert Oesterlin, Deputy Flotilla Commander, flew to Naxos to take charge of the remnants of the unit.

Amid the chaos, innocent Naxian civilians were caught in the crossfire, whether struck by aircraft or anti-aircraft ordnance remains disputed. Levogiannis explained that Dimitris Valvis, a tailor, was cut down outside his shop as deadly projectiles swept the street. Nearby, Nikiforos G. Legakis, a 36-year-old school gymnast, was killed while trying to reach safety.[21]

For all these people, it was already over – yet those in the battle fought on.

Still unaware of *Flying Caisson*'s fate, Keith continued on a 150° heading at 170 miles per hour (270km/h). Meanwhile, Fletch saw *'S' for Sugar* '*make for the clouds*' – his last sight of Hayter and Harper.

Keith then called all aircraft. There was silence, until Fletch spoke: '*I caught him up and told him over the VHF what had happened ...*'[22]

Most of the flak now converged on *'S' for Sugar*. Even as *GA-54* erupted in flames below, its gunners struck true: the starboard wing was shredded, the main tank ripped away, trailing unexploded fuel and vapour. '*Repeated jars made the whole aircraft shudder and I feared that she might disintegrate.*' Losing altitude rapidly, Hayter somehow struggled clear of the harbour; one wing in tatters, oil pressure failing, and fuel lost – catastrophe inevitable.

'*"S" for Sugar had met her fate, an Aegean graveyard, and it was up to me to prevent Tom and me from going down with her.*'

Only the enemy saw what happened next. Smith notes, '*the missing Beaufighter might have made off to the west, close inshore and out of our view*'.[23] *GA-01* reports: '*Another machine showed a smoke trail from the right engine and flew at a decreasing altitude directly under the coast of Naxos to the north.*'[24]

Under continuing flak, Keith and Fletch circled the site where *Flying Caisson* had gone down. An oil slick spread below. '*There was no wreckage except what looked like a torn piece of life raft. No persons were seen in the water*,' Keith reports.[25] With fuel low and *'S' for Sugar* astray, they had no choice but to turn south-west for North Africa.

Hayter was left coaxing every ounce of life from his crippled Beaufighter. Passing low over a schooner, he assumed it to be harmless. Only later did he realise the lost opportunity. '*Which was a pity*,' he writes, '*because it was right in our line of fire, and we would have had the almost certainly unique experience of sinking an enemy ship in the condition we were in.*'

With altitude bleeding away and their remaining engine on the verge of failure, Hayter and Harper faced their only option – a ditching. Hayter wrestled the cockpit canopy open, a logical move that instantly engulfed him in a choking cloud of Saharan sand. The *'S' in Sugar* now took on a darker meaning as they fought to stay on course, flying blind, hearts pounding, bracing for an unseen impact.

The trailing smoke had marked their path directly over the German schooner. *GA-01* reports: '*The motor sailer N.K.A. SA-89 of the M.N.O./ Syros, with Oberleutnant [Lt] Harckenbusch on board, arrived from the north at this moment and saw the aircraft crash with its engine on fire.*'[26] The Germans had seen everything – and realised a British aircraft was down.

And yet, as we now know, it was only the beginning of their extraordinary story.

Epilogue

METAL OR METTLE?

Epilogue (n): from Greek *ἐπίλογος* (epilogos); *epi* 'in addition' + *logos* 'speech'.

Many Nazi structures still stand across Europe: Atlantic Wall casemates, U-boat pens, countless bunkers, and even the *Kehlsteinhaus* (Eagle's Nest) – now a tourist attraction with its gilded lift and sweeping views. Concentration camps such as Auschwitz and Dachau endure as solemn memorials to persecution and mass murder. Military sites, including Peenemünde, where the V2 was developed, link wartime innovation to later achievements such as the Apollo space programme.

War always leaves a mixed legacy of ingenuity, devastation, and human endurance.

Although WWII produced war materiel on an unprecedented scale, surprisingly little survives. Museums preserve aircraft, tanks, and other artefacts, yet operational examples are rare. Despite their size, naval vessels fared no better: thousands were lost, scrapped, or sunk in post-war testing, their wrecks now silent monuments on the seabed.

Of some 1,350 Tiger I tanks, only a handful remain, with just one operational. Over 7,300 Avro Lancasters were built, yet fewer than 20 survive, only two airworthy. Of more than 15,000 P-47 Thunderbolts, fewer than 20 remain flight-worthy, and of over 5,900 Beaufighters, only a handful survive, none able to fly. Some machines saw later service – Syrian Panzer IVs fought in the Six-Day and Yom Kippur Wars – but most others were destroyed, scrapped, sold, or simply left to rot.

This stark contrast highlights a paradox of total war: industrial ingenuity fuelled mass destruction, yet so little endures. When the machines that shaped history vanish, what does it say about how we honour those who fought and died using them? Should wars – and the lives they cost – be so utterly disposable?

A few are dedicated to salvaging the past – historians, authors, filmmakers, YouTube creators, and game developers. Accuracy varies, but together they make history accessible, revealing human stories and the machines of war, keeping the past alive.

Shipwreck hunting – an evocative name for a pursuit both arduous and costly, yet driven by the thrill of discovery and the promise of understanding – is one of the most exacting forms of this endeavour.

Greece, particularly the Aegean, offers a vast field for exploration. Control of these waters shaped access to the Dardanelles, the Black Sea, and Eastern Mediterranean shipping, which explains the Nazi U-boat base at Salamis near Athens. The Axis invasion in April 1941, Operation Accolade in September 1943, and the German withdrawal in October 1944 each left traces on the seabed – silent, submerged witnesses to history.

Few embody this pursuit better than commercial diver Kostas Thoctarides, who has located eight submarines to date, including HMS *Perseus*,[1] HMS *Triumph*,[2] and HMS *Trooper*,[3] as well as independently discovering and identifying *U-133*.[4] Finding *Triumph* took 25 years; he and his daughter Agapi traced it through Mk VIII torpedoes from a 1942 attack on an Italian freighter, resolving an 81-year-old mystery and giving long-awaited closure to the Triumph Association, led by former Royal Navy officer Gav Don, and to the families of the 64 lost aboard.

Among countless other wrecks, Thoctarides also located the missing bow of RHN *Adrias*,[5] the Greek destroyer that struck a mine off Kalymnos during Operation Accolade, and HMS *Hurworth*,[6] sunk while attempting to assist her. *Adrias*' return to Alexandria on 6 December 1943 became a symbol of defiance. Remarkably, Thoctarides achieved all this without institutional or financial support, relying chiefly on a modified off-the-shelf fish finder.

Many others also devote their largely unpaid, often unrewarded efforts to piecing the past together. Among them are divers, authors, and researchers, as well as our good friends: Platon Alexiades, Aris Bilalis, W/Cdr Chris Goss (RAF ret'd), Dimitri Galon, George Karelas, Vasilis

Mentogiannis, Dr Kimon Papadimitriou, Nikolaos Sidiropoulos, and the late Byron Tezapsidis, all of whom have been indispensable in preserving these histories.

Virgin wrecks continue to be found, often at shallow depths. In 2024, Papadimitriou and Sidiropoulos discovered a Junkers Ju 88 at 82ft (25m) off Psara, the seventh such aircraft in Greek waters. It had lain there since 13 December 1943, inadvertently discovered while they were researching the documentary *Thalatta – Secrets of the Aegean.*[7]

In 2007, diver Manolis Bardanis discovered a Bristol Beaufighter off Naxos at 105ft (32m), initially thought to be *'S' for Sugar*, JM317, but later identified as 'Y', LX998, from No. 603 Squadron RAF. Part of an eight-aircraft sortie from Nos. 603 and 47 Squadrons against shipping in Naoussa port and Yanni Bay on Paros, the mission faced heavy anti-aircraft fire and attacks from Bf 109s and Arado 196s. After strafing barges and caïques and reportedly downing an Arado, LX998 was damaged and ditched on 6 November 1943. P/O K.I.E. Hopkins and W/O K.V. Roget[8] survived in their inflatable dinghy, drifting nearly 30 nautical miles (55km) south-east past Heraclea and Schinousa amid November's Meltemi winds.

HMS *Unrivalled*'s[9] log notes: '*6 Nov 1943: At 1803 hrs, picked up two RAF pilots of a Beaufighter of 603 Squadron and their rubber dinghy near position 36°40'N, 25°47'E.*'[10]

A typically laconic RAF report adds: '*Aircraft "Y" was forced to ditch after having shot down another ARADO; the crew, however P/O Hopkins and W/O Roget, were subsequently picked up by a submarine and landed at Malta, returning to the squadron a week later.*'[11]

A more human account appeared in *The Age* newspaper, Australia, on 18 December 1943:

> MELB. AIRMEN SURPRISED
> Rescue at Sea
>
> LONDON. Dec. 17 (A.A.P.).
> Pilot-Officer Keith E. Hopkins, of Melbourne, who recently was awarded the D.F.C., was shot down while participating in an attack on a U-boat. Announcing this, the Air Ministry states

> that Pilot-Officer Hopkins, with his navigator, Keith Roget, also of Melbourne, had been in a rubber dinghy for several hours when a British submarine came to the surface alongside them. The commander of the submarine had seen the airmen take to the dinghy, and he waited until dusk to rescue them. Pilot-Officer Hopkins said: 'I could not have been more surprised if Hitler came down the chimney dressed as Santa Claus.'

Although U-boats were never involved, you have to agree that Hopkins' personal comment breathes life into the story. His words capture what a good story does best: preserving emotion, colour, and immediacy, even as the physical traces begin to fade.

Unlike LX998, the wreck of *'S' for Sugar*, JM317, remains officially undiscovered, plundered by man and sea – scattered, buried, and unrecognisable. In 2007, Bardanis reportedly recovered two instruments, including a gyrocompass, in under 40ft (12m) off north-west Naxos, yet time and tide have erased almost all other traces of its fall.

What endures, however, is Bill Hayter's account – untouched by salt, tide, or time – preserving not just the aircraft's last moments, but the human experience behind them. The sea may have reclaimed wreckage, but memory and testimony endure – long after the metal is gone …

But only if we let it.

ACKNOWLEDGEMENTS

Special thanks to Dimitri Galon for *Kriegsmarine* reports, Brendan O'Carroll for LRDG materials and images, and Kostas Thoctarides for additional *Kriegsmarine* and SOE files; George Hayter, Mali Hayter, Richard Harper, Elizabeth Hirst, Antonis Karidis, Vasilis Mentogiannis, Mathilde Plet, Patricia Staunton, Emilia Steliarou, Victoria Timsit, and Anne Timsit-Hayter for their respective contributions including images/image processing; and Dr Kimon Papadimitriou for map creation.

Cover Image Credits

Artwork: Antonis Karidis
LRDG Badge: Brendan O'Carroll
Logbook: Victoria Timsit
Beaufighter LX998: Vasilis Mentogiannis

Appendix 1

BILL HAYTER'S OPERATIONAL SORTIES (NORTH AFRICA)

Excerpts from RAF ORBs.

No. 114 Squadron RAF

Hayter posted 04.07.42; Sqdn flew Bristol 'Bisley' Blenheim Mk V.

22.11.42: Blida; Bisley BA729; P/O W.E. Hayter (p); Up/Down 1255/1830 hrs; 1 a/c; two ships bombed, Bizerta harbour.

Night 23/24.11.42: Blida; Bisley BA804; P/O Hayter (p); Up/Down 0220/0740 hrs; 4 a/c; docks and shipping bombed, Bizerta harbour.

Night 30.11/01.12.42: Blida; Bisley BA804; P/O Hayter (p); Up/Down 0210/0725 hrs; 6 a/c; Bizerta/Sidi Ahmed bombed; 2 a/c with engine failure, one crashed (crew survived), other landed safely.

Night 02/03.12.42: Blida; Bisley BA804; P/O Hayter (p); Up/Down 0240/0830 hrs; 7 a/c; Tunis bombed.

Night 04/05.12.42: Canrobert; Bisley BA744; P/O Hayter (p); Up/Down 0415/0800 hrs; 4 a/c; Bizerta docks bombed; 1 a/c engine failure, F/Sgt Baikie (p) killed when chute failed.

Night 14/15.12.42: Canrobert; Bisley BA817; P/O Hayter (p); Up/Down 0435/0745 hrs; 4 a/c; Tunis docks bombed; 1 a/c crash-landed, crew uninjured.

Night 17/18.12.42: Canrobert; Bisley BA822; P/O Hayter (p); Up/Down 1740/2035 hrs; 5 a/c; bombed Bizerta docks, Hayter brought payload back.

Night 28/29.12.42: Canrobert; Bisley BA727; P/O Hayter (p); Up/Down 0437/0730 hrs; 3 a/c; MT Pont du Fahs-Tunis bombed.

Night 22/23.02.43: Canrobert; Bisley BA733; P/O Hayter (p), Sgt D.L. Jeffery (nav/obs), P/O R. Almond (w/op ag); Up/Down 0435/0650 hrs; 11 a/c; MT concentration bombed, Thala-Kasserine Pass.

Night 23/24.02.43: Canrobert; Bisley BA882; P/O Hayter (p), Sgt Jeffery (nav/obs), P/O Almond (w/op ag); Up/Down 0455/0700 hrs; 10 a/c; road junction bombed (no MT found).

Sqdn requipped with Douglas Boston Mk III.

21.04.43: King's Cross; Boston Z2284; P/O Hayter (p), P/O Almond (w/op ag), Sgt Robinson (ag); Up/Down 1315/1420 hrs; 6 a/c; Longstop Hill bombed.

22.04.43: King's Cross; Boston Z2284; P/O Hayter (p), P/O Almond (w/op ag), Sgt Robinson (ag); Up/Down 1408/[unspecified] hrs; 6 a/c; failed to rendezvous with fighter escort, aborted.

22.04.43: King's Cross; Boston Z2284; P/O Hayter (p), P/O Almond (w/op ag), Sgt Robinson (ag); Up/Down 1616/1710 hrs; 12 a/c; Longstop Hill obscured (payloads returned).

23.04.43: King's Cross; Boston Z2284; P/O Hayter (p), P/O Almond (w/op ag), Sgt Robinson (ag); Up/Down 0544/0622 hrs; 12 a/c; recalled due to fog (difficult landing, minor damage).

23.04.43: King's Cross; Boston Z2284; P/O Hayter (p), P/O Almond (w/op ag), Sgt Robinson (ag); Up/Down 1440/1540 hrs; 12 a/c; wadi bombed 'excellent pattern'.

25.04.43: King's Cross; Boston Z2284; P/O Hayter (p), P/O Almond (w/op ag), Sgt Robinson (ag), Sgt Scott (obs); Up/Down 1640/1735 hrs; 12 a/c; attacked by ME 109s before target, 3 a/c damaged, payloads returned.

26.04.43: King's Cross; Boston AL749; P/O Hayter (p), P/O Almond (w/op ag), Sgt Robinson (ag); Up/Down 1235/1330 hrs; 12 a/c; Ksartyr village bombed.

27.04.43: King's Cross; Boston Z2284; P/O Hayter (p), P/O Almond (w/op ag), Sgt Robinson (ag), Sgt Scott (obs); Up/Down 1500/1550 hrs; 12 a/c; wadi bombed, 2 a/c hit by flak.

28.04.43: King's Cross; Boston Z2284; P/O Hayter (p), P/O Almond (w/op ag), Sgt Robinson (ag); Up/Down 1702/1755 hrs; 6 a/c; ridge bombed.

29.04.43: King's Cross; Boston Z2284; P/O Hayter (p), P/O Almond (w/op ag), Sgt Robinson (ag), Sgt Goodfellow (obs); Up/Down 1620/1715 hrs; 6 a/c; enemy troops bombed, 1 a/c hit by flak.

30.04.43: King's Cross; Boston AL749; P/O Hayter (p), P/O Almond (w/op ag), Sgt Robinson (ag); Up/Down 1545/1630 hrs; 12 a/c; enemy troops bombed.

05.05.43: King's Cross; Boston Z2284; P/O Hayter (p), P/O Almond (w/op ag), Sgt Robinson (ag); Up/Down 1540/1635 hrs; 11 a/c; wadi bombed, 10 a/c hit by flak.

06.05.43: King's Cross; Boston Z2284; P/O Hayter (p), P/O Almond (w/op ag), Sgt Robinson (ag), P/O Humphry-Baker (obs); Up/Down 1707/1758 hrs; 12 a/c; MT bombed on St Cyprien-La Mornaghia-Tunis road.

07.05.43: King's Cross; Boston AL755; P/O Hayter (p), P/O Almond (w/op ag), Sgt Robinson (ag), Sgt Jeffery (obs); Up/Down 1120/1215 hrs; 12 a/c; Bizerta-Tunis bombed.

08.05.43: King's Cross; Boston AL749; P/O Hayter (p), P/O Almond (w/op ag), Sgt Robinson (ag), F/O Hall (obs); Up/Down 1400/1515 hrs; 12 a/c; road into Cape Bon bombed, observer in another a/c wounded by flak but continued.

08.05.43: King's Cross; Boston AL749; P/O Hayter (p), P/O Almond (w/op ag), Sgt Robinson (ag), F/O Jeffery (obs); Up/Down 1635/1805 hrs; 11 a/c; road into Cape Bon bombed after ships not found, 1 a/c badly hit by flak returned safely.

09.05.43: King's Cross; Boston Z2284; P/O Hayter (p), P/O Almond (w/op ag), Sgt Robinson (ag), F/O Jeffery (obs); Up/Down 0950/1100 hrs; 12 a/c; derelict ship off Bizerta attacked, all bombs overshot.

10.05.43: King's Cross; Boston Z2284; P/O Hayter (p), P/O Almond (w/op ag), Sgt Robinson (ag), F/O Humphry-Baker (obs); Up/Down 1255/1435 hrs; 12 a/c; bridge south of Korba bombed, missed but road hit.

10.05.43: King's Cross; Boston AL749; P/O Hayter (p), P/O Almond (w/op ag), Sgt Robinson (ag), F/O Hall (obs); Up/Down 1645/1830 hrs; 11 a/c; Menzel Temimi airfield bombed, highly successful. Hayter's final squadron operation in Tunisia.

No. 13 Squadron RAF

Hayter posted 13.05.43; Sqdn flew Bristol 'Bisley' Blenheim Mk V.

06.06.43: Blida; Bisley BB163; P/O W.E. Hayter (p), F/Sgt D.L. Jeffery (nav/obs), P/O R. Almond (w/op ag); Up/Down 1357/1745 hrs; 3 a/c; U-Boat hunt.

09.06.43: Blida; Bisley EH322; P/O Hayter (p), F/Sgt Jeffery (nav/obs), P/O Almond (w/op ag); Up/Down 0845/1250 hrs; 1 a/c; U-Boat hunt.
11.06.43: Blida; Bisley BA806; P/O Hayter (p), F/Sgt Jeffery (nav/obs), P/O R. Almond (w/op ag); Up/Down 1330/1745 hrs; 1 a/c; staggered 9 a/c U-Boat hunt.
12.06.43: Blida; Bisley BB165; P/O Hayter (p), F/Sgt Jeffery (nav/obs), P/O Almond (w/op ag); Up/Down 0535/0940 hrs; 2 a/c; staggered 9 a/c U-Boat hunt.
18.06.43: Blida; Bisley BB165; P/O Hayter (p), F/Sgt Jeffery (nav/obs), W/O R.H. Hooker (ag); Up/Down 1514/1914 hrs; 1 a/c; convoy escort.
20.06.43: Blida; Bisley EH322; P/O Hayter (p), F/Sgt Jeffery (nav/obs), W/O Hooker (ag); Up/Down 0626/1040 hrs; 2 a/c; staggered 8 a/c U-Boat hunt.
22.06.43: Blida; Bisley BA733; P/O Hayter (p), F/Sgt Jeffery (nav/obs), W/O Hooker (ag); Up/Down 1318/1738 hrs; 2 a/c; staggered 6 a/c U-Boat hunt.
14.08.43: Blida; Bisley BB149; P/O Hayter (p), F/Sgt D.L. Jeffery (nav/obs), Sgt S.W. Knight (ag); Up/Down 1345/1815 hrs; 1 a/c; staggered 4 a/c convoy escort.

No. 47 Squadron RAF

Hayter posted 27.08.43; Sqdn flew Bristol Beaufighter Mk X, TF variant.
02.09.43: Protville II; Beaufighter 'Q'; F/O W.E. Hayter (p), F/Sgt D.L. Jeffery (nav/obs); Up/Down 1432/2025 hrs; 10 a/c; strike on sighting shipping (43°24′N 10°08′E); 1 a/c crashed, killing aircrew, another ditched, aircrew survived.
10.09.43: Protville II; Beaufighter 'W'; F/O Hayter (p), F/Sgt Jeffery (nav/obs); Up/Down 1600/2135 hrs; 2 a/c; escort for Air Sea Rescue Catalina (three men rescued from water).
30.10.43: El Adem; Beaufighter 'S'; F/O Hayter (p), W/O J.S. Harper (603 Sqdn, nav/obs); Up/Down 1347/1812 hrs; 4 a/c; Naxos harbour strike with B-25Gs; one B-25G lost, 'S' hit, ditched, aircrew escaped.
25.11.43: Gambut III; Beaufighter 'E'; F/O Hayter (p), F/O F.C. Miles (nav/obs); Up/Down 1310/1730 hrs; 4 a/c; southern Aegean sweep, no attacks.

27.11.43: Gambut III; Beaufighter 'J'; F/O Hayter (p), F/O Miles (nav/obs); Up/Down 1006/1506 hrs; 4 a/c; shipping strike Nilaria, no sightings.

04.12.43: Gambut III; Beaufighter 'G'; F/O Hayter (p), F/O Miles (nav/obs); Up/Down 1124/1618 hrs; 6 a/c; eastern Aegean sweep, Hayter returned with W/T unserviceable, others engaged Arados and damaged a HSL.

05.12.43: Gambut III; Beaufighter 'Z'; F/O Hayter (p), F/O Miles (nav/obs); Up/Down 1219/1643 hrs; 3 a/c; eastern Aegean sweep, no sightings. Hayter's final combat sortie.

Appendix 2

TOM HARPER'S OPERATIONAL SORTIES

Excerpts from RAF ORBs

No. 604 Squadron RAF

Harper posted 07.04.42; Sqdn flew Bristol Beaufighter Mk I.

07.04.42: Middle Wallop; Beaufighter 7747; S/L Skinner (p), F/Sgt Larony (nav/obs), Sgt Harper; Up/Down 1500/1545 hrs; 1 a/c; NFT.

10.04.42: Middle Wallop; Beaufighter 7556; Sgt Atkinson (p), Sgt Sanders (nav/obs), Sgt Harper; Up/Down 1500/1545 hrs; 2 a/c; NFT.

13.04.42: Middle Wallop; Beaufighter 7556; Sgt Atkinson (p), Sgt Sanders (nav/obs), Sgt Harper; Up/Down 1500/1620 hrs; 4 a/c; NFT.

17.04.42: Middle Wallop; Beaufighter 6626; Sgt Ward (p), Sgt Harper (nav/obs); Up/Down 1725/1900 hrs; 1 a/c; local flying.

18.04.42: Middle Wallop; Beaufighter 7556; Sgt Fraser (p), Sgt Bird (nav/obs), Sgt Harper; Up/Down 1455/1605 hrs; 2 a/c; NFT.

20.04.42: Middle Wallop; Beaufighter 2208; Sgt Ward (p), Sgt Harper (nav/obs); Up/Down 1720/1825 hrs; 1 a/c; local flying.

23.04.42: Middle Wallop; Beaufighter 4626; Sgt Ward (p), Sgt Harper (nav/obs); Up/Down 1645/1740 hrs; 1 a/c; local flying.

24.04.42: Middle Wallop; Beaufighter 4623; Sgt Ward (p), Sgt Harper (nav/obs); Up/Down 1520/1630 hrs; 4 a/c; AI practice.

25.04.42: Middle Wallop; Beaufighter 2146; Sgt Ward (p), Sgt Harper (nav/obs); Up/Down 1645/1800 hrs; 1 a/c; AI practice.

28.04.42: Middle Wallop; Beaufighter 2188; Sgt Ward (p), Sgt Harper (nav/obs); Up/Down 1455/1615 hrs; 2 a/c; AI practice.
29.04.42: Middle Wallop; Beaufighter 2188; Sgt Ward (p), Sgt Harper (nav/obs); Up/Down 1255/1350 hrs; 1 a/c; circuits and landings.
04.05.42: Middle Wallop; Beaufighter 4626; Sgt Ward (p), Sgt Harper (nav/obs); Up/Down 1225/1355 hrs; 1 a/c; local flying. Up/Down 17:10/18:15 hrs; 1 a/c; local flying.
06.05.42: Middle Wallop; Beaufighter 4626; Sgt Ward (p), Sgt Harper (nav/obs); Up/Down 1250/1410 hrs; 2 a/c; local flying.
07.05.42: Middle Wallop; Beaufighter 2091; Sgt Ward (p), Sgt Harper (nav/obs); Up/Down 1240/1410 hrs; 1 a/c; local flying.
08.05.42: Middle Wallop; Beaufighter 2186; Sgt Ward (p), Sgt Harper (nav/obs); Up/Down 1745/1950 hrs; 2 a/c; AI practice.
11.05.42: Middle Wallop; Beaufighter 7550; Sgt Ward (p), Sgt Harper (nav/obs), LAC Smith; Up/Down 1500/1650 hrs; 4 a/c; AI practice.
14.05.42: Middle Wallop; Beaufighter 4626; Sgt Ward (p), Sgt Harper (nav/obs); Up/Down 1240/1410 hrs; 1 a/c; AI & NFT.
15.05.42: Middle Wallop; Beaufighter 4623; Sgt Ward (p), Sgt Harper (nav/obs), Cpl Hill; Up/Down 1455/1600 hrs; 1 a/c; air firing.
16.05.42: Middle Wallop; Beaufighter 4623; Sgt Ward (p), Sgt Harper (nav/obs); Up/Down 1620/1800 hrs; 1 a/c; AI & NFT.
Up/Down 22:15/22:55 hrs (a/c '2188'); dusk landings.
19.05.42: Middle Wallop; Beaufighter 7550; Sgt Ward (p), Sgt Harper (nav/obs); Up/Down 1520/1615 hrs; 2 a/c; AI & NFT. Up/Down 2010/2100 hrs; 2 a/c; AI & NFT. Up/Down 2255/0115 hrs; 3 a/c; Sopley practice.
22.05.42: Middle Wallop; Beaufighter 7556; Sgt Ward (p), Sgt Harper (nav/obs); Up/Down 1830/1930 hrs; 1 a/c; NFT. Up/Down 2245/0055 hrs; 3 a/c; Sopley practice.
25.05.42: Middle Wallop; Beaufighter 4626; Sgt Ward (p), Sgt Harper (nav/obs); Up/Down 2150/2230 hrs; 7 a/c; AI & NFT.
26.05.42: Middle Wallop; Beaufighter 4626; Sgt Ward (p), Sgt Harper (nav/obs); Up/Down 1845/1950 hrs; 8 a/c; AI & NFT.
Up/Down 2245/0115 hrs; 1 a/c; staggered 3 a/c patrol.
28.05.42: Middle Wallop; Beaufighter 7811; Sgt Ward (p), Sgt Harper (nav/obs); Up/Down 1235/1425 hrs; 2 a/c; AI practice.

No. 603 Squadron RAF

Harper posted 02.02.43; Sqdn flew Bristol Beaufighter Mk IC & VIC

15.03.43: El Magrum; Beaufighter KL504; Sgt T.R. Beattie (p), Sgt T.J. Harper (nav/obs); Up/Down 0700/1200 hrs (landed Misurata); 3 a/c; staggered 7 a/c convoy escort 'Survey', Ju 88s seen.

16.03.43: El Magrum; Beaufighter KL504; Sgt Beattie (p), Sgt Harper (nav/obs); Up/Down 1420/1845 hrs; 2 a/c; convoy escort 'Poker'.

21.03.43: El Magrum; Beaufighter KL504; Sgt Beattie (p), Sgt Harper (nav/obs); Up/Down 0945/1510 hrs; 2 a/c; convoy escort 'Liquid'.

29.03.43: El Magrum; Beaufighter KL504; Sgt Beattie (p), Sgt Harper (nav/obs); Up/Down 1200/1700 hrs; 1 a/c; staggered 5 a/c convoy escort 'Anger'.

03.04.43: Misurata West; Beaufighter 'L' KL504; Sgt Beattie (p), Sgt Harper (nav/obs); Up/Down 0735/1110 hrs; 2 a/c; staggered 4 a/c convoy escort 'Outwit', 'L' returned early with engine trouble.

11.04.43: Misurata West; Beaufighter 'A' J5724; F/Sgt Beattie (p), Sgt Harper (nav/obs); Up/Down 0930/1305 hrs; 1 a/c; staggered 5 a/c convoy escort 'Curly'.

17.04.43: Misurata West; Beaufighter 'A' JL724; Sgt Beattie (p), Sgt Harper (nav/obs); Up/Down 1210/1705 hrs; 1 a/c; staggered 4 a/c convoy escort 'Heavy', 1 a/c retired with engine trouble.

27.04.43: Misurata West; Beaufighter 'T' X7772; Sgt Beattie (p), Sgt Harper (nav/obs); Up/Down 0920/1240 hrs; 2 a/c; staggered 6 a/c convoy escort 'Nation', 1 a/c retired with ill pilot.

04.05.43: Misurata West; Beaufighter 'T' X7772; F/Sgt Beattie (p), F/Sgt Harper (nav/obs); Up/Down 1210/1700 hrs; 2 a/c; staggered 4 a/c convoy escort 'Brilliant', not located (acquired later).

11.05.43: Misurata West; Beaufighter 'T' X7772; F/Sgt Beattie (p), F/Sgt Harper (nav/obs); Up/Down 1530/2050 hrs; 2 a/c; staggered 4 a/c convoy escort 'Brilliant'.

20.05.43: Misurata West; Beaufighter 'J' KL517; F/Sgt Beattie (p), F/Sgt Harper (nav/obs); Up/Down 1355/1850 hrs; 2 a/c; staggered 4 a/c convoy escort 'Venus'.

23.05.43: Misurata West; Beaufighter 'H' X7741; F/Sgt Beattie (p), F/Sgt Harper (nav/obs); Up/Down 1620/1640 hrs; 2 a/c; staggered 5 a/c convoy escort 'Nutshell', 'H' retired with engine trouble, changed a/c.

Up/Down 1705/2000 hrs; 'J' KL517; 1 a/c; resumed convoy escort 'Nutshell'.

29.05.43: Misurata West; Beaufighter 'B' JL516; F/Sgt Beattie (p), F/Sgt Harper (nav/obs); Up/Down 1320/1800 hrs; 2 a/c; staggered 6 a/c convoy escort 'Blanket'.

04.06.43: Misurata West; Beaufighter 'O' KL448; F/Sgt Beattie (p), F/Sgt Harper (nav/obs); Up/Down 0425/0905 hrs; 2 a/c; staggered 4 a/c convoy escort 'Swing'.

06.06.43: Misurata West; Beaufighter 'O' KL448; F/Sgt Beattie (p), F/Sgt Harper (nav/obs); Up/Down 0515/0920 hrs; 2 a/c; staggered 4 a/c convoy escort 'Sampler', later a hospital ship.

08.06.43: Misurata West; Beaufighter 'B' JL516; F/Sgt Beattie (p), F/Sgt Harper (nav/obs); Up/Down 0500/0755 hrs; 2 a/c; convoy escort 'Paper'.

09.06.43: Misurata West; Beaufighter 'B' JL516; F/Sgt Beattie (p), F/Sgt Harper (nav/obs); Up/Down 1755/2145 hrs; 2 a/c; staggered 4 a/c convoy escort 'Mammoth'.

18.06.43: Misurata West; Beaufighter 'B' JL516; F/Sgt Beattie (p), F/Sgt Harper (nav/obs); Up/Down 1455/1925 hrs; 2 a/c; staggered 4 a/c convoy escort 'Decade'.

23.06.43: Misurata West; Beaufighter 'B' JL516; F/Sgt Beattie (p), F/Sgt Harper (nav/obs); Up/Down 0935/1345 hrs; 2 a/c; staggered 6 a/c convoy escort 'Across'.

26.06.43: Misurata West; Beaufighter 'B' JL516; F/Sgt Beattie (p), F/Sgt Harper (nav/obs); Up/Down 1730/1815 hrs; 2 a/c; staggered 5 a/c convoy escort 'Nonce'.

08.07.43: Misurata West; Beaufighter 'O' KL448; F/Sgt Beattie (p), F/Sgt Harper (nav/obs); Up/Down 0530/0910 hrs; 2 a/c; staggered 11 a/c convoy escort 'Investigate'.

12.07.43: Misurata West; Beaufighter 'F' X7762; F/Sgt Beattie (p), F/Sgt Harper (nav/obs); Up/Down 0715/1250 hrs; 2 a/c; staggered 19 a/c convoy escort 'Bowary', 1 a/c belly-landed, aircrew uninjured.

25.08.43: Misurata West; Beaufighter 'J' KL517; F/O C.B. Megone (p), F/Sgt Harper (nav/obs); Up/Down 1045/1615 hrs; 2 a/c; staggered 4 a/c convoy escort 'Untrue'.

09.09.43: Borizzo; Beaufighter 'J' KL517; F/O Megone (p), W/O Harper (nav/obs); Up/Down 1557/1837 hrs; 2 a/c; convoy escort 'Elicit', not located.

12.09.43: Borizzo; Beaufighter 'D' JL731; P/O P.H. Miller (p), W/O Harper (nav/obs); Up/Down 1909/2035 hrs; 4 a/c; convoy escort 'Monica', not located.

16.09.43: Borizzo; Beaufighter 'T' X8105; P/O Miller (p), W/O Harper (nav/obs); Up/Down 1250/1805 hrs; 3 a/c; aircraft recce sweep, 'T' and another a/c detached to cover 2 convoys.

17.09.43: Borizzo; Beaufighter 'E' JL761; W/Cdr H.A. Chater (p), W/O Harper (nav/obs); Up/Down 0625/0840 hrs; 3 a/c; recce sweep led by 'E', no unescorted convoys found.

30.10.43: Gambut III; No. 47 Sqdn aircraft; W/O Harper (nav/obs); 'aircraft failed to return'.

Sqdn flew Bristol Beaufighter Mk X

25.02.44: Gambut III; Beaufighter 'H' NK400; F/Sgt C.J. Gould (p), W/O Harper (nav/obs); Up/Down 1325/1815 hrs; 4 a/c; central Aegean sweep (Kaso Straits, Santorini, Nios, Amorgos, Stampalia, Kaso St.).

02.03.44: Gambut III; Beaufighter 'Q' NH363; F/Sgt Gould (p), W/O Harper (nav/obs); Up/Down 1215/1515 hrs; 4 a/c; central Aegean sweep, early return due to bad weather.

14.03.44: Berka; Beaufighter 'B' NH282; F/Sgt Gould (p), W/O Harper (nav/obs); Up/Down 1050/1540 hrs; 4 a/c; convoy escort.

20.03.44: Gambut III; Beaufighter 'D' LX872; F/Sgt Gould (p), W/O Harper (nav/obs); Up/Down 1030/1520 hrs; 6 a/c; central Aegean sweep, attacks on 4 caïques at Port Panom, Mykonos; 2 hits on caique at Paros.

23.03.44: Gambut III; Beaufighter 'D' LX872; F/Sgt Gould (p), W/O Harper (nav/obs); Up/Down 1050/1510 hrs; 4 a/c; eastern Greek coast sweep.

27.03.44: Gambut III; Beaufighter 'D' LX872; F/Sgt Gould (p), W/O Harper (nav/obs); Up/Down 1250/1650 hrs; 6 a/c; convoy escort.

07.04.44: Gambut III; Beaufighter 'B' NE282; F/Sgt Gould (p), W/O Harper (nav/obs); Up/Down 1000/1315 hrs; 1 a/c; staggered 2 a/c convoy escort 'Rubicon'.

10.04.44: Gambut III; Beaufighter 'F' LZ272; F/Sgt Gould (p), W/O Harper (nav/obs); Up/Down 1325/1830 hrs; 4 a/c; central Aegean sweep, attacks on caïques.

13.04.44: Gambut III; Beaufighter 'F' LZ272; F/Sgt Gould (p), W/O Harper (nav/obs); Up/Down 0640/1120 hrs; 6 a/c; Gulf of Lakonia sweep, engagement with Me 109s; aircraft 'N' shot down, 'F' damaged.
16.04.44: Gambut III; Beaufighter 'A' LZ489; F/Sgt Gould (p), W/O Harper (nav/obs); Up/Down 1325/1545 hrs; 4 a/c; central Aegean sweep, all returned early.
18.04.44: Gambut III; Beaufighter 'J' LZ522; F/Sgt Gould (p), W/O Harper (nav/obs); Up/Down 1515/1950 hrs; 1 a/c; staggered 6 a/c U-boat hunt.
21.04.44: Gambut III; Beaufighter 'H' NE400; F/Sgt Gould (p), W/O Harper (nav/obs); Up/Down 1400/1900 hrs; 1 a/c; U-boat hunt.
Harper's final combat sortie.

ENDNOTES

Chapter 1

1. Munich Crisis, Sep. 1938: Chamberlain met Hitler three times, ending with the Munich Agreement at the *Führerbau*, Munich (building survives today).
2. The *Sturmabteilung* (SA or Brownshirts) and *Schutzstaffel* (SS) paramilitaries; 1934 Night of the Long Knives purged SA, consolidating SS power.
3. Translations: '*Heil Hitler!*' (Hail Hitler!), '*Sieg Heil!*' (Hail Victory!), '*Deutschland über Alles!*' (Germany above all!).
4. Poland: borders shifted frequently; disappeared 1795–1918 due to partitions, regained in-dependence after WWI.

Chapter 2

1. Churchill speech, House of Commons, 20 Aug. 1940: Hansard 364.
2. Hayter's British Forces Middle East ID card specifies 'Green'.
3. Hartley Wintney in Southampton (now Hampshire); renamed 1950s.
4. Anne Timsit-Hayter: emails 2023–25.
5. BCATP: Canada; EATS: Empire; JATS: South Africa.
6. May 1940 to Mar. 1945: 157,600 trained in Canada; 83.4 per cent graduated; 37.8 per cent pilots.
7. *A Man Called Intrepid* (1976), biography of Sir William Stephenson by William Stevenson (no relation).
8. Allberry, C.R.C.A., *Manichaean Psalm Book II*, CUP, 1938.
9. David Allberry: emails 2024.

10. Lewis, Charles Allberry: *A Portrait.*
11. Patricia Staunton: emails 2023–25.

Chapter 3

1. LAC Kenneth F. Davis (S/N R89395) and LAC Alexander F. Switzer (R95519): Des Moines, Iowa, and Pembroke, Ontario; both 27 years old.
2. Hayter promoted to F/Sgt, 21 Dec. 1941.
3. David Allberry: emails 2024.
4. F/O Charles R.C.A. Allberry (127293, RAFVR): 31; buried Eindhoven (Woensel) General Cemetery, NL.
5. *Oberleutnant* Eckart-W. von Bonin: 6./NJG1; survived WWII with 37 victories.
6. Beam Approach Beacon System (BABS): radio system guiding low-visibility landings.
7. AIR-27-882-53.
8. Raid also propaganda coup; Harris launched 1,047 aircraft plus ~100 intruder sorties.
9. Harris' quote: *Hosea* 8:7, inspired by the Blitz.
10. Twente Airfield, Enschede, NL: expanded by Germans into radar-linked night-fighter base.
11. AIR-27-882-57.

Chapter 4

1. AIR-27-882-62.
2. Ibid.
3. Dec. 1942, 114 Sqdn records handwritten, omitting crew. Later ORBs suggest P/O J.L. Steele with P/O R.J. Phillips (nav) and F/Sgt G. Gregory or F/Sgt D.V. Symindson (W/AG).
4. AIR-27-882-63.
5. Bisley BA744: F/O W.R. Gellatly (pilot), Sgt E.K. Stringer (nav), Sgt J.D. Hammill (W/AG).
6. Bisley BA991: F/Sgt D.F. Gilbert (pilot), Sgt W.T. Wiggall (nav), Sgt F.E. Hughes (W/AG).

7. AIR-27-882-63.
8. AIR-27-882-65.
9. Ibid.
10. Ibid.
11. AIR-27-882-66.
12. AIR-27-882-65; AIR-27-882-66.
13. AIR-27-882-66.
14. Ibid.
15. Ibid.
16. AIR-27-882-65.
17. Ibid.
18. Ibid.
19. Ibid.

Chapter 5

1. AIR-27-882-67.
2. AM Sir Arthur Coningham (1895–1948), WDAF commander at El Alamein (Nov. 1942).
3. AVM Sir Laurence Sinclair (1908–2002), GC; commanded 110 Sqdn, served North Africa/Balkans.
4. British (and Commonwealth) honours: AFC (Air Force Cross), CB (Companion of the Order of the Bath), CBE (Commander of the Order of the British Empire), DFC (Distinguished Flying Cross), DSO (Distinguished Service Order), GC (George Cross), MC (Military Cross).
5. Douglas A-20 Havoc (RAF: Boston Mk III).
6. AIR-27-882-67.
7. Longstop Hill, Tunisia, Apr. 1943: 78th Division and Churchill tanks broke German resistance.
8. AIR-27-882-67.
9. 'Wadi': dry riverbed in North Africa, floods only after rain.
10. AIR-27-882-67.
11. AIR-27-244-21.
12. AIR-27-882-69.
13. Ibid.
14. Ibid.

Chapter 6

1. AIR-27-181-37; AIR-27-882-69.
2. ACM Sir Kenneth 'Bing' Cross (1911–2003), RAF commander; led No. 46 Sqdn in Norway 1940, earned Norwegian War Cross, survived sinking of HMS *Glorious*; in 1943 commanded Nos. 212 and 242 Groups, North Africa.
3. AIR-27-181-37.
4. *23. U-Flottille* (23rd U-boat Flotilla), based on Salamis, Greece; *29. U-Flottille* (29th U-boat Flotilla), based in La Spezia, Italy.
5. AIR-27-181-40.
6. Timeline: 22 Feb.–18 Jun. 1943. No. 114 Sqdn ORBs (Nov.–Dec. 1942) omit crews, but Jeffery and Almond likely flew with Hayter on seven sorties.
7. AIR-27-181-43.
8. AIR-27-464-26.
9. AIR-27-181-43.

Chapter 7

1. 'Mae Wests': yellow inflatable life jackets, named after actress Mae West's curvaceous figure.
2. AIR-27-464-28.
3. Ibid.
4. Ibid.
5. Ibid.
6. Churchill, *The Second World War*, Vol. 5, p.168.
7. Ibid, p.167.
8. George Jellicoe (1918–2007), 2nd Earl Jellicoe; Coldstream Guards, No. 8 Commando/SAS, later SBS commander. Worked with Greek Sacred Band, led Aegean operations (Heraklion 1942; Rhodes, Kos, Leros 1943), later First Lord of the Admiralty and Leader of the House of Lords.
9. 'Cyclades' from Greek *kyklós* ('circle'), reflecting the islands' ring around Delos, sacred to Apollo and Artemis.
10. No. 47 Sqdn RAF ORBs (Sep.–Oct. 1943) misidentified B-25Gs as 310th BG USAAF; actually 445th and 446th Sqdns, 321st BG, until 30 Oct.

11. ADM 199/1818.
12. Ibid.
13. German Naval Staff War Diary, Oct. 1943, p.439.
14. *Kriegsmarine* War Diary, Oct. 1943, p.440.
15. F/O John Dixon (47785, RAFVR) (22 y.o.), Capt. George & Norah L.W. Dixon, Clifton, Bristol; Alamein Memorial, col. 268, Egypt.
16. F/O George Alec Terry (132857, RAFVR), Alamein Memorial, col. 269, Egypt.

Chapter 8

1. Simonides, epitaph for Athenians at Plataea, 479 BCE.
2. Hayter pencilled in: '*After a few weeks in the desert, you begin talking to yourself. Soon after, you begin talking to the lizards. After a fortnight, they begin talking to you. After that, you find yourself listening to them.*'
3. 'The man' identified as Vic Borrowdale – later crossed out.

Chapter 9

1. Tobruk changed hands four times in WWII: Italy (1940), Allies (1941 siege), Axis (1942), Allies (1942).
2. CO: commanding officer.
3. Gabes, Tunisia, Axis airbase, retaken 1943; now Int'l Airport.
4. Misurata, Libya's third largest city, on Via Balbia (coastal highway).
5. MO: medical officer.
6. 1937 Marble Arch (*Arco dei Fileni*), marking Tripolitania-Cyrenaica border.
7. George Formby OBE (1904–61), top UK entertainer, ENSA wartime tours.
8. 'Libyans': Cyrenaeans.
9. Cyrene, Greek colony (631 BCE), later Roman; namesake of Cyrenaica (eastern Libya).
10. RAF El Adem (LG 144), now Libyan airbase.
11. 'Shooting up': RAF low pass.
12. Navy, Army and Air Force Institutes (NAAFI): canteens and recreation for British forces, since 1920.

13. No. 47 Sqdn ordered from Tunisia to Gambut III Oct. 1943, but often used El Adem.
14. RAF Gambut, 31 miles (50km) from Tobruk, comprised six airfields: LG-159, LG-142, LG-143, LG-156, LG-159, LG-158.
15. Kos (Dodecanese): Italian airfield, German-held from 1943; now airport.
16. 'Gharri': car.
17. 'Erk': junior RAF airman.
18. Non-commissioned officers (NCOs), RAF ranks from corporal to warrant officer (Cpl-WO).
19. F/Sgt A. Woodfield (pilot), RAFVR.
20. F/O Lewis 'Ross' Rossner (pilot) (131150), RAFVR.
21. F/O John 'Dicky' Dixon (pilot) (47785), RAFVR.
22. F/O John Bratt 'Fletch' Fletcher (pilot) (128593), RAFVR.
23. F/O Joseph Arthur Unwin (pilot) (129568), RAFVR; ORB clerical errors in initials; known as Arthur.
24. Translation: There are as many opinions as there are people.
25. F/O George Alec Terry (nav/obs) (132857), RAFVR.
26. F/O John Stephens 'Titch' Hayden (pilot) (130938), RAFVR; 'Titch' a nickname for someone diminutive in stature.
27. F/O Joseph Arthur Unwin (129568), RAFVR, (22 y.o.), John and Annie Unwin, Dagenham; Alamein Memorial, col. 279, Egypt.
28. Victoria Cross (VC): highest gallantry award.
29. 13 Feb. 1944, No. 47 Sqdn ORB: Unwin's Beaufighter (with F/ Sgt K. Farmer), near Milos, seen '*doing violent turns on the deck with smoke pouring from the starboard engine, hemmed in by three ME-109s*'. Both KIA.
30. Entertainments National Service Association (ENSA): wartime entertainment organisation.
31. Green Mamba modern version: Midori melon liqueur, Bacardi 151, club soda, and sweet-and-sour mix.
32. F/O D.A. 'Duggy' Smart (pilot), RAFVR.
33. F/O Anthony David 'Tony' Bond (pilot) (125666), RAFVR.
34. F/O Athol George 'Nobby' Greentree (pilot) (414974), RNZAF.
35. 26 Oct. 1943: Hayden's guns jammed vs Ju 52; flew again 29 Oct.

36. 'Flight fantastic': death.
37. 24 Aug. 1943: Beaufighter hit mast, ditched off Tunisia; crew rescued. See Chapter 6.
38. Lord Byron (1788–1824), *Childe Harold's Pilgrimage*; poet died in Greece.
39. Hayter last flew with F/Sgt D.L. Jeffery (nav/obs) 10 Sep. 1943.
40. 5 Nov. 1943: W/Cdr Lee-Evans DFC shot down near Athens; succeeded by Lewis then Filson-Young.
41. A 25 Feb. 1944 letter from the US 445th Bomb Sqdn, 321st BG, to CG Twelfth Air Force (APO 650, Foggia, Italy) details B-25G 42-64579's mission: '*Attack merchant vessels in Naxos Harbour, Klodes Island, Greece; departed Gambut, Libya, flying 209° for 210 mi (1 h 15 min), 360° for 20 mi (7 min), 330° for 130 mi (40 min).*'

Chapter 10

1. Invasion of Crete began 20 May 1941: largest airborne invasion to date; fell after 11 days, 18,600 British/Dominion troops evacuated, 12,000 and thousands of Greeks remained, many joined resistance.
2. Radar.
3. Translation: 'Descent to hell is easy!' – Vergil, *Aeneid* (70–19 BCE).
4. Lord Byron (1788–1824), *Don Juan* (1819); '*The Isles of Greece*', Canto III.
5. Paros famed for white marble, exported since 6th BCE; horizontal quarries survive.
6. Praxiteles (c. 360 BCE): leading forth-century Athenian sculptor; first life-sized nude female statue in Paros marble.
7. Demeter, goddess of agriculture/harvest/fertility: worshipped in Greece as 'Saint Demetra' after 380 CE.
8. Dionysius (also spelt Dionysus) (Bacchus): Greek god of wine, festivity, theatre, ecstasy, madness; Dennis/Denise derived from his name.
9. Excerpt from *Into Battle* (1915), Julian H.F. Grenfell (1888–1915); British captain and poet, died of wounds May 1915.
10. W/Cdr Brendan 'Paddy' E.F. Finucane DSO, DFC and two bars (1920–42): RAF ace, 28 victories, youngest W/Cdr; killed 15 Jul. 1942 ditching Spitfire, English Channel.

11. See Chapter 22 for full description of attack.
12. Location of Hayter/Harper's Beaufighter JM317 (33–39ft (10–12m) depth off north-east of Naxos) never publicly disclosed; little remains.
13. See *Stars and Stripes*, Chapter 6.
14. 'Morphia': antiquated term for morphine.

Chapter 11

1. Craven 'A' cigarettes: launched 1921; wartime favourite in red packs with 'throat-friendly' slogans; ironically, 'craven' means 'cowardly'.
2. WWII RAF emergency packs: included food, Horlicks, gum, Halazone (water purification), Benzedrine (amphetamine), matches, compass, maps; Harper's kit likely similar. (IWM Catalogue EPH 3833)
3. Mykonos and Delos: ~18.5 miles (30km) north-west of Naxos.
4. Lapis lazuli: semi-precious rock prized since antiquity for deep blue colour.
5. Amethyst: quartz stone notable for striking violet colour.
6. Horlicks tablets: high-energy malted milk included in WWII RAF emergency packs.
7. 'A nation of shopkeepers': coined by Barère 1794, wrongly attributed to Napoleon; mocked Britain's commerce, though trade/naval strength secured post-Waterloo (1815) dominance.
8. Algernon Charles Swinburne (1837–1909): English poet/critic; *A Forsaken Garden* (1876) explores love, mortality, ocean, and time.
9. John Keats (1795–1821): 'Ode on a Grecian Urn', 'Heard melodies are sweet, but those unheard are sweeter.'
10. Xenophon: *Anabasis* (c. 370 BCE) recounts the Ten Thousand mercenaries' 401 BCE expedition for Cyrus, perilous retreat, ultimate sighting of the Black Sea: '*Thalassa! Thalassa!*' (The Sea! The Sea!)
11. Plato (c. 428–348 BCE): maxim highlighting practical knowledge alongside intellectual learning.
12. 'Narpoo' (or 'napoo'): WWI British slang for 'dead' or 'gone', likely from French *il n'y a plus* ('there is no more').
13. 'Sanfareyan': British soldier slang from French *Ça ne fait rien*, meaning 'it does nothing'.

Chapter 12

1. 'Alex': Alexandria, Egypt.
2. Nikiforos Levogiannis: Maria Levogianni, daughter of Nikiforos and Varvara Chorianopoulou-Levogianni, recalled her father's composure under pressure, removing all traces of the airmen's presence, even burying cigarette butts.
3. 8 Oct. 1944: F/Lt Volonakis and F/Os Mitrakis and Margaritis, No. 335 Sqdn RAF, landed Spitfires at Araxos (near Patras), first RHAF pilots on Greek soil since 1941; one paid 135 million drachmae (5/- or 60p) for 2.7lb (1.3kg) of apples; a month later, monetary reforms valued 1 post-war drachma at 50 billion wartime drachmas, highlighting extreme hyperinflation.
4. Paros: ~8 miles (13km) off north-west coast of Naxos.
5. Melos also spelt Milos.
6. Leto: goddess whose concealed beauty Zeus saw; bore Apollo (god of light/music) and Artemis (goddess of hunting); Hera forbade all lands to shelter her; Leto fled to Delos, considered unattached to seafloor, giving birth safely.
7. Terrace of the Lions (c. 600 BCE): nine marble lions along Delos' Sacred Way, north of Apollo's sanctuary, overlooking the Sacred Lake.
8. Ariadne: daughter of King Minos; helped Theseus escape Minotaur, abandoned on Naxos, found/married by Dionysus; crown became Corona Borealis.
9. Translation: 'Ariane, my sister, of what wounded love, You died on the shores where you were left.' – Racine, *Phèdre* (1677), reworking Euripides' *Hippolytus*.
10. Daedalus and Icarus: escaped Crete with wax-and-feather wings; Icarus flew too close to the sun, melting the wax, and fell tragically into the sea.
11. Cos also spelt Kos.
12. Rome: fell to the Allies on 5 Jun. 1944.
13. Verey pistol (also spelt Very pistol): single-shot flare gun named after Edward W. Very, used for distress signalling.
14. Joel Chandler Harris, *Uncle Remus* (1881): line '*Lounging around and suffering*' warns that passivity strengthens enemies and worsens situations.

15. *Volga Boatman*: traditional Russian song, first published by Mily Balakirev in 1866.
16. *Mother Machree*: 1910 American-Irish song by Ernest Ball and Rida Johnson Young, originally sung by Chauncey Olcott; 'Machree' means 'my heart' in Irish-Gaelic.
17. *Loch Lomond*: short for *The Bonnie Banks o' Loch Lomond*, Scottish song first recorded in prose by Andrew Lang (1876).
18. 'Colleen': meaning girl; appears in *Mother Machree*: '*There's a spot in my heart, which no colleen may own.*'
19. Tennyson, *Ulysses* (1833): inspired by Homer's *Odyssey*, declares '*I am a part of all that I have met.*' The poem affirms that a heroic spirit endures despite weariness.
20. Dr Emmanuel Bardanis.
21. Translation: 'mountain doctor': village or country physician serving locals through practical experience, unlike urban specialists.
22. Dornier Do-24 'CH+EX' *Werknummer* (Work No.) 105, *Reichsluftfahrtministerium* (RLM, Serial No.) 0032.
23. German Naval Staff War Diary, Oct. 1943, p.455: '*On 29 Oct. a Do-24 sea-rescue plane sank in Naxos harbour; nine men missing.*'
24. Ikaria: named after Icarus; ~23 miles (37km) south-west of Naxos.
25. Varvara Chorianopoulou: George's adopted niece, married Nikiforos Levogiannis; three children; George died at 47, Varvara lived to 100; granddaughter Areti married Manolis Bardanis, diver who found scattered remains of Hayter/Harper's Beaufighter JM317 in 2007.
26. Tricoteuse: vengeful women knitting by guillotine during French Revolution (1789–99), immortalised by Dickens' *Madame Defarge*.

Chapter 13

1. Reproduction of this note: see Chapter 17.
2. A.A. Milne, *Now We Are Six* (1927): children's verse collection; extract about 'bad King John'.
3. LRDG patrol (R1): men on Naxos monitoring shipping, aircraft, and garrison activity; reported by W/T (radio). See Chapter 17.

4. 'Mad' Carew: from J. Milton, *The Green Eye of the Yellow God* (1911); impulsive officer steals the Green Eye, fatally wounded, dies in Nepal; Hayter draws analogy with his carefree night beneath the stars.

Chapter 14

1. Mk IV AI radar: early Beaufighter radar (190–195 MHz), range 4 miles, key for night interceptions.
2. Ground Controlled Interception (GCI): radar system guiding fighters with headings and altitude during night or low-visibility operations.
3. RAF Sopley: first mobile GCI station (1940), active until 1974.
4. *Gee & Oboe*: Gee for navigation; Oboe guided bombers via radio beams in poor weather/night.
5. AIR-27-2083-30.
6. Ibid.
7. AIR-27-2083-32.
8. Ibid.
9. John Cunningham (1917–2002): Gp Capt. CBE, DSO and two bars, DFC and bar, AE; post-war test pilot, helped develop de Havilland Comet.
10. Cecil 'Jimmy' Rawnsley (1904–1965): S/Ldr, DSO, DFC, DFM and bar; post-war Auxiliary Air Force, co-authored *Night Fighter* (1957).
11. AIR-27-2083-32.
12. He 111 H-6, *Werknummer* (Work No.) 4627, 6N+FR.
13. AIR-27-2083-32.
14. AIR-27-1578-3.

Chapter 15

1. HMS *Wasp* (CV-7), Capt. J.W. Reeves Jr, USN.
2. AIR-27-2079-42.
3. AIR-27-2079-44.
4. AIR-27-2079-45.
5. AIR-27-2079-47.
6. AIR-27-2079-48.

7. Ibid.
8. AIR-27-2079-52.
9. HMS *Warspite* (03), Capt. H.A. Packer, RN; HMS *Valiant* (02), Capt. L.H. Ashmore, RN; and aircraft carrier HMS *Formidable* (67), Rear-Admiral A.G. Talbot DSO, RN.
10. AIR-27-2079-52.
11. AIR-27-2079-56.

Chapter 16

1. Also known as Koronis.
2. Kostas Stavropoulos (1900–74), born in Egypt to a wealthy Greek family, joined the Hellenic Broadcasting Corporation in 1939.
3. Leon Trotsky (1879–1940), Russian revolutionary and Red Army founder, argued history is shaped by class and imperialism, not individuals.
4. The Asia Minor campaign (1919–22) saw Greek forces advance into Anatolia before defeat by Turkish nationalists, ending with the 1923 Treaty of Lausanne.
5. Conversation with Nikos Levogiannis, Greek philologist, former MP, and an expert on the modern history of Naxos, Dec. 2024.
6. Sideris' request for reinstatement in Apr. 1945 followed the instalment of the Venizelist Voulgaris government, which may hint at his own political alignment.
7. RHN *Georgios Averof* uniquely took part in both the 1911 and 1937 Coronation Naval Reviews at Spithead, England. She is now a museum at Flisvos Marina, Athens.
8. Delfino, *Tenente di Vascello* (Lt) G. Aicardi, Regia Marina.
9. RHN *Elli*, Capt. A. Chatzopoulos, RHN.
10. ULTRA: Allied decryption of Axis codes, including Enigma, at Bletchley Park.
11. HMS *Decoy* (H75), Cdr E.G. McGregor, RN.
12. Levogiannis, *Georgios Ioannis Sideris*, Vol. 3, p.303.
13. Ibid.
14. SOE: Sideris, G., 17 Apr. 1945.

Chapter 17

1. Brig. Ralph Bagnold, OBE (1896–1990), desert explorer and LRDG founder (1940); his expertise shaped Allied desert tactics and influenced Earth/Mars research.
2. 'Jerry can': 4.4 gal (20l) German fuel container (1930s), later adopted by Allies. It remains a classic of wartime industrial design.
3. Lt Col. David Stirling DSO, OBE (1915–90), Scottish officer, SAS founder (1941); proposed L-Detachment, destroyed +250 Axis aircraft; captured 1943.
4. Smith, B., LRDG Association Newsletter, 1979.
5. LRDG: WO-201-818 (1077).
6. Portolago, Italian naval base and model town with fascist youth centre (1923–1930s), renamed Lakki in 1947.
7. HMS *Intrepid* (D10), Cdr C.A. de W. Kitcat, RN.
8. RHN *Vasilissa Olga* (H86), Lt Cdr G. Blessas DSO, RHN.
9. Lt Gen. F.W. Müller (1897–1947), German officer, infamous for Greek reprisals; replaced by Maj. Gen. Kreipe; executed 20 May 1947.
10. *Ierós Lóchos* (Sacred Band), Greek special forces formed 1942, trained with SAS/SBS; specialised in amphibious/airborne raids until 1945.

Chapter 18

1. Charalambidis, *The Experience of Occupation and Resistance in Athens*.
2. SOE: George Sideris, #G1797, 11 Aug. 1954.
3. Mackenzie, Lt K.J., Report on Operations 'Primer' and 'Grotesque II' (1943).
4. Mackenzie called Psaras an 'old friend'; they worked on several missions, and Mackenzie became *koumpáros* (godfather) to Psaras' grandson.
5. Sideris, G., personal diary, unpublished, 1944.
6. Levogiannis, *Georgios Ioannis Sideris*, Vol. 3, p.303.
7. Ibid.
8. German Naval Staff War Diary, Aug. 1944, pp.571–572.

9. Churchill, *The Second World War,* Vol. 6, p.252.
10. HMS *Ajax* (22), Capt. J.W. Cuthbert, RN.
11. The Royal Air Forces Escaping Society (RAFES), founded in 1946, supported civilians who aided downed Allied airmen and maintained ties with MI9 and SOE veterans.
12. SOE: George Sideris, #G1797, 11 Aug. 1954.

Chapter 19

1. HQ 321st BG USAAF War Diary, Oct. 1943.
2. HMS *Panther* (G41), L/Cdr the Viscount Jocelyn, RN.
3. HMS *Carlisle* (D67), Capt. H.F. Nalder, RN.
4. Churchill, *The Second World War*, Vol. 5, p.180.
5. HQ 321st BG USAAF War Diary, Oct. 1943.
6. *Flying Caisson* aircrew KIA: pilot 2nd Lt Gordon J. Black (O-742663), co-pilot 2nd Lt William (mi) Golden (O-674485), cannon loader S/Sgt Richard E. Wenrich (38224757), radio operator S/Sgt Arthur W. Lang (31174614), engineer S/Sgt Edwin E. Ramsburg (33238203), and armament operator S/Sgt Felton E. Horton (15077105).
7. AIR-27-464-32.
8. Hastings, *Bomber Command*, p.175.
9. F/O Lewis Rossner (131150, RAFVR); Phaleron War Cemetery, Plot 23.B.20, Athens, Greece.
10. AIR-27-464-32.
11. F/O John Stephens Hayden (130938, RAFVR) (20 y.o.), Leslie John and Dora Marian Hayden, Crownhill, Plymouth; Alamein Memorial, col. 268, Egypt.
12. AIR-27-464-32.
13. F/O Athol George Greentree (414974, RNZAF) (31 y.o.), Henry Arthur and Alice May Greentree; husband of Winifred Annie Greentree, Invercargill, Southland, NZ; Alamein Memorial, col. 277, Egypt.
14. AIR-27-464-31.
15. Ibid.
16. Ibid.
17. AIR-27-464-32.

18. F/O Anthony David Bond (125666, RAFVR) (21 y.o.), Charles George and Nellie Bond, Doncaster, Yorkshire; Alamein Memorial, col. 267, Egypt (sqdn ORBs as F/O G. Bond).
19. F/O William Walker Thwaites (50176, RAF) (22 y.o.), William Walker and Elizabeth Thwaites, Southwick, Sunderland, Co. Durham; Alamein Memorial, col. 269, Egypt.
20. F/O John Edwin Lovell (136381, RAFVR) (22 y.o.), Mr and Mrs Frank Lovell; husband of Vera Rose Lovell, New Bradwell, Buckinghamshire; Alamein Memorial, col. 268, Egypt.
21. F/O John Bratt Fletcher (128593, RAFVR) (20 y.o.), Frederick William and Dorothy Fletcher, Ipswich, Suffolk; Alamein Memorial, col. 268, Egypt.
22. Sgt Jack Dale (1516617, RAFVR) (21 y.o.), James and Bertha Dale, Ashton-under-Lyne, Lancashire; Alamein Memorial, col. 270, Egypt.
23. AIR-27-464-34.

Chapter 20

1. Prinzregentenplatz 16, München, Deutschland.
2. Thomas Wolfe (1900–38), American novelist.
3. Château de Sermet (13th–14th century), now houses the Club des Autos.
4. Patricia Staunton: emails 2023–25.
5. Hayter family: discussions/emails 2023–25.

Chapter 21

1. 'Keep Calm and Carry On': 1939 British morale poster, little used then, later iconic.
2. RPs: 25lb (11.3kg) introduced late 1943 (No. 603 Sqdn first use 8 Nov.); 60lb (27.2kg) introduced mid-1944.
3. Danube lighters: shallow-water barges repurposed in WWII for troops and supplies.
4. Cape Matapan (Cape Tainaron): southernmost point of mainland Greece, site of a decisive WWII naval battle in Mar. 1941, linked to Poseidon and the mythical entrance to Hades.

5. AIR-27-2080-7.
6. Art Stacey: email 7 May 2023.
7. Richard Harper: emails 2023–24.

Chapter 22

1. Smith, B., LRDG Association Newsletter, 1979.
2. *Kriegsmarine* War Diary, 30 Oct. 1943, p.441.
3. *GA-01* Combat Report, 30 Oct. 1943.
4. *GA-54* Combat Report, 30 Oct. 1943.
5. USAAF Missing Air Crew Report (MACR) #1137, 30 Oct. 1943.
6. *GA-01* Combat Report, 30 Oct. 1943.
7. USAAF MACR #1137, 30 Oct. 1943.
8. *GA-54* Combat Report, 30 Oct. 1943.
9. USAAF MACR #1137, 30 Oct. 1943.
10. Ibid.
11. Smith, B., LRDG Association Newsletter, 1979.
12. *GA-01* Combat Report, 30 Oct. 1943.
13. USAAF MACR #1137, 30 Oct. 1943.
14. Ibid.
15. *GA-01* Combat Report, 30 Oct. 1943.
16. *GA-54* Combat Report, 30 Oct. 1943.
17. *Kriegsmarine* War Diary, 30 Oct. 1943, p.441.
18. *GA-01* Combat Report, 30 Oct. 1943.
19. Ibid.
20. *Kriegsmarine* War Diary, 30 Oct. 1943: '*After completing the most necessary repairs and replacing the damaged weapons, GA-01 and GA-54 set sail again for Naxos on 11/08, 18:00 hrs.*'
21. Nikolas Levogiannis: discussion, Dec. 2024.
22. USAAF MACR #1137, 30 Oct. 1943.
23. Smith, B., LRDG Association Newsletter, 1979.
24. *GA-01* Combat Report, 30 Oct. 1943: Hayter noted port engine oil loss, not fire; flak likely hit port, not starboard (right), wing.
25. USAAF MACR #1137, 30 Oct. 1943.
26. *GA-01* Combat Report, 30 Oct. 1943.

Epilogue

1. HMS *Perseus* (N36), Lt/Cdr E.C.F. Nicolay, RN; mined Dec 1941, one survivor; wreck found 26 Dec. 1997, 107ft (32m).
2. HMS *Triumph* (N18), Lt J.S. Huddart, RN; sank 14 Jan. 1942, all 64 crew lost, likely torpedo; wreck found 7 Jun. 2023, 666ft (203m).
3. HMS *Trooper* (N91), Lt J.S. Wraith, RN; sank 17 Oct. 1943, all 64 crew lost, likely EMF mine; wreck found 6 Oct. 2024, 830ft (250m), Icarian Sea.
4. Type VII U-133, *Leutnant* (Lt) Eberhard Mohr; sank one hour into commander's first patrol, 14 Mar. 1942, mine at Salamis, all crew lost, posthumous promotion to *Kapitänleutnant* (Lt Cdr); wreck at 236ft (72m).
5. RHN *Adrias* (L67), Cdr I. Toumbas, RHN; mined off Kalymnos 22 Oct. 1943, bow blown off, ship reached Alexandria 6 Dec. Bow wreckage found 2004.
6. HMS *Hurworth* (L28), Cdr R.H. Wright DSC, RN; mined and sunk 22 Oct. 1943 while aiding Adrias. Wreck at 335ft (102m), found 2004.
7. Thalatta: ancient Greek for 'the Sea'.
8. P/O Keith I.E. Hopkins DFC (AUS400924) and W/O Keith V. Roget (AUS401153), RAAF.
9. HMS *Unrivalled* (P45), Lt H.B. Turner, RN.
10. ADM 199/1821.
11. AIR-27-2079-60.

SELECT BIBLIOGRAPHY

Primary Sources

Kriegstagebuch Admiral Ägäis (Admiral Aegean War Diary), Oct. 1943, German Navy Archives.

Dillon, B.E., some notes on operations by Station Lillian, Mount Elikon, Voiotia, Greece, Sep.–Dec. 1944, by Major Brian Dillon MBE, R. Norfolks, station commander. Unpublished.

GA-01 Gefechtsbericht (Combat Report), 30 Oct. 1943.

GA-54 Combat Report, 30 Oct. 1943.

London Gazette, 28 Jan. 1941, issue 35057, p.561; 4 Apr. 1941, issue 35127, p.1959; 29 Apr. 1941, supplement 35148, p.2445; 22 Aug. 1941, issue 35254, p.4870; 19 Sep. 1941, issue 35279, p.5420.

Kriegsmarine War Diary, 30 Oct. 1943, p.440–441. German Navy Archives.

TNA:

ADM 199/1818, ADM 199/1821

AIR 27/244/13

AIR-27-181-33, AIR-27-181-37, AIR-27-181-39

AIR-27-2079-1, AIR-27-2079-2, AIR-27-2079-42, AIR-27-2079-43, AIR-27-2079-44, AIR-27-2079-45, AIR-27-2079-46, AIR-27-2079-47, AIR-27-2079-49, AIR-27-2079-50, AIR-27-2079-52, AIR-27-2079-53, AIR-27-2079-57, AIR-27-2079-60, AIR-27-2079-61

AIR-27-2080-3, AIR-27-2080-4, AIR-27-2080-7

AIR-27-2120-15, AIR-27-2120-17

AIR-27-244-22

AIR-27-464-26, AIR-27-464-27, AIR-27-464-28, AIR-27-464-29, AIR-27-464-30, AIR-27-464-31, AIR-27-464-32, AIR-27-464-33, AIR-27-464-34

AIR-27-882-59, AIR-27-882-60, AIR-27-882-62, AIR-27-882-63, AIR-27-882-64, AIR-27-882-65, AIR-27-882-66, AIR-27-882-67, AIR-27-882-68, AIR-27-882-69, AIR-27-882-70
AIR-27-1334-44
AIR-27-1675-34
AIR-27-1733-55, AIR-27-1735-39

LRDG: Diary and Narrative (26 Sep.–5 Nov. 1943) WO-201-818 (1077).
SOE Record Sheet, Sideris, G., (Ref: AL/Cyclds/186), 17 Apr. 1945.
SOE: Internal Assessment: George Sideris, #G1797, 11 Aug. 1954.

US National Archives:
USAAF, Deceased Personnel File; Gordon Black (O-742663).
USAAF, Missing Air Crew Report (MACR) No. 1137, 30 Oct. 1943.

German Naval Staff War Diary (Operations Division); Pt A, Vols. 50 and 60 (Aug.–Oct. 1943).

Literature/Websites

'Airmen Surprised', *The Age,* Melbourne, Vic., 18 Dec. 1943, p.1. Retrieved 1 Jul. 2025, from http://nla.gov.au/nla.news-article206352983.
Atkinson, R., *An Army at Dawn: The Liberation Trilogy*, Little, Brown Book Group, Kindle edition, p.327, 2002.
Bagnold, R.A., *The Physics of Blown Sand and Desert Dunes*, Methuen, London, 1941.
Broughton, D.J., 'The History of Oshawa Airport', *Flying News,* 27 Jun. 1994.
Carter, K.C. & Mueller, R., *U.S. Army Air Forces in World War II: Combat Chronology 1941–1945*, Center for Air Force History, Washington, DC, 1991.
Charalambidis, Menelaos, *The Experience of Occupation and Resistance in Athens*, Alexandria, Athens, 2012.
Chionidou, Violetta, *Famine and Death in Occupied Greece 1941–44*, Estia, Athens, 2011.
Churchill, W.S., *The Second World War: Volume V, Closing the Ring*, The Reprint Society, London, UK, 1952.

Churchill, W.S., *The Second World War: Volume VI, Triumph and Tragedy*, Houghton Mifflin, Boston, p.252, 1953.

Commonwealth War Graves Commission, online casualty database. www.cwgc.org (Accessed Jun.–Aug. 2025).

Daphnes, Grigorios, *Greece Between Two Wars 1923–1940*, Kaktos, Athens, 1997.

Fitzgerald, John T., SMSgt, USAF (ret.), *321st BG History: October 1943* [MS]. Compiled from HQ and Squadron War Diaries, AFHRA, Maxwell AFB, Alabama, n.d.

Foreman, J., Mathews, J. & Parry, S., *Luftwaffe Night Fighter Claims 1939–1945*, Red Kite, Walton on Thames, UK, 2004.

Forsgren, J., *The Junkers Ju 52 Story*, Fonthill Media, Stroud, UK, 2017.

Golley, J., *John 'Cat's-Eyes' Cunningham: The Aviation Legend*, Airlife Publishing, Shrewsbury, UK, 1999.

HAGs/DID (Hellenic Army General Staff/Directorate of Army History), *The Hellenic Army in WWI and the Asia Minor Campaign*, Vols. I–II, 1–2; Concise History of the Asia Minor Campaign 1919–1922, Athens, 1958–2018.

Hastings, M., *Bomber Command*, Zenith Military Classics, Quarto Publishing Group USA, Kindle edition, 2013.

Hatch, F.J., *The Aerodrome of Democracy: Canada and the BCATP, 1939–1945*, Canadian Department of National Defence, 1983.

Hillmer, N., Hatch, F.J. & Myers, P., *British Commonwealth Air Training Plan*, The Canadian Encyclopedia, Historica Canada, 6 Feb.; updated 30 Jun. 2023, 2006.

Higham, Robin, *Diary of a Disaster: British Aid to Greece 1940–1941*, University Press of Kentucky, Lexington, 1986.

Howe, G.F., *Northwest Africa: Seizing the Initiative in the West*, Center of Military History, Washington, DC, anniversary edition published 1993, 1957.

Kennedy Shaw, W.B., *Long Range Desert Group: Its Work in Libya 1940–43*, Collins, London, 1945.

Leon, George, *Greece and the First World War 1917–1918*, Columbia University Press, Boulder, 1990.

Levogiannis, N. (ed.), *Georgios Ioannis Sideris – His Actions During 1940–44: The Occupation of Naxos, in Komiaki Naxos*, Vol. 3, Koronida Naxos Association, Athens, 2005.

Lewis, Patricia K.G., *Charles Allberry: A Portrait*, privately published. Printed by E&E Plumridge Ltd., Cambridge, UK, 1984.

Macintyre, Ben, *SAS: Rogue Heroes*, Viking, London, 2017.

Maurer, I., *Air Force Combat Units of World War II*, US Government Printing Office, Washington, DC, 1961.

Margaritis, Giorgos, *Harbinger of Stormy Winds: The Albanian War and Early Occupation*, Vivliorama, Athens, 2009.

Mazower, Mark, *Inside Hitler's Greece 1941–1944*, Yale University Press, New Haven, 1993.

Mazower, Mark, *Greece and the Interwar Economic Crisis*, MIET, Athens, 2009.

Michailidis, Iakovos, *The National Defence Movement – Thessaloniki in WWI*, University Studio Press, Thessaloniki, 2015.

Met Office, Historic Station Data, Met Office. www.metoffice.gov.uk/research/climate/maps-and-data/historic-station-data (Accessed 24 Aug. 2025).

Miller, D., *Submarines of the World*, Salamander Books, London, UK, 1991.

Molony, C.J.C. (Brig.), *The History of World War Two*, United Kingdom Military Series Vol. 5: The Mediterranean and Middle East, H.M. Stationery Office, 1973.

Naval Encyclopedia, *WW2 Italian Submarines*. https://naval-encyclopedia.com (Accessed 20 Jul. 2025).

Naxos 1943: *A Shocking Incident in Komiaki*. YouTube video, 28 Feb. 2020. www.youtube.com/watch?v=UiHta4A2Sx8 (Accessed Apr. 2025).

O'Carroll, Brendan, *The Long Range Desert Group in Action 1940–43*, Pen & Sword, Barnsley, 2020.

O'Carroll, Brendan, *The Long Range Desert Group in the Aegean*, Pen & Sword, Barnsley, 2021.

O'Hara, V.P., *Naval Operations in the Mediterranean Sea*, in S.C. Tucker (ed.), *World War II at Sea: An Encyclopedia*, Vol. II: L-Z, pp.490–494, ABC-CLIO, LLC, 2011.

Paterson, L., *U-Boats in the Mediterranean, 1941–1944*, Skyhorse Publishing, USA, 2019.

RAF Museum, BABS Mk1C Still Air: Collection Ref: X001-6746. www.rafmuseum.org.uk/research/archive-exhibitions/worth-a-thousand-words-air-diagrams/babs-mk1c-still-air (Accessed 16 Aug. 2024).

Rawnsley, C.F. & Wright, R., *Night Fighter*, Collins, London, 1957.
Reaping the Whirlwind: A Symposium on the Strategic Bomber Offensive 1939–45. Bracknell Paper No. 4. Royal Air Force Historical Society and RAF Staff College, Bracknell, 26 Mar. 1993.
Robertson, R.J., '"S" for Sugar, "S" for Survival', *Britain at War magazine,* Issue 196, Aug. 2023.
Robertson, R.J., 'The Erudite Airman', *Britain at War magazine*, Issue 209, Sep. 2024.
Robertson, R.J., *The Milos Marines*, *The Sheet Anchor*, No. 1, Royal Marines Historical Society, Portsmouth, UK, pp.66–75, 2024.
Robertson, R.J., *Back in the fold: Finding a Ju 88 in the Aegean*, Divernet UK. Jun. 2025, https://divernet.com/world-dives/europe/back-in-the-fold-finding-a-Ju 88-in-the-aegean (Accessed 7 Sep. 2025).
Sharpe, R., *Wings Above the Skyline: The Story of No. 5 Service Flying Training School, Brantford, Ontario, 1940–1944*, Tate Publishing, 2015.
Smith, P.C. & Walker, E.R., *War in the Aegean: Campaign for the Eastern Mediterranean in WWII*, Stackpole Books, USA, 2008.
Sopley Rotor Radar Station. Subterranea Britannica. www.subbrit.org.uk/sites/sopley-rotor-radar-station (Accessed 20 Jul. 2025).
Spiliotopoulou, Maria, *Allied Missions in the Cyclades: Resistance and Liberation in Naxos, Paros, and Irakleia, Modern Greek Historical Studies*, Vol. 4, Academy of Athens, 2016.
Stars and Stripes, Algiers Daily, Vol. I, No. 96, Thursday, 26 Aug. 1943.
Voglis, Polymeris, *Greek Society During the Occupation 1941–1944*, Alexandria, Athens, 2010.
Van Wijngaarden, P. & Staal, P., *Dornier Do-24*, Bergen, Bonneville, 1992.
Wessels, A., *The South African Air Force, 1920–2012: A Review of Its History and an Indication of its Cultural Heritage*, Scientia Militaria, 40(3), 2012.

INDEX